THE
GOTHIC REVIVAL
& AMERICAN CHURCH
ARCHITECTURE

Seals of the Cambridge Camden Society and the New York Ecclesiological Society

Phoebe B. Stanton

THE GOTHIC REVIVAL & AMERICAN CHURCH ARCHITECTURE

An Episode in Taste

1840-1856

The Johns Hopkins University Press

Baltimore and London

Copyright © 1968 by The Johns Hopkins Press
All rights reserved
Printed in the United States of America on acid-free paper

First published in a hardcover edition by The Johns Hopkins Press, 1968
Johns Hopkins Paperbacks edition, 1997
06 05 04 03 02 01 00 99 98 97   5 4 3 2 1

The Johns Hopkins University Press
2715 North Charles Street
Baltimore, Maryland 21218-4319
The Johns Hopkins Press Ltd., London

ISBN 0-8018-5622-1

Library of Congress Catalog Card Number 68-16273

A catalog record for this book is available from the British Library.

To D. J. S.

Preface to the 1997 Edition

This book began when, as I was working on a study of the English Gothic Revival, I found in the *Ecclesiologist* a statement that the Ecclesiological Society had sent plans for a small parish church of good design "suitable for the Colonies" to the United States and that a church in Philadelphia and one near Baltimore were under construction from these plans. The doctrinaires who were then in command of the society were proud of this achievement, for they believed their advice could only improve quality of taste in America.

My interest in the past, present, and future of Baltimore architecture, my affection for the remarkable urban character of the city, my wish to do what I could to preserve the human scale and singular character it had acquired over time, caused me to be alert to this assertion. One fact led to another, and shortly after I had learned of this model church I went to see the Church of St. James the Less in Philadelphia.

On a cold snowy day, the rector and his wife welcomed me and, to my amazement, St. James the Less proved to be an exquisite little building, reminiscent of churches—indeed a particular medieval church, St. Michaels in Longstanton, Cambridgeshire—that I had studied on my travels around England. On that first visit I took the pictures of the exterior of St. James the Less that appear in this book.

The Gothic Revival and American Church Architecture was born that day. I wondered which Baltimore church had, according to the Ecclesiological Society, been built from the plan it had provided, how the plans had been sent, whether other churches in this "colony" had been built from this pattern, where they were, and which features and qualities of St. Michael's had survived the transplantation of the design. I knew at once that the richness of St. James the Less must be unique.

Working beyond my study of St. James the Less—which I did not "discover," for its attractiveness was well known to ecclesiastical historians and students of Philadelphia architecture—I began to uncover matters that took me afield, into another of my art-historical interests, the routes along which tastes were transmitted in the nineteenth century. I found that I was able to link persons ecclesiastical, English and American— among them Bishop Doane of New Jersey and Bishop Whittingham of Maryland—and artistic—Frank Wills, J. W. Priest, and Richard Upjohn—who contributed to the revival of the English parish church form in the nineteenth century and that these people were interesting in their own right. The English ecclesiologists, the movement they produced, the architectural and decorative style they fostered, and their opinions—many of which were contentious—were also representative of their time and its tastes. Finally I sought out and visited American churches and their records.

I soon realized that the geographical extent of the style was too large for me to cover in its entirety. At this point in my research I decided that my study should define the style, its sources and its manifestations, so that subsequent research could identify buildings that were its progeny, wherever they might be. *The Gothic Revival and American Church Architecture* was to be a case study in how to handle materials of this sort and an invitation to others to find and identify buildings that I could not visit but that showed signs of the influence of the parish church model.

For me chapter 5 is the most significant, for in it I describe what the Americans accepted of English ideas and tastes and what, because of their own ideas, needs, and architectural requirements, they rejected or modified.

I was able to use the Enoch Pratt Free Library and the George Peabody Library in Baltimore, where, when I was working, the library and many papers of Bishop Whittingham were lodged. They are now at the General Theological Seminary in New York, where I hope the books have been kept as a separate collection, a record of the mind of the bishop and the time when he assembled them.

I found materials in magazines an invaluable source of information on taste and its expressions, for often a first and lively announcement of preferences appeared there rather than in books.

The title I chose for this book was *Ecclesiology Abroad,* but because my advisors felt few readers would know what that meant, it was changed to *The Gothic Revival and American Church Architecture.* I remain convinced that I was right and they were wrong.

Contents

List of Figures

Facing title page. The upper seal was designed in 1844 for the Cambridge Camden Society by A. W. Pugin, whose monogram appears at the lower left, below St. John. The saints in tabernacle work are St. George and St. Etheldreda, patron saints of England and Ely, respectively, on either side of the Virgin and child; St. John the Evangelist, patron of architecture, holding a chart of the New Jerusalem; and St. Luke, patron of painting and the fine arts, holding a picture. At the extreme left, a detail of a ruined church; at the extreme right, a detail of the church restored. At the bottom, S. Sepulchre's, Cambridge, restored by the Cambridge Camden Society. Below it, an angel bearing a scroll with the legend *Quam Dilecta,* from Psalm 83. The lower seal was designed in 1848 for the New York Ecclesiological Society by Frank Wills.

Photographs not otherwise identified were taken by the author.

LIST OF FIGURES

LIST OF FIGURES

LIST OF FIGURES

LIST OF FIGURES

Introduction

The wish to copy Gothic architecture and the thoughts about building which developed as a result were singularly expressive of the respect and nostalgia for the past which were characteristic of the nineteenth century. One can look back upon Gothic revivalism from the twentieth century, however, and see that, though they were still inchoate, the statements on architectural aesthetics made by the revivalists and their contemporaries also contributed to the constellation of theories from which modern architectural thought and the buildings based upon it would later grow. A particular form of Gothic revivalism appeared in North America between 1840 and 1856, and it is this occurrence, and the progressive architectural ideas which it encouraged, with which this study is concerned.

Because of my interest in the growth of "Gothic rationalism" in America, I was pleased when Peter Collins' *Changing Ideals in Modern Architecture, 1750–1950* was published in 1965,[1] for in it the European origins of these American events are presented with exemplary clarity, and the assumptions and interpretation of events upon which the present book is based are corroborated. The reader will find in *Changing Ideals in Modern Architecture* a full discussion of the European background of the ideas whose American mani-

[1] (Montreal: McGill University Press, 1965).

festation is explored here. My term, "Gothic rationalism," is borrowed from Professor Collins: he defines it as the "belief that architecture derives its finest expression from the most economical use of structural forms."[2] Though his book is notable for its consistent breadth and originality, Chapter 19 is particularly recommended for its account of an aspect of American architectural taste and thought in the critical years of the mid-nineteenth century.

Gothic revivalism arrived in North America in the form of the English Gothic revival, with its preference for the English medieval parish church as a model for ecclesiastical architecture. In order to understand when and how this influence appeared, the sources from which it sprang, the reception it was given, the system of thought which came with it, the confrontation which ensued between the Cambridge Camden Society, the primary English sponsor of the revival, and its American adherents, and the ways in which American ideas about art and architecture were altered by contact with this foreign taste, the history of a number of North American buildings in which English models are reflected has been presented and opinions expressed in commentaries on architecture and Gothic revivalism by American writers have been extracted. When, in the nineteenth century, a set of European artistic ideas crossed the Atlantic and there faced the predispositions of an intelligent American audience, the events which followed illuminated both the meaning of the doctrines which had emigrated and the true nature of American thought and taste.

The English conviction that it was desirable to build copies of medieval English parish churches was a secondary plot in a much larger nineteenth-century drama; for this reason, the parish church revival in England and abroad would seem merely idiosyncratic without some explanation of the identity of the other and larger movements whose presence it reflected and whose motives it amplified. Whatever their concern and however large their role, all the participants shared certain attitudes: first, the instinctive nineteenth-century rejection and fear of secularism in the Church and in art; second (particularly true of those in the arts), dislike of the Classical revivals which were associated with that secularism; third, a desire for greater formal richness in

[2] *Ibid.*, p. 208.

the Episcopal liturgy and visual opulence in Church architecture. Distaste for the immediate past and its influence upon the present, then, was the source from which all these reformers finally drew their energy.

The Oxford Movement was the largest and most important contemporary counterpart of the parish church revival in England. By 1800 demands for reform and restoration within the Church in England were frequent and justified. Behind lay nearly three centuries of struggle, in which power had passed back and forth between a High Church party which represented the continuation of the Catholic tradition and a Protestant sector. Parliament gave every sign of its willingness to intercede in the affairs of the Church to correct abuses, and disestablishment seemed a possibility. At this point, in 1833, John Keble, in a sermon on "National Apostasy," called for internal spiritual renewal and return to the truths which had been put forward by seventeenth-century divines such as William Laud. The Oxford Movement was, in fact, a rejection of the Protestant domination over the Church in the eighteenth century and a plea for the earlier High Church position. By 1839, under the leadership of John Henry Newman, Edward B. Pusey, James A. Froude, and many others, the Movement had become widely known and had gained not only a following but a vigorous opposition which felt and feared its pro-Roman import. The addition of new members and continuing development in the thought of Newman characterized the years from 1839 to 1841, when Newman's *Tract 90* appeared. In 1845, after a deep personal crisis and further self-questioning, Newman became a Roman Catholic, a step in which he was followed by a few members of the Movement. The majority, led by Pusey and Keble, remained in the Church, continuing their attempts to reform from within. The Oxford Movement has been correctly described as a "quiet Anglican 'Counter-reformation,'" which was based on the conviction that "'Protestantism,' by drawing Anglicans away from that sure foundation of apostolic succession and apostolic tradition on which the English Church had stood firm through all the storms of the Reformation, had exposed the Church to the onslaughts of 'Erastianism' and 'Liberalism.'"[3]

The similarities between the objectives of the Oxford Movement and those

[3] Eugene R. Fairweather, ed., *The Oxford Movement* (New York: Oxford University Press, 1964), p. 9.

of the parish church revival are obvious; Peter Collins has said that the Cambridge Camden Society (later the Ecclesiological Society), whose particular interest it was, "put into effect" the "architectural programme" of the Oxford reformers. The chronology of critical events within the Movement and that of the parish church revival in the Church of England coincide so closely that the connection between the two seems more than fortuitous. The Society was organized in the period of the Oxford Tracts in the late 1830's, and it moved to consolidate its position and policies just as the Movement entered its time of crisis with the publication of Newman's *Tract 90* in 1841. At the same time, it should be recognized that neither the Oxford leaders nor the Society publicly admitted the connection which Collins describes. The men at Oxford eschewed artistic and ritualistic preoccupations, and the Cambridge revivalists preferred to believe that they were independent but sympathetic observers of religious developments at Oxford. It would, perhaps, be best to think of Tractarianism and the architectural revival as coeval phenomena rising from common sources in the thought and attitudes of the 1830's and 1840's. Persons interested in the one were likely to be equally concerned with the other; such was the case with those members of the American clergy who sponsored the English parish church style.

The proposal that the medieval parish church be accepted as the model for church builders was at once an artistic expression of the reformist impulses which had inspired Newman, Keble, Pusey, and the others at Oxford, an acknowledgment of the authority and appropriateness of Gothic revivalism, and a peculiarly English solution. The many local churches which survive from the Middle Ages in England constitute a unique inheritance. The division of England into parishes was not regularized until the twelfth century, when the priests, who had originally been attached to landowners, by degrees became recognized as freeholders whose first loyalty was to the bishops from whom their spiritual faculties came. Parishes were composed of the lands within a reasonable distance of a church. They were essentially the result of rural land-holding arrangements and the administration of the tithes. These local churches belonged to the Church and were subject only to its authority, but their buildings were the responsibility of the parishioners and the priest. The wealthier members of the parish, who were often the lords of the manor or manors nearby, frequently contributed the money necessary for major additions and repairs. The comparatively small size of the landholding units which were established after the Conquest, combined with the fact that each unit tended to have its own parish church, made it possible for many of these small, vernacular structures to survive into the period after the Reformation. From the early sixteenth century to the beginning of the nineteenth, though they were used and sometimes abused, neglected, or remodeled, they were rarely added to in conflicting styles or replaced. There were, as a result, hundreds of these churches, some large and richly appointed, others so modest as to be plain, which the nineteenth-century enthusiast of Gothic architecture could study. All contained at least a nave and chancel, were constructed of local materials, and seemed deliberately and gracefully related to the countryside in which they were set.

To those who wished to restore the Church in England as an institution and to withdraw it from corrupting secular attachments, the return to this traditional English building type and to the ceremonial connected with it seemed not only reasonable but necessary, suggestive of a splendid moment in the national past. The renewal of interest in Gothic heightened curiosity about these local churches; the burgeoning scholarship about it provided the knowledge which was needed to catalogue their qualities. John Rickman, for example, had supplied the stylistic definitions "Early English" (period ending about 1290, characterized by traces of Norman influence, lancet windows, and vaults which had not attained quadripartite form), "Decorated" (1290 to 1350, characterized by rich ornament and spatial complexity, singularly English), and "Perpendicular" (from 1350 on, characterized by verticality, linearity, slenderness, increasing complexity in rib patterns, and repetitive paneling). Such definitions could be applied to parish churches as well as to the cathedrals with which England was also richly endowed.

The decision to recommend the parish church as a model was, thus, only a specialized manifestation of the Gothic revival, which had long been in progress. Appreciation of medieval art and architecture had been part of English taste for at least a century when opinions about Gothic changed in temper and intent in the 1830's because of its association with ideas of social and religious reform. Before 1835 designers and architects had not attempted to copy medieval art. Instead, fascinated by its decorative possibilities, they had used it as they had Chinese and other foreign arts, utilizing its strangeness and potential as applied ornament.[4] Enthusiasm for the parish church was one facet of the new, scholarly, intense, and reformist Gothic revival of the 1840's.

In addition to reflecting the Oxford Movement and the Gothic revival, American Gothic revivalism was influenced by the Roman Catholic revival which was in progress in England. No matter how authentic and earnest the connections between the revivalists and the Church might be, it was perfectly clear to everyone involved that the buildings they admired and proposed to copy had been built in a Roman Catholic age for Roman Catholic purposes. Recommendation of this style and these models necessarily raised the embarrassing specter of guilt by association with "Romanism." That A. W. Pugin, the youthful and talented designer in Gothic and the leading publicist of the revival, was a recent convert to Catholicism did nothing to allay these fears, which were particularly lively in England. In North America, though the revival was of course opposed by those who disliked High Church policies, it generated no such violent tension.

Finally, the parish church revival was intimately connected with the nineteenth-century rejection of the simplifications of liturgical practice which had been in progress since the Reformation. In their admirable book, *The Architectural Setting of Anglican Worship*, G. W. O. Addleshaw and Frederick Etchells describe the revisions in the service which were made in the seventeenth and eighteenth centuries and call the parish church revivalists "romantic medievalists."[5] Whatever the overt reasons the revivalists gave in defense of their position, it now seems that it had two immediate sources. Whenever they were faced with a problem which required amelioration, mid-nineteenth-century leaders in any field were likely to retreat into the past in search for a workable solution. Return to an earlier liturgy was such a retreat. And yet changes in taste had taken place, and the bald, declarative, open arrangements of eighteenth-century churches were no longer satisfactory. The revivalists' desire to convert England "by repeating the architectural triumphs of the

[4] See Kenneth Clark, *The Gothic Revival* (London: Constable, 1928); Henry-Russell Hitchcock, *Early Victorian Architecture in Britain*, 2 vols. (New Haven: Yale University Press, 1954), and *Architecture, Nineteenth and Twentieth Centuries* (Baltimore: Penguin, 1958); and N. Pevsner, "Richard Payne Knight," *Art Bulletin*, 31 (December, 1949):309–11.
[5] (London: Faber and Faber, 1948), p. 204.

INTRODUCTION

Middle Ages and by placing the Prayer Book service in a setting of medieval ceremonial"[6] was an expression of early Victorian artistic sentiment, dispositions, and taste.

The observations and conclusions contained in *The Architectural Setting of Anglican Worship* and in R. W. Albright's *A History of the Protestant Episcopal Church*[7] have been accepted without qualification as background for this study. I had already embarked upon the research on the American parish church revival when I first read Addleshaw and Etchells and was able, because of their evidence, to connect Bishop Doane of New Jersey with the English church builders. Fortunately, Albright's book appeared in 1964, in time for me to find, in his chapter entitled "The Oxford Movement and Party Spirit," an account of the men whose churches I was studying in my preliminary examination of buildings. James F. White's *The Cambridge Movement* and A. G. Lough's *The Influence of John Mason Neale*, both published in 1962, released me from the responsibility of recapitulating the history of the Ecclesiological Society in detail. Neither book stressed the architectural missionary activities of the Society which were my particular concern.

Everyone writing about this period in England is in debt to Henry-Russell Hitchcock, Sir Kenneth Clark, Sir John Summerson, and Nikolaus Pevsner. I have also referred to John P. Coolidge's 1935 honors thesis for Harvard, "Gothic Revival Churches in New England and New York," which in some ways resembles my project, though Coolidge limits his topic to New England and New York and does not impose the strict chronological limits which I was determined to maintain.

The notes to this study are sufficiently complete to allow the reader to reconstruct the sources of the evidence presented and the way in which fragments of factual and visual evidence were unearthed and combined. A full bibliography of the normal sort would simply duplicate the excellent listings in White and the nineteenth-century items in the bibliography in Addleshaw and Etchells. The new material added is largely in the form of articles in English and American periodicals, manuscript material in vestry records and various university

[6] Ibid., p. 204.
[7] (New York: Macmillan, 1946).

collections, and the photographs which accompany the text, all of which are discussed in the notes.

I am indebted to the libraries of Duke University, Yale University, The Johns Hopkins University, Bryn Mawr College, The General Theological Seminary, The Union Theological Seminary, the State of Connecticut, and the Peabody Institute, and to the Library of Congress, as well as to the many clergymen who showed me their churches and answered my questions with patience and kindness.

Finally, I wish to pay tribute to the nineteenth-century ecclesiologists who are, for one with a feeling for the Victorian period, among the most appealing groups of their time. Their contentiousness and self-righteousness is both brilliant and puzzling. The insoluble problems they set themselves were characteristic of their fascinating age. They were not humorless and knew full well what they were about, and this awareness can occasionally be detected between the lines of their argument. In 1849, for example, they noted in passing that "we have been honoured by a present of the handbills of the Vegetarian Society. We beg leave to have it understood that we are not in connection with Punch, nor do we profess to deal with idiosyncratic religionisms. The old Egyptians, however, worshipped the onion, and if the society in question have any intention of reviving the worship, and erecting a temple to their deity, the criticism of the plans and arrangements might, as a favour, be brought within the scope of the *Ecclesiologist*."

South door, St. Anne's Chapel, Fredericton, N.B.
Frank Wills. Cornerstone laid 1846.

I

The Background

In the 1840's mature Gothic revivalism appeared in American church architecture largely because the Cambridge Camden Society (later the Ecclesiological Society), an English and eminently Anglican group, had resolved to do what it could to influence the design of churches outside the British Isles. Though a number of American Gothic revival churches had been built after 1800, they were separated from the churches of the 40's and 50's by the astonishing accuracy and authenticity of the latter. The earlier churches had been symmetrical in plan; their ornament had been applied decoration, unrelated to structure; their building materials had been those of the Georgian and Classical revivals. Because they were copies of specific English Gothic and Gothic revival examples, the later churches were frequently asymmetrical; their ornament was extracted from English books on Gothic and it was used as it had been in medieval building; they were more often than not built of stone rather than brick and, because of this material and their proportions, they, like their medieval prototypes, fitted comfortably into the landscape in which they were set. The new Gothic revival made that which preceded it seem primitive and old-fashioned.

By the time that the Cambridge Camden Society had resolved to expand its activities to include what it quaintly termed "the Colonies," it had also decided

3

to recommend the English parish church as *the* model for revival. When the first churches in this foreign type and style appeared in America, they seemed but a tasteful, unobtrusive, and specialized addition to an already eclectic architectural scene. The parish church revival was, for one thing, limited to ecclesiastical building, and even within that narrow category it was the property of a single denomination. Churches in the English manner satisfied the requirements and sentiments of those clergy and laymen of the Protestant Episcopal Church who possessed High Church preferences. Other Episcopal churchmen who were not concerned with matters of ritual were able to find churches in this English style appealing because they suggested the English background and the distinguished lineage of their Church. Montgomery Schuyler, an astute critic and observer of American nineteenth-century architecture, was correct when, in 1908, he observed that "the impulse to the Gothic revival in this country came from the Protestant Episcopal Church and was necessarily 'Anglican.' "[1]

Though superficially it was parochial, the revival was destined to influence American architecture, for the buildings produced under its aegis led perceptive Americans to a deepened understanding and appreciation of medieval art, and taught lessons and raised questions about the aesthetics of architecture which were applicable to architecture in any style. The Cambridge Camden Society and others in England who were concerned with the revival interpreted their responsibilities seriously. They chose with care and intelligence the models they proposed to their followers, suggesting only buildings which were of the highest quality and yet simple enough to be copied effectively in faraway places. When it was necessary to employ an architect to adapt the design of a medieval church for exportation, they hired talented men to do the work. They were equally careful when, as was sometimes necessary, they proposed an English Gothic revival church as a model. The results of this devoted and informed direction were constructive; as soon as a few churches which conformed to the English suggestions were built in the United States and Canada, they made a profound impression, for they were architecture of good to excellent quality. Discrimination and competence in the practice and appreciation of design were fostered by what was essentially a specialized, ecclesiastical stylistic preference.

[1] *American Architecture and Other Writings*, ed. William H. Jordy and Ralph Coe, 2 vols. (Cambridge, Mass.: Harvard University Press, 1961), 1:145.

The parish church revival challenged American taste, lifted it out of its provincialism, increased its self-consciousness, and introduced fully developed ideas about the profession of architecture and the larger responsibilities of the architect.

It did not take long for Americans to recognize that these new churches possessed attributes which were desirable in architecture for other purposes and in other styles. In medieval parish churches the undisguised texture and color of the building materials had enriched the whole composition. Their exterior masses and elevations expressed both the form of their interior spaces and the purpose they were to serve. There was a certain logic in the use of a style and a building type that had, in the past, been evolved in response to a need which the nineteenth century was also experiencing; Gothic for churches not only made good historical sense, but it was expressive of function. Though the parish church revival was influential in North America because it introduced a manner which was appealing, evocative, new, it was even more significant because, first, it caused architects and laymen to explore, more deeply than they might otherwise have, the ideas being generated in England; second, it introduced principles of design and a style which made those of the Classical revival obsolete; and third, it forced Americans to accept or reject what the Cambridge Camden Society told them. Though they were ready to investigate and even develop the ideas and models which came from abroad, the Americans were not prepared to accommodate to each detailed English specification. The disparity which emerged between English doctrine and the use Americans made of it reveals a good deal about both sides of this transatlantic exchange.

By the time that the Cambridge Camden Society had acquired an American following, it was already firmly established as a vocal, powerful, and dogmatic party in English architectural affairs. Its multifarious activities and the rigidity of its policies are comprehensible only if they are seen in the context of the whole English Gothic revival. About 1835 an earlier, fanciful medievalism went out of favor in England, to be replaced by a new Gothic revival which was more earnest than stylish. Its advocates admired not only the art but also the social structure of the Middle Ages. At this moment two ideas emerged which were to play an important part in subsequent architectural theory and practice. Neither was invented by the new revival; both were clarified by it.

Though he was intensely preoccupied with the life and artistic achievements of the Middle Ages, this new revivalist was even more involved with his hopes and grave fears for his own time. The study of history had increased his uneasiness about the condition of life and art in the nineteenth century, and for this reason it was easy for him to conclude that the brilliant artistic attainment of certain past ages had been possible because the society of which it was an expression had been "good." His decision about what art had been beautiful was, of course, as subjective as his definition of "good." Both were conditioned by distress about the art and social situation of "the Age" and the wish to bring about reforms. The conviction that "bad" societies had produced "bad" art was ultimately a comment upon the shortcomings of the nineteenth century, the theme with which the revivalist had begun and to which he invariably returned. At no point did the social implications of the revival obscure genuine admiration for medieval art and architecture. The two were combined; each augmented the power of the other.

Comparisons between past and present made in a climate of opinion such as this were inevitably emotionally charged and sometimes fanatically partisan. What began as a modest party of Gothic enthusiasts and scholars with diffuse ideas suddenly became a large, insistent, and vocal body of believers who were convinced that the presence of "good" art from a "better" age would improve contemporary life. The study of medieval art, the restoration and preservation of its extant monuments, and the revival of the style became a cause to which a variety of persons and organizations were attracted. Each had specific objections to the nineteenth century and specific plans for its reform. The restoration of medieval ceremonial and of the churches which had been designed to house it were the province of the Cambridge Camden Society.

In this hothouse atmosphere the study of medieval art and understanding of its details grew astonishingly; the constructive social effects which it was hoped the revival might produce were believed to reside, at least in part, in the capacity to reproduce Gothic exactly. Knowledge was more than a necessity: it was an obligation. The theoreticians and critics of the revival equated inadequate information with social irresponsibility. By 1835 antiquarian, archeological, and topographical literature on the Middle Ages had begun to proliferate, for the new breed of enthusiast demanded and was provided with ever more voluminous, more accurate, and more selective information on the monuments he admired. By no means all of those who specialized in the study of medieval art or the design of Gothic revival architecture participated in the zealous pursuit of reforms of one kind or another. All were affected, however, by the presence of those who did.

One enduring product of the Gothic revival was the conviction that the architecture of an age illustrates its inner nature, strengths, and weaknesses, and that the architect may influence, for good or bad, the lives of those around him. The second lasting contribution of the revival was its insistence that the function of a building should be expressed in its appearance. Expanded knowledge of the history of architecture had demonstrated that in buildings of quality and in periods of artistic creativity use had indeed been visible in and had directed design. This was no new idea, but it was one which flourished in an age dominated, as was the nineteenth century, by historical studies, for a panoramic view of past architectural achievement offered an artificially simple set of connections between styles and their uses. The demand that buildings in some way reflect the use to which they are to be put was an expression of distaste for the ubiquitous Classical revival, which, used as it was for every conceivable architectural purpose, had come to seem monotonous and unattractive.

Vitruvius and all who followed him had stressed the role of function in architectural design. The nineteenth century, which inherited this assumption, had begun to reconsider it long before the Gothic revival made its appearance. Samuel Taylor Coleridge, reflecting upon the problem, defined architectural genius as "the power of aptly, becomingly, and proportionally inclosing, subinclosing and applying in all its dimensions a given space, the place of which remains the same, for a given end or ends; and of producing a unity of the exterior surface, expressing at once the greater or less manifoldness of the Spaces contained and the characteristic purpose of the whole, not without a correspondency and reciprocity of effect on the object."[2]

The Cambridge Camden Society adopted the identification of "good" art with "good" societies and the belief that the function of a building should

[2] *Inquiring Spirit, a New Presentation of Coleridge from His Published and Unpublished Prose Writings*, ed. K. Coburn (London: Routledge and Paul, 1951), p. 216 (from an unpublished manuscript).

influence its design, and adapted these principles to its Anglican requirements. In search of a way to state "the characteristic purpose of the whole" in church architecture, it proposed to resurrect a particular medieval building type, the English parish church of the fourteenth century. Because no original church style was available in the 1840's and because the exalted nature of church buildings tended to provoke a conservative treatment, this decision seemed well founded. The parish church was Christian and English. Its native charm and the ease with which it could be reproduced in the nineteenth century were hard to resist. In any event, the leaders of the Society reasoned, replicas of Gothic would at least recall the virtues of an earlier and better time.

The system of thought developed by the Cambridge Camden Society was called "ecclesiology," and its members proudly accepted the title of "ecclesiologists." The meaning of these terms and the method of reasoning they implied were best described by the Reverend George Ayliffe Poole, in *The Appropriate Character of Church Architecture*, a slim but important book published in 1842.[3] Poole was never a member of the Society, but he and the Cambridge men were thinking along similar lines, using the same sources, and moving toward the same conclusions. Though Poole's later books displeased the ecclesiologists, they never altered their decision that *The Appropriate Character of Church Architecture* was "the earliest treatise upon systematic ecclesiology."[4]

---

[3] (Leeds and London: T. W. Green and Rivington's, 1842). The book was composed of lectures Poole delivered in 1841 before the membership of the Leeds Church of England Library. When first published as articles in the *Christian Miscellany* for March, 1841, they came to the attention of A. W. Pugin, who mentioned them favorably in the *Dublin Review* (23 [February, 1842]) in an article subsequently included in his *The Present State of Ecclesiastical Architecture in England* (London: Charles Dolman, 1843), pp. 67–73. Poole (1809–1883), a priest and author, was graduated from Emmanuel College, Cambridge, in 1831 and entered the Church in 1838. He became curate of St. James', Leeds, in 1839, where he remained until he became rector of Winwick, near Rugby, in 1843. Poole was a High Churchman whose major avocational interest was the study of Gothic architecture. He wrote numerous books. The ecclesiologists found his *History of Ecclesiastical Architecture in England*, published in 1848, "prolix and filled with minute anecdote and incorrect in its conclusions," but the editors also admitted to a certain bias, stating that they felt Poole had somehow acquired "a strong antipathy against our Society" (*Ecclesiologist*, 10 [October, 1849]:141; hereafter cited as *E.*).

[4] "Mr. Poole and Mr. Freeman. No. I," *E.*, 10 (October, 1849):123. The *Ecclesiologist* had also recommended *Appropriate Character* when it was published (*E.*, 1 [June, 1842]: 125–26).

THE BACKGROUND

Poole provided a succinct definition of the Anglican admiration for medieval architecture: "There arose in the west, in the middle ages, or in the dark ages, as we complacently call them, a style of Architecture growing, in all its parts and characters, out of the wants of the church; and adapting itself to the expression of the very things which the church desires to express, in all her methods of embodying herself to the eyes of the world, and to the hearts of her sons."[5] This passage is significant because it challenged those who denigrated medieval artistic achievement and because it declared Gothic to be a visible statement of the "wants" of the Church. "So entirely," Poole said, "did this style arise out of the strivings of the church to give a bodily form to her teaching, that it seems to have clothed her spirit, almost as if the invisible things had put forth their energies, unseen, but powerful and plastic, and gathered around them on all sides the very forms and figures which might best serve to embody them to the eye of sense." Having established this image, he then went on to describe Gothic and "the invisible things" which supply its form:

A Gothic church, in its perfection, is an exposition of the distinctive doctrines of Christianity, clothed upon with a material form; and is, as Coleridge has more forcibly expressed it, 'the petrifaction of our religion.' The greater mysteries concerning the divine objects of our worship are symbolized in the fundamental design of the structure; other Christian verities are set forth in the minor arrangement, and in the ornamental details.[6]

At this point the characteristic nineteenth-century interpretation of the relationship between architectural function and design emerges. Poole had come

---

[5] *Appropriate Character,* pp. 40–41.

[6] *Ibid.* The meaning of this quotation depends upon Coleridge's choice of the word "petrifaction," for clearly he did not intend to imply numbness, deadness, stiffness. He wished to convey the idea that the medieval churches remaining in England preserved in their form and their ornament a record of the religious life of the Middle Ages. Coleridge's admiration for Gothic can be documented. In *Table Talk* for June 29, 1833, he said: "The principle of the Gothic architecture is Infinity made imaginable. It is no doubt a sublimer effort of genius than the Greek style; but then it depends much more on execution for its effect. I was more than ever impressed with the marvelous sublimity and transcendent beauty of King's College Chapel" (*The Complete Works of Samuel Taylor Coleridge,* ed. Professor Shedd, 7 vols. [New York: Harper and Brothers, 1854], 6:461). His lectures of 1818 also contain comments on Gothic which reveal his sensitivity to the style and his indebtedness to A. W. von Schlegel (*Coleridge's Miscellaneous Criticism,* ed. T. M. Raysor [Cambridge, Mass.: Harvard University Press, 1936], pp. 7–17).

upon the *Rationale divinorum officiorum* of Durandus[7] and through it had learned to see the church as an image, a representation of doctrine, and its style as "theological, ecclesiastical and mystical, in all its parts and characters." The Trinity and the Atonement were expressed in "the ground plan, and in the more important lines of the elevation . . . the Doctrine of Regeneration in Holy Baptism, and the Communion of Saints, find their expression in the subordinate arrangements. . . . the precepts of the moral law, and some of the more important parts of Ecclesiastical History, afford endless varieties of decorative details."

Thus to Poole, the ecclesiologists, and some other followers of the Gothic revival, architecture was more than an arbitrary aesthetic exercise. At its best, and at its worst, building was a record in stone of the age that produced it. By praising England's Gothic churches, such men were able to discount the work of non-Gothic periods. This insistence that the teachings of the Church were embodied to the "eye of sense" by architecture was characteristic of ecclesiology, and gave the Society its militant character.

Poole's wistful admiration for Gothic and the ecclesiologists' vigorous program for its revival represented more than nostalgia for a great past age. They were reactions against changes in ecclesiastical design and ceremony that had been introduced in the seventeenth and eighteenth centuries. In *The Architectural Setting of the Anglican Worship* G. W. O. Addleshaw and Frederick Etchells describe the practices to which the ecclesiologists were opposed. In

---

[7] William Durandus (*ca.* 1230–1296), canonist, commentator on the liturgy, papal officer, and Bishop of Mende, died in Rome where he had been called to serve Clement IV. Durandus wrote two major books, the *Speculum judiciale* (1271), and the *Rationale divinorum officiorum* (1289), the latter consisting of eight books which described the Roman rite, its laws and forms. Book I explains the symbolism of the architecture of the church; the other books do the same for the vestments and the service. The *Rationale divinorum officiorum* enjoyed continuous popularity. In the fifteenth century editions were prepared at Mainz (1459), Ulm (1473), Naples (1478), and Strasbourg (1486).

Book I was translated and annotated by John Mason Neale and Benjamin Webb (see nn. 10 and 12 below) and published in 1843 under the title, *The Symbolism of Churches and Church Ornaments: A Translation of the First Book of the Rationale Divinorum Officiorum, Written by William Durandus. Sometime Bishop of Mende* (Leeds: T. W. Green, 1843). In their preface Neale and Webb said that they had worked from a Roman edition of 1473, which they described as "a magnificent specimen of typography: the words are excessively contracted; and there are double columns to each page. Our copy is partially illuminated and the binding is ornamented with a border of the Evangelistic Symbols" (p. x).

the eighteenth century, under the influence of Protestant religious requirements, architects and clergymen had sought, when they built new churches or
remodeled old ones, to "place the people near the minister, so that even at the
cost of some dignity and propriety they could see what was happening and
follow the service."[8] New churches in this style were wider in proportion to
their length than medieval examples. They had no aisles, and galleries were
introduced at the sides and across the back. The chancels which resembled the
medieval kind—a smaller, lower, eastern chamber, continuous with the long
dimension of the nave but cut off from it by a screen—were omitted altogether.
When an old church had such a feature, it was often abandoned as a ceremonial center. Natural light from large windows filled with clear glass replaced
medieval dimness.

The ecclesiologists found all these changes distasteful. Modern revisions in
the service seemed to them symptomatic of the secularization of the Church,
which had, in their view, caused it to lose its constructive social influence. The
medieval parish church had been designed to house the liturgy which the
Society approved. Its form, features, diluted light, organization, and color were
directly opposed to those of the architecture of the modern ceremonial pattern.
It is difficult to discern whether the liturgical or the architectural objective
came first into the Society's program. Both were attempts to reform the nineteenth-century Church, and both expressed the artistic and social restlessness
which characterized the Gothic revival. The ecclesiologists had a taste for the
rich decoration and the dark but brilliant colors of Gothic, and they admired
the confinement of the ritual to the chancel, sheltered from the public gaze, in
the medieval churches. Most nineteenth-century ceremonial buildings, whatever their style, were oriented inward, and thus the ecclesiologists' determination to reverse the direction in which church design had been moving for more
than a century was in accord with an instinctive early Victorian preference for
enclosure of interior spaces in architecture. The ecclesiologists belonged to
their time.

The Cambridge Camden Society was unable to separate events in England
from those abroad. The conflicts and rivalries in which it was involved at

[8] (London: Faber and Faber, 1943), p. 203; see esp. chaps. 6 and 7.

home influenced the decisions it made in its American affairs, with the result that the Society took umbrage and behaved in a dictatorial, illogical, and high-handed manner whenever its American friends showed the least independence of mind. The stormy character of the Society's missionary activities is incomprehensible without knowledge of the English background and some awareness of the relationship between the Society and other groups within the English revival. Full descriptions of the Society and its history are available,[9] and this review will stress only what is relevant to the transatlantic connection.

Tension, irascibility, and dogmatism marked the life of the Society. It had begun in 1836 as an association of undergraduate students at Trinity College, Cambridge; John Mason Neale[10] and Edward Jacob Boyce[11] were its founders. They shared an avocational interest in medieval art, to which they were attracted because they had resolved to enter the priesthood. Other men of similar

[9] There is a recent and detailed history of the Cambridge Camden Society (after 1846 the Ecclesiological Society) by James F. White, *The Cambridge Movement, the Ecclesiologists and the Gothic Revival* (Cambridge: Cambridge University Press, 1962). The chapter on the movement in Sir Kenneth Clark's *The Gothic Revival* (London: Constable, 1928), fits the Society into the picture of the whole revival. There are numerous and illuminating references to the Society and its influence on architecture in Henry-Russell Hitchcock's *Early Victorian Architecture in Britain*, 2 vols. (New Haven: Yale University Press, 1954), and his *Architecture, Nineteenth and Twentieth Centuries* (Baltimore: Penguin Books, 1958). A recent biography of John Mason Neale (see n. 10 below) by A. G. Lough, *The Influence of John Mason Neale* (London: Society for the Propagation of Christian Knowledge, 1962), is essential for the history of the Society. M. H. Port's *Six Hundred New Churches, a Study of the Church Building Commission, 1818–1856, and Its Church Building Activities* (London: S.P.C.K., 1961) covers the work of the English church building societies.

[10] Neale (1818–1866) entered Trinity College, Cambridge, in 1836 and was made deacon and chaplain of Downing College, Cambridge, in 1841. Finding the latter position not to his liking, he resigned. Ordained a priest in 1842, he became rector of Crawley, in Sussex, but left the post because of ill health after a short tenure. In 1846 he became Warden of Sackville College, East Grinstead, and remained there for twenty years. Neale was deeply interested in the role of religious orders and established the Society of St. Margaret. He was a poet and wrote many hymns, including some for special groups of workers, such as iron founders and glass blowers. He was also a student of the history of the Eastern Orthodox Church. Neale's life was a masterpiece of a kind of mid-nineteenth-century mentality. He was scholarly, persistent, deeply religious, intelligent, tolerant and brutally intolerant, emotional and disdainful of emotion.

[11] Boyce later became rector of Houghton, Stockbridge, Hampshire. He was residing there when he wrote *A Memorial of the Cambridge Camden Society, Instituted May, 1839 and the Ecclesiological (Late Cambridge Camden) Society* (London and Cambridge: Palmer and Bell, 1888). He was the author of various religious tracts and sermons.

inclination soon joined them—Benjamin Webb,[12] who entered Trinity[13] in 1838, Harvey Goodwin from Caius, and F. A. Paley from St. John's were first members of this group, which initially organized walking trips to churches worthy of study in the Cambridge region and began to accumulate information about medieval architecture. Their findings were far from reassuring and sometimes downright alarming, for the buildings they visited were poorly maintained and often brutally remodeled and services were conducted in a perfunctory manner. Moved by these discoveries, the Society from its inception decided to do what it could to reform church ceremony and to restore and preserve medieval buildings. These ambitions were easily enlarged. When the Society declared that it would attempt to control the design of new churches, its contentious career had begun. A generation of churchmen fell under its influence, and those who refused to accept its tenets were involved with the Society in spite of themselves, because of their position as members of the opposition.

[12] Webb (1819–1885) is known for his work with the Cambridge Camden Society, his attainments as a critic and historian of architecture, and his achievements as rector of St. Andrew's, Wells Street, London. He entered Trinity College, Cambridge, in 1838 and received his degree in 1842. He was curate to the Venerable Thomas Thorp at Kemerton, and it was while he was there that he translated, with Neale, the first book of Durandus. The postscript to *The Symbolism of Churches* was written from Kemerton in August, 1843. By 1849 Webb was at Brasted, Kent, where he commissioned William Butterfield as architect and ordered stained glass windows from A. W. Pugin. There are letters from Pugin in connection with this order describing Webb as "a capital man and the editor of the *Ecclesiologist.*" In 1851 Webb became perpetual curate of Sheen, Staffordshire, and in 1862 went to St. Andrew's, Wells Street, as rector, where his energetic leadership resulted in constructive educational activities and improvements in church ceremony. Like others of his associates, Webb was interested in church music and composed hymns. In addition to his collaboration with Neale on *The Symbolism of Churches*, he was the sole author of *Sketches of Continental Ecclesiology: or, Church Notes in Belgium. Germany, and Italy* (London: Joseph Masters, 1848).

Webb assisted the architect George Edmund Street to secure the patrons and commissions which launched his career. (The details of this association have been described by H. R. Hitchcock in an article on Street in the *Journal of the Society of Architectural Historians*, 19 [December, 1960].) In the course of his life within the Church Webb also employed the architect R. C. Carpenter to plan the restoration and additions to St. Nicholas, Kemerton. The consecration of the restored church took place in 1847, and the *Ecclesiologist* (8 [December, 1847]) carried a description of the building.

[13] Trinity College was a likely center for the study of medieval art; it had a tradition of religious and artistic activity. Kenelm Digby and Ambrose Phillips de Lisle, converts to Roman Catholicism and amateurs of medieval art, were at the college in the 1820's. Trinity ultimately gave more men to the Oxford Movement than did any college at Oxford (Bernard Holland, *Memoirs of Kenelm Henry Digby* [London: Longmans', 1919], p. 48).

Events of these early years are somewhat confused.[14] Boyce, who became the official historian of the Society, says that, although first called the Ecclesiological Society, the organization changed its name almost immediately to the Camden Society. In 1839, when another organization by that name was founded, the ecclesiologists again changed the name of their group to the Cambridge Camden Society. In spite of the informal arrangements which at first prevailed, the membership grew rapidly, for its leaders had expressed opinions welcomed by their contemporaries. In 1839, a sudden upheaval over a blackballing incident, the details of which are not clear in any account of the Society's history, demonstrated the need for a revised constitution to govern the organization. Neale, Webb, and Boyce appealed to the Venerable Thomas Thorp, Fellow and Tutor of Trinity College and Archdeacon and Chancellor of Bristol, to become President and assist in the reorganization. With the aid of Thorp a new constitution was prepared, and because of his presence among the officers, prominent clerics and officials of the University joined as members and officers.[15] The new constitution established honorary memberships and provided for the election of patrons to encourage further distinguished participants. At the time of the installation of the constitution of 1839, forty-three new regular members joined the rank and file. Trinity and St. John's were heavily represented.

[14] White's *Cambridge Movement* and Boyce's *Memorial* are the sources from which the narrative of these years is taken.
[15] After 1839, Professors Corrie, Isaacson, Whewell, and Smith became vice-presidents, and the list of patrons included the bishops of Gloucester, Bristol, Ely, and Nova Scotia (the membership is given and discussed in Boyce, *Memorial*). Professor William Whewell (1794–1866) was an intellectual leader of his generation. He entered Trinity College in 1812 and was elected a Fellow of the College in 1817. He was intimately associated with Julius Hare, George Peacock, and Hugh James Rose, members of a group of Cambridge scholars who were studying German literature. Whewell's first publications were in the field of mathematics, but by 1822 he had become engrossed with the subject of medieval architecture. He escorted parties of students abroad, and Kenelm Digby was among those so favored. Whewell's *Architectural Notes* appeared in 1830 and was expanded in subsequent editions. In 1841 he became Master of Trinity College. His connections with the Cambridge Camden Society began in 1839, but by 1843 his name had disappeared from the membership list. Professor George E. Corrie (1793–1885) was Norrisian Professor of Divinity (1838–54) and Master of Jesus College. He wrote on historical and theological subjects, and he was founder and president of the Cambridge Antiquarian Society, which was established when the Cambridge Camden Society left Cambridge.

THE BACKGROUND

The constitution defined the aims of the Society, established the number and duties of its officers, and declared that it had resolved to "promote the study of Ecclesiastical Architecture and Antiquities, and the restoration of mutilated Architectural remains."[16] The most important administrative change introduced in 1839 was the creation of a committee of fourteen, "composed of the President, Vice-Presidents and six ordinary members," to attend to the day-to-day work of the association and direct development of policy.[17] As might have been anticipated, Neale, Boyce, and Webb were elected Chairman, Treasurer, and Secretary, respectively, and in return for performance of these tasks they were given considerable power. Though in the course of its long life the Society was to undergo further reorganizations and periods of conflict and ominous disagreement, Neale and Webb never lost their positions of authority. When Boyce left the inner circle of the Committee in 1844, he was replaced by A. J. B. Hope,[18] who, with Neale and Webb, formed a triumvirate. Alterations in the Society merely consolidated their strength. Committee members came and went, regular members resigned and others joined; everyone in the Society either agreed with these three or withdrew in defeat.

The reorganization of 1839 had eased a tense situation only temporarily, for the Committee it established set out to expand the Society's ambitions and to redefine its antiquarian and preservationist preoccupations to include the statement that Gothic was the only Christian style. The vice-presidents, whose

---

[16] Boyce, *Memorial*, p. 36.

[17] *Ibid.*, p. 37.

[18] Alexander James Beresford-Hope (1820–1887), ecclesiologist, politician, connoisseur, son of Thomas Hope, graduated from Trinity College, Cambridge, in 1841. An enemy of Disraeli, he entered Parliament as a conservative member from Maidstone and remained there until 1852, after which he was not returned for Maidstone until 1857. In 1865 he was elected for Stoke-upon-Trent. From 1868 until his death he represented the University of Cambridge. A devoted churchman, Hope drew upon his sizable personal fortune to build and repair churches; St. Augustine's Abbey, Canterbury, and All Saints', Margaret Street, London, both by William Butterfield, were among his benefactions. In 1839 Hope was a member of the Cambridge Camden Society, and he became a member of the Committee in 1840, appeared again in its membership list in 1844, and was its chairman from 1845 to 1849, after the Ecclesiological Society was formed. In 1846 he declared before the Oxford Architectural Society that a turning point in English ecclesiological science had occurred when the English parish church of the Decorated period was recognized as a monument of critical importance.

positions were honorary and who tended to play a passive role, became alarmed as they perceived this growing concern with the traditions of ceremony, a topic reminiscent to some of the development of Tractarianism at Oxford.

Neale and Webb had suggested that the Society should produce a publication which would reach those members who had graduated and left Cambridge, and it was they who assumed the burdens of editorship when the *Ecclesiologist* began publication in November, 1841.[19] The long-postponed and often threatened break between the Committee and the conservative element in the Society came when the policies of Neale and Webb were set forth in print for everyone to read. In the first issue of the *Ecclesiologist* the editors announced the subjects with which they proposed to concern themselves: "Church Building at home and in the Colonies: Church Restoration in England and abroad: the theory and practice of Ecclesiastical Architecture: the investigation of Church Antiquities: the connection of Architecture and Ritual: the science of Symbolism: the principles of Church Arrangements: Church Musick and all the Decorative Arts which can be made subservient to Religion: the exposing and denouncing of glaring cases of Church Desecration: Criticisms upon Designs for and upon New Churches."[20] Determined to take at the outset a positive stand in support of their declared principles, the editors published a harsh review of a new church in Cambridge. An acrimonious dispute began: twelve prominent honorary and regular members protested, saying, with justice, that "there exists in some quarters a desire to convert the Society into an engine of polemical theology, instead of an instrument for promoting the study and practice of Ecclesiastical Architecture."[21]

Though they were not as dramatic as the resolution to "expose," "denounce," and "criticize," which had inspired the attack on the church in Cambridge, two of the stated objectives of the *Ecclesiologist* were to be of the

---

[19] Boyce, *Memorial*, p. 17. Of the 159 contributions in the first volume of the *Ecclesiologist*, Neale was responsible for 47, Webb for 46, and Paley for 36.

[20] *Ibid.*, p. 11.

[21] See White, *Cambridge Movement*, pp. 117–18; a full discussion of the dispute is given there. The account of it in the *Ecclesiologist* is specific and revealing ("Report of the Twenty-Third Meeting of the Cambridge Camden Society, Monday, December 6, 1841," *E.*, 1 [December, 1841]:22–26).

utmost importance to the future of the whole ecclesiological enterprise. The first was the editors' expression of interest in church building in the "colonies," for it was to bring the influence of the Society to North America. The second was the rather mystifying reference to "the science of Symbolism," which was, in fact, an allusion to a translation of Book I of the *Rationale divinorum officiorum* by Durandus on which Neale and Webb were hard at work in 1841. When this book appeared in 1843, under the title *The Symbolism of Churches and Church Ornaments,* it contained not only Book I from Durandus, but the first and second chapters of *The Mystical Mirror of the Church* by Hugh of St. Victor, portions of Book V of Durandus, and an appendix of notes taken from Martene.[22] In a revealing Introduction of one hundred and twenty-five pages Neale and Webb explained their theories and set forth their opinions of other writers on medieval architecture and architects working in the field of church design. At last the full pattern of ideas which had been developed by the *avant-garde* of the Society was available in coherent, printed form.

In order to understand the meaning of this statement and appreciate its importance as a document of ecclesiological theory, one must have some knowledge of the architectural scene upon which its authors hoped to impose their views. Neale and Webb claimed that the superiority of Gothic was a product of its "sacramentality," a quality which they defined as "the idea that, by the outward and visible form, is signified something inward and spiritual; that the material fabric symbolizes, embodies, figures, represents, expresses, answers to, some abstract meaning."[23] There was, of course, little difference between this statement and the one Poole had made a year earlier,[24] which explains why *The Appropriate Character of Church Architecture* received the

---

[22] See White, *Cambridge Movement,* pp. 68–77, for a discussion of this important book. All page references to *The Symbolism of Churches* here are to the third edition (London: Gibbings and Company, 1906). It should be noted that the postscript to the first edition is dated August 16, 1843, which dates Neale and Webb's work on the translation (see also n. 7 above). *The Symbolism of Churches* enjoyed an international reputation. A French translation was made in 1847, *Du Symbolisme dans Les Églises Du Moyen Age par J. Mason Neale et Benj. Webb M.A. de l'Université de Cambridge traduit de l'Anglais par M. V. O. Avec Une Introduction, Des Additions et Des Notes par M. l'Abbé J.-J. Bourassé* (Tours: Mame et Cie., 1847).

[23] *The Symbolism of Churches,* p. xxvi.

[24] See p. 9 above.

endorsement of Neale and Webb, who usually disapproved of the work of almost every other writer in the field.

The Introduction also announced that two ecclesiological policies, which had been earlier discussed in the *Ecclesiologist,* had become doctrine. It pronounced the Decorated style to be Gothic at its finest and recommended the English parish church of the fourteenth century as the model for revival. Reasoning that the rule of "sacramentality" linked the design of churches with the quality of the religion they were built to serve, Neale and Webb concluded that art had been at its best in the fourteenth century because the Church, as an institution, was immature before that date and decadent after it. "The Anglican architect" needed only to know enough "of the earlier styles to be able to restore the deeply interesting churches which they left us as precious heirlooms; enough of the Debased styles, to take warning from their decline." Architects should "choose the glorious architecture of the fourteenth century; and, just as no man has more than one handwriting, so in this one language alone will he express his architectural ideas."[25] In support of this decision the Committee, which was in fact Neale and Webb, persuaded the Society to sponsor the preparation of measured drawings of selected medieval churches in the best style of the best period, that they might be made available to clergymen and their architects.

Though they had arrived on the scene rather later than others, Neale and Webb did not propose to accept passively a secondary place among the champions of the Gothic cause. *The Symbolism of Churches and Church Ornaments* opened, therefore, on a negative note, as its authors went to great lengths to enumerate the errors which had been made by those who had earlier explained Gothic and advocated its revival. As they discussed the works of eleven authors and the publications of the Oxford Society for Promoting the Study of Gothic Architecture, a group with which the Cambridge Society had had sometimes friendly and sometimes unfriendly relations, Neale and Webb found the observations of all wanting when they were compared with the ecclesiological theory of Gothic.

George R. Lewis had trespassed upon the domain to which Neale and Webb proposed to lay claim when, in 1842, the year before the appearance of *The Symbolism of Churches and Church Ornaments,* he published his *Illustrations*

[25] P. xxiv.

of Kilpeck Church, Herefordshire . . . with an Essay on Ecclesiastical Design,[26] for in it he had included a translation of portions of Durandus, Book I. Though Lewis had modestly attributed his translation to "the kindness of a friend," he had every right to consider himself the person who had brought the thirteenth-century authority out of obscurity. Durandus had been known before 1842; a singularly intelligent critic had, in fact, quoted him unsympathetically but at some length in the *Quarterly Review* as early as 1822. But Lewis' inclusion in his book of the extensive extract from the *Rationale divinorum officiorum* occurred at just the time when the revivalists were ready to accept him. Neale and Webb, who could hardly have been pleased when Lewis usurped any claim they might have had to exclusive sponsorship of a Durandus revival, brought their heaviest artillery into action. They disposed of Lewis by saying that "his book excited some attention at the time of publication, and was met by considerable ridicule in many quarters," and they put particular stress on the inaccuracy of his assumption that "*all* church architecture was *intentionally* symbolical.*" "Till church architecture was fully developed," they said, "we do not think that its real significance was understood to its full extent by those who used it." In other words, Lewis had not recommended the Decorated style.

A. W. Pugin[27] was less easy to refute, for as the most gifted and best

[26] *Illustrations of Kilpeck Church, Herefordshire: In a series of Drawings made on the Spot with an Essay on Ecclesiastical Design, and A Descriptive Interpretation* (London: William Pickering and G. R. Lewis, 1842). George Robert Lewis (1782–1871), a painter, topographer, and author of works on architecture, with his brother, F. C. Lewis, executed aquatint illustrations for twenty-two books, among which were Combe's *History of Westminster Abbey* and *History of Oxford* and Varley's *Principles of Landscape Design.* Lewis studied under Henry Fuseli, had exhibited at the Royal Academy, and accompanied Thomas Frognell Dibdin as a draftsman-assistant in the preparation of the latter's *Bibliographical and Picturesque Tour through France and Germany* (1821). Lewis may have become acquainted with Durandus through his employment by Dibdin, since the *Rationale* is mentioned in Dibdin's bibliographical notes. He came to the study of Gothic late in life, and followed the book on Kilpeck Church with one on Shobden, Herefordshire.

[27] Augustus Welby Pugin (1812–1852) was an architect, a designer in the decorative arts, author, and a leader in the Gothic and Catholic revivals in England (he became a Roman Catholic in 1835). He established his reputation as a controversial architect in 1836, when he published his first book, *Contrasts,* in which he attributed the decline in the arts to the Reformation. As an architect Pugin usually practiced within the Roman Catholic Communion, though his largest single commission was to give Charles Barry decorative assistance in the design of the Houses of Parliament. There are two biographies of Pugin, one written shortly after his death by Benjamin Ferrey, *Recollections of A. N. W. Pugin and His Father, Augustus Pugin: with Notices of their Works* (London: Stanford, 1861), and that of M. Trappes-Lomax, *Pugin, a Medieval Victorian* (London: Sheed and Ward, 1932).

known of the partisans of Gothic, he occupied an all but impregnable position, and he had earlier independently and publicly reached every conclusion to which the ecclesiologists were laying claim in 1843. Since Gothic art and architecture had been products of a Roman Catholic society, the existence of Pugin among them was a perpetual threat to Protestant Gothic revivalists: Pugin was an outspoken convert to Roman Catholicism whose presence reminded Anglican believers in Gothic that they might, by their own historical logic, be forced to acknowledge the institutions which had inspired the art they so admired. Before the publication of *The Symbolism of Churches* the Society had made no secret of its approval of Pugin's architecture and writing. His relations with the ecclesiologists had been friendly; in 1842 he had toured Ely with a party of the members of the Society.[28] Neale and Webb were in no way restrained by their association with Pugin, however, when they set out to describe the weaknesses in the position he had adopted in the brilliant and pioneering books he had published between 1836 and 1843.[29] In defense of Neale and Webb it should be noted that Pugin had, in fact, given them every opportunity to pick his ideas to pieces, for, though he was by nature forthrightly logical, his religious convictions and his architectural acumen had led him in two directions at the same time.

Pugin was in a dilemma which he chose to overlook rather than resolve. His admiration for medieval architecture and his recommendation that, for social, religious, and artistic reasons it be revived were contradicted by his observations on the principles of design and the relationships which necessarily united the art of building and the society of which it was a part. Through his study of Gothic Pugin had arrived at basic observations on architecture which were not identified with any historical style. In 1841 in *The True Principles of Pointed or Christian Architecture* he had declared that "there should be no features about a building which are not necessary for convenience, construction or propriety," that "all ornament should consist of enrichment of the essential con-

---

[28] Diary of A. W. Pugin, May 3, 1842.
[29] Particularly his *Contrasts: or a Parallel Between the Noble Edifices of the Fourteenth and Fifteenth Centuries, and Similar Buildings of the Present Day: Showing the Present Decay of Taste,* which by 1843 had appeared in two editions, the first published in Salisbury by the author in 1836, the second (London: Dolman, 1841) containing additional plates, and *The True Principles of Pointed or Christian Architecture: Set Forth in Two Lectures Delivered at St. Marie's Oscott* (London: John Weale, 1841).

struction of the building," that "the smallest detail should have a meaning or serve a purpose," and that construction "should vary with the material employed." Pugin perceived that these rules contained no positive recommendation of Gothic, his chosen style, and he hastened to unite his proposal to revive Gothic with his principles of design by adding that "in pointed architecture alone . . . these principles had been carried out" and that "the architects of the Middle Ages were the first who turned the natural properties of the various materials to their full account and made their mechanism a vehicle for their art." No amount of enthusiasm for Gothic could obscure the fact that the principles could also be used to justify any building in any style which measured up to their criteria, and this was exactly the weakness which Neale and Webb were pointing out when they said that Pugin's principles, and his notion that buildings in which they were realized possessed a "reality" which others did not, were open to many and perhaps unorthodox interpretations. They might, in fact, actually encourage architects to employ styles other than Gothic. What Pugin defined as "reality," they said, was not enough, for "what can be more *real* than a pyramid, yet what less Christian?" In the eyes of the ecclesiologists, Pugin had failed to recognize the great principle of "sacramentality," which separated Gothic from other historical styles. Even his buildings demonstrated this fatal shortcoming, said the authors of *The Symbolism of Churches*, and they added that if they cared to do so they could easily detail the cases in which "bold expedients and fearless licence" had caused Pugin to go wrong. Having delivered this opinion, one of the two, probably Webb, who was the milder in nature and was closer to Pugin, must have felt some misgivings, for in a postscript the authors admitted that "persons" who had read the proofs had questioned "whether the writers had given Mr. Pugin sufficient credit for several passages in his works which seem to *involve* the principle now contended for." The apology was awkward, asserting as it still did that Pugin had proposed no adequate substitute for the authors' own view.

Though they preferred not to share their conclusions with anyone, least of all Pugin, Neale and Webb were clearly in the embarrassing position of having to do so. As early as the winter of 1840, Pugin had remarked in the manuscript of *True Principles* which he was then preparing that the loss of emphasis on "*height* or the *vertical* principle" had marked the onset of decadence in Gothic design. He had also described height as an expression of the Resurrection. In his pamphlet on his Church of St. Oswald, Liverpool, which was published in 1842, he had indicated that he knew and appreciated the writing of Durandus. To make matters worse he had observed in a long footnote in *True Principles* that "from the various symptoms of decline which I have shown to have existed in the later pointed works, I feel convinced that Christian architecture had gone its length, and it must necessarily have destroyed itself by departing from its own principles in the pursuit of novelty, or it must have fallen back on its pure and ancient models." To evade charges of sympathy with Roman Catholicism and validate their claim of originality, the Anglican partisans had to rid themselves, once and for all, of the association with Pugin. The matter was made even more pressing by Pugin's naïvely enthusiastic praise of the Society in an article he published in the *Dublin Review* in 1842, in which he implied that the Society's convictions coincided with his own in every fundamental way.[30] An added source of embarrassment was St. Oswald's itself, for in it Pugin had produced the first polished example of the very parish church style the ecclesiologists were proposing to call their own[31] (Fig. I–1).

Other victims of Neale and Webb's attack included the Reverend John Lewis Petit,[32] whose *Remarks on Church Architecture* had appeared in 1841. They

[30] Pugin's comments about the ecclesiologists were contained in an article which appeared in "On the Present State of Ecclesiastical Architecture in England" (*Dublin Review*, 23 [February, 1842]), which was later republished as the second article in Pugin's *The Present State of Ecclesiastical Architecture in England* (London: Dolman, 1843). In the same article Pugin also discussed Durandus at length in a footnote (pp. 117–20).

[31] See Pugin, *Description of the Catholic Church of Saint Oswald, Old Swan, Liverpool* (Liverpool: Rockliff and Ellis, 1842): "Most persons labor under the erroneous impression that these decorations have been revived by the mere arbitrary whim of an individual, as a matter of taste; but were they to examine with attention the work of Catholic artists, while they worked in accordance *with tradition* they would readily perceive that, however varied their talents and power of expressive delineation they never departed from the common rules to which their greatest efforts were subservient." On the importance of St. Oswald's to English Gothic revival church design, see Hitchcock, *Early Victorian Architecture*, pp. 73–74.

[32] Petit (1810–1868), priest and historian of Gothic, was educated at Eton and Trinity College and admitted to Holy Orders in 1824. Petit never undertook pastoral duties but instead devoted his energies to artistic and archeological work and writing. He illustrated his own books, but he was an artist rather than a proficient architectural draftsman. Between 1839, the year in which he wrote *Remarks on Church Architecture* (2 vols. [London: Burns, 1841]), and 1854 he published a book a year. Many were short studies of individual buildings, that on Tewkesbury Abbey being typical. His most elaborate publication was *Architectural Studies in France* (1852), on which he collaborated with Professor Dela-

Figure I-1. St. Oswald's, Liverpool. Southeast view. A. W. Pugin. 1839–42. (Now destroyed.)
Of this church Henry-Russell Hitchcock says, "Here in this tiny suburban Roman Catholic
church . . . Pugin first established a new model, almost a new building type, quite
discontinuous with Georgian church architecture."

also challenged the whole approach employed by Thomas Hope[33] in his *Essay on Architecture,* which had been published in 1835 after the death of its author. They described Francis Grose,[34] John Milner,[35] and John Carter[36] as important, though primitive, writers who had mistakenly assumed that one could understand medieval art simply by knowing all there was to know about

---

motte. He was the founder of the British Archeological Institute at Cambridge in 1844 and an honorary member of the Institute of British Architects.

The *Ecclesiologist* never approved of Petit. In 1842 the reviewer of his *Remarks* said: "It may surely be with reason remarked, that to fill volume after volume with dull theories on the history of Romanesque, or the revived Roman or Lombardic, or Italian styles, can be of little use to English church builders, unless it be the wish and intention on the part of writers, that our own most pure and beautiful models, so admirably adapted to, because reared by, the genius of our Church, our nation, and our climate, should be superseded by the semi-pagan varieties imported from lands and people differing widely from our own" (*E.,* 1 [March, 1842]:88).

[33] Hope (1770–1831), connoisseur and author, was born of an English family resident in Holland. He settled in England in 1796 after extensive travel in the Near East. He was wealthy and a devoted patron of the arts; John Flaxman, Antonio Canova, and A. B. Thorvaldsen were among the artists he assisted. Hope wrote a number of important books: *Household Furniture and Interior Decoration,* a central document of the Classical influence in decorative design in England, appeared in 1807; *Costume of the Ancients* in 1809; and a romance, *Anastasius,* published anonymously, was acknowledged by Hope as his own when it was enthusiastically received. Two books of his were published posthumously, *An Essay on the Origins and Prospects of Man* and *An Essay on Architecture.* The latter, which was important in the development of the taste for architecture in pre-Gothic styles, appeared in 1835 in two volumes, one of text and one of plates which were drawn by the author. It gave a chronological account of Early Christian, Byzantine, and Italian Romanesque styles. Hope explained the transition to Gothic by flatly stating that England had invented it.

[34] Grose (1731–1791) was an antiquary and draftsman whose comments on medieval architecture in England formed a part of his books on historical topography. His *Antiquities of England and Wales,* published from 1783 to 1787 in four folio volumes, established his reputation as an authority on medieval building.

[35] Milner (1752–1826) was a Roman Catholic bishop, the Vicar Apostolic of the Western District of England. Trained at the English College in Douay, he served as a priest in England after 1777. In 1792, while living in Winchester, he directed the construction of a chapel in the Gothic style. He was an antiquary of ability. After 1802 he resided at Wolverhampton as Bishop of Castabala. His *History, Civil and Ecclesiastical, and Survey of Antiquities of Winchester* (1798–1801) is a masterpiece of topographical literature. Pugin admired Milner greatly, in particular his *Letters to a Prebendary* (1800).

[36] Carter (1748–1817) was an architectural illustrator employed by the Society of Antiquaries, by Richard Gough, a notable topographical author, and by Horace Walpole, to whom Carter's *Specimens of Ancient Sculpture and Painting* (1780) was dedicated.

it. They paused long enough to reconsider the contributions of George A. Poole, and concluded that he had failed to comprehend the scope of the principles of symbolism and interpretations he had earlier put forward. They found the publications and policies of the Oxford Architectural Society inadequate for the monumental tasks at hand, and Thomas Rickman[37] was called a "separatist" unable to understand the symbolic system of Gothic. Even Matthew H. Bloxam,[38] an authority with whom they might have agreed without endangering their reputation, appeared to Neale and Webb to have reached only partially satisfactory conclusions.

This discussion of Neale and Webb's *The Symbolism of Churches* will provide a glimpse of the ecclesiological leaders whom the Americans were to encounter. Jealous of their authority, they were unwilling to share their North American following with anyone. They were embattled and defensive about the originality of their ideas, and they feared the taint of Roman Catholicism. But it was precisely because the Society was preoccupied with its precarious position that it actively sought an audience abroad: the rapidity with which ecclesiological ideas spread in America was, at least in part, a result of the

[37] The major contribution of Rickman (1776–1841), an architect and draftsman, was his early study of English Gothic and his classification of its periods and styles. His descriptive nomenclature, which he first published in 1817, is still in use. By the late 1830's it was usual for Rickman to be thought of as a pioneer but far from an expert; he was often called "Rickman the Quaker," and his own Gothic revival designs, such as the New Court, St. John's College, Cambridge, of 1827 to 1831, were felt to be feeble and primitive, if not entirely incorrect.

[38] Matthew Holbeache Bloxam (*ca.* 1804–*ca.* 1886) and his brother John Rouse Bloxam were associated with religious and artistic affairs in the Anglican community of the early nineteenth century. J. R. Bloxam, a friend and associate of John Henry Newman, was curate at Littlemore (1837) and, as a Fellow at Magdalen College, Oxford, was on friendly terms with Ambrose Phillipps de Lisle and Pugin. M. H. Bloxam was an antiquary and an authority on medieval architecture. He resided at Rugby, where he was employed at Rugby School. In 1843 he was made an honorary member of the Cambridge Camden Society. His books included *The Principles of Gothic Ecclesiastical Architecture Elucidated by Questions and Answers*, first published in 1829, which went into ten more editions, the last of which appeared in 1859. His other major work was *A Glimpse at the Monumental Architecture and Sculpture of Great Britain* (1834). Bloxam was convinced that the Decorated style was the finest expression of English Gothic. In the fourth edition of his *Principles* (1844), he asserted that it was "justly considered the most beautiful style of English ecclesiastical architecture." The ecclesiologists hinted that Bloxam had modified and improved his theories as a result of their work (Neale and Webb, *The Symbolism of Churches*, p. xxxii).

beleaguered position in which the ecclesiologists found themselves in England. It was also inevitable that some of the tensions which characterized the life of the Society would affect its attitude toward American ecclesiology.

After the publication of *The Symbolism of Churches* it became painfully clear that the Society could not continue as it had been constituted, for the zeal of the Committee had alienated many of its more prominent and more conservative members, who were within the University faculties. The younger members, the larger number of whom had left the University, tended to support and follow the Committee. In January and February, 1845, a struggle for power ensued between these two groups, and a dissenting minority set out to curb the Committee and its policies. Secure in its feeling that the majority of the rank-and-file members would follow, the Committee withdrew from Cambridge and the battle for authority and moved the offices of the organization to London. An impressive number of members resigned in protest. Neale and Webb acquired the copyright to the *Ecclesiologist* and continued to publish it independently until May, 1846, when the Society was officially revived under the new name of the Ecclesiological Society (late Cambridge Camden Society), and resumed responsibility for its periodical.

Purged of persons who would not accept the theories of Neale, Webb, and Hope, the Society was prepared to do all it could to make its ambitious program a reality. The statement of its aims was formally revised, and it announced that it was dedicated to the promotion and study of "Christian Art and Antiquities" and "the restoration of Ecclesiastical remains." This was the transformed, belligerent Society with which the Americans were to associate themselves.

Old scores now had to be settled. Though Neale and Webb had already declared their independence of Pugin, the Venerable Thomas Thorp, who had remained within the Society through the turmoil of 1845 and 1846, wanted all association with Pugin formally terminated. In January, 1846, while the *Ecclesiologist* was being published by Neale and Webb, it printed a truly damaging critique of Pugin's works and reputation. The Society had its reasons for severing all challenging relationships with Roman Catholic enthusiasts of Gothic. In 1844, Charles-Forbes-René, Comte de Montalembert,[39] had refused

---

[39] Montalembert (1810–1870) was an author, polemicist, associate of Lammenais, expert on medieval art, and a political figure. Son of a Scottish mother and a French father,

an honorary membership offered him by Neale. In a long letter to Neale
Montalembert carefully described a situation which, though tacitly understood,
had never before been articulated. He said that he could not tolerate in silence
the Society's "unwarrantable and most unjustified assumption of the name of
Catholic by people and things belonging to the actual Church of England."
Montalembert did not mince his words. The activities of the Society, he said,

---

Montalembert lived in England and France in his early life and maintained significant contacts with the developing Catholic revival in England. He was closely associated with
Ambrose Phillipps, Kenelm Digby, the Earl of Shrewsbury, and A. W. Pugin. Between 1830
and 1833, until the latter broke with the Church, Montalembert worked with Lammenais.
He continuously questioned the government on Catholic rights, the defense of Catholics
abroad, and the position France should take in relation to the Papacy. At first he supported
Napoleon III but became disappointed in him and withdrew from participation in the
government.

Montalembert's major effort was expended on the cause of freedom of education in
France, the scholarly pursuit of medieval history, and the encouragement of the study of
medieval art. His great ambition, never realized, was to write a life of St. Bernard. However, he did write a number of books, of which *The Monks of the West*, published in France
in 1860, was best known. The re-establishment of monasticism in England in the course of
the Catholic revival was in part due to his influence upon Ambrose Phillipps and the Earl
of Shrewsbury. In the course of his career he made a number of important statements on
art, the earliest of which was a public letter to Victor Hugo, in the *Revue des Deux Mondes*
of March 1, 1833, entitled "Du Vandalisme en France," describing the treatment of
medieval buildings and art in France. In 1838 he praised the Nazarenes and Overbeck. In
1845 he fought a successful personal battle to obtain funds from the French government
to repair the Cathedral of Notre Dame, and he continued to check upon and report errors
in the works of restoration and preservation. It was largely because of his efforts that the
Comité Historique des Arts et des Monuments was founded in 1837. His views on art were
profoundly influenced by those of his friend and teacher A. F. Rio, the art historian.

Montalembert's letter to Neale was printed in various places at various times. It first
appeared as *A Letter Addressed to a Reverend Member of the Camden Society, on the
Architectural, Artistical, and Archaeological Movements of the Puseyites* (Liverpool:
Booker and Co., 1844). Subsequently it was picked up and used for their own ends by
persons opposed to ecclesiology, as *A Re-Print of a Letter Addressed to a Revd. Member
of the Cambridge Camden Society by M. le Comte de Montalembert, Accompanied by a
Few Remarks and Queries* (Cheltenham, 1845). In the *Oeuvres de M. Le Comte de
Montalembert*, from which the quotations in the text are taken, it appears in volume 6
(Paris: Le Coffre at Cie, 1861), pp. 366–87.

At least a year before Montalembert's letter to Neale, Pugin had commented in the
Dublin Review on English High Churchmen who were not associated with the ecclesiologists in exactly the terms Montalembert was to use. He said of an author in the *Christian
Remembrancer*, "He evidently belongs to that class of persons who assume the title of
Catholic as a *nom de guerre*, the better to forward certain heretical designs in which they
are engaged, and while professing to revive truth and antiquity, are proved by their writings
to be the promulgators of dangerous errors and foolish conceits" (p. 117).

were "an attempt to steal away from us and appropriate to the use of a faction of the Church of England the glorious title of Catholic. . . ."

Free of Pugin, disdained by Montalembert, embroiled in endless arguments with fellow members of the Anglican Communion, the Ecclesiological Society set out in 1846 to realize its missionary program. The *Ecclesiologist* expanded its coverage of church building in "the Colonies" and entered into cordial correspondence with Lassus and Viollet le Duc concerning their work in the restoration and preservation of medieval art and architecture in France. It also attempted to maintain an affectionate but stern paternal relationship with the youthful ecclesiological party in North America.

No association with the English ecclesiologists could endure for long without strain. The Americans were constitutionally unable to follow orders dutifully and to exclude from their ideas and practices the insights of authorities who, though they were not in the ecclesiological inner circle, were contributing creatively to the English Gothic revival. From the outset the American architect and his patron modified ecclesiological dogma and eliminated the idiosyncrasy, provincialism, and crankiness acquired in the course of the Ecclesiological Society's quarrels. From the beginning the Americans' principles and observations on the nature of building differed radically from those of their mentors and form a revealing profile of American architectural inclinations.

By 1853 communication between the Ecclesiological Society and American ecclesiologists had ended; the Society allowed its transatlantic contacts to dissolve. The ecclesiologists, however, had left their mark: though they withdrew from an alliance which was no longer tenable, the Americans had absorbed much that was constructive in the program the Society offered them. For more than a decade a group of distinguished architects were influenced by ecclesiology because they had worked within or close to it. Though the Protestant Episcopal Church was not large, it constituted a privileged and intellectually distinguished group which was able to publicize the doctrines in which it believed.

The American events and buildings described in Chapter II belong to the years 1841 to 1847, a period which, in English ecclesiological affairs, begins with the first publication of the *Ecclesiologist* and ends with the removal of the

Society to London, the change in its name, and the beginning of active missionary work. Chapter III discusses the years 1845 to 1847, when Neale and Webb were carrying on the *Ecclesiologist* without the support of the Society. A New York Ecclesiological Society, with a journal of its own, the *New York Ecclesiologist*, was founded in 1848. This organization retained its power only until 1853, at which point its influence rapidly waned and its publication was discontinued. In England from 1848 to 1853 the Ecclesiological Society was settling into an active middle age in which it consolidated its position and doggedly continued to assert its objectives.

Through the critical years 1841 to 1853 communications between American and English clergymen were frequent and friendly, for a surprisingly large number of Americans traveled abroad for pleasure and further education. When these travelers visited churches and universities in England, they were presented with only the successes of the ecclesiological enterprise. They were not there long enough to ascertain that internecine struggles sometimes attended the rites of ecclesiology. When news of such conflicts reached the United States, the Americans, if they understood the issues at all, tended to sympathize with their embattled friends. American followers were never able to comprehend the rigid orthodoxy of the English, for they had no direct experience of the pressures under which the Ecclesiological Society carried on its operation. Finally, it is profoundly significant that the years of ecclesiological assertiveness in England and abroad were also those of the growth of the Oxford Movement. American architectural proclivities, especially their interest in ecclesiological theory, reveal the depth and the breadth of the influence that significant episode in the English Church had on its American counterparts.

II

Ecclesiology in the United States: The First Phase, 1841–1847

In November, 1841, in the first issue of the *Ecclesiologist*,[1] the Cambridge Camden Society announced that it had missionary aspirations and that the Right Reverend George Washington Doane, Bishop of New Jersey,[2] had been elected a patron member. Bishop Doane was but the second North American so honored; the Right Reverend J. Inglis, Bishop of Nova Scotia, had become

---

[1] "Report of the Twenty-First Meeting of the Cambridge Camden Society," *E.*, 1 (November, 1841):70.

[2] Doane (1799–1859), hymnologist, educator, and author, was born in New Jersey and graduated from Union College, Schenectady. Doane was ordained deacon in 1821 and priest in 1823. He taught at Trinity College, Hartford, from 1824 to 1828; he became rector at Trinity Church, Boston, in 1830. Doane and William Crosswell, who shared Doane's High Church sympathies, founded the *Banner of the Cross*, a journal which was one of the major voices of the Church in the 1830's and 40's. Doane was called to be Bishop of New Jersey in 1832; he accepted the diocese though he knew it was poor and in need of leadership. He became rector of Burlington and from there embarked on a successful campaign to strengthen his diocese. Under his administration the number of parishes was raised from twenty-seven to eighty-eight. Doane was financially independent because of the wealth of his wife, but his venturesome investments in the interests of the Church caused him difficulty, and in 1852 he was tried by the House of Bishops for his management of the funds of St. Mary's Hall. He was called "the John Keble" of the American Church. His hymns included "Fling Out the Banner" and "Softly Now the Light of Day."

a patron in 1839. In 1845 a third American, the Bishop of Newfoundland, was brought into the Society.[3] Election of these and other colonial prelates— the Bishops of Tasmania and New Zealand joined the patrons in 1841 and 1842, respectively, when their bishoprics were created—was in accord with the Society's desire to influence church design abroad and followed the pattern of its growth in England. The social, intellectual, and clerical status of the honorary members and patrons of the Society rose abruptly between 1839 and 1843.[4]

The members of the Society had met the Bishop of New Jersey when he traveled to England in 1841, in response to an invitation from Walter Farquhar Hook, Vicar of Leeds,[5] whose new church, St. Peter's, Kirkgate, was to be consecrated in September. Though the Archbishop of York and the bishops of Ripon and Ross and Argyll were to be present at the ceremony, Doane was asked to preach the sermon of consecration. It was significant that an American bishop should appear in so stellar a role. The ban that had prevented American bishops from preaching in English churches at long last had been lifted; Doane's sermon would inaugurate the formal renewal of the relationship between the Churches of England and the United States. There were good reasons why the Bishop of New Jersey was chosen. Doane was famous as a preacher, but he had been known to High Churchmen in England since 1834, when his American edition of John Keble's *Christian Year* appeared. He had

[3] "Report of the Forty-First Meeting of the Cambridge Camden Society," *E.,* 5 (March, 1845):70.
[4] In 1843 the list of patrons included the Archbishop of Canterbury and the Bishops of Bangor, Lincoln, Exeter, Ely, Norwich, Saint David's, Hereford, Worcester, and Edinburgh.
[5] Hook (1798–1875), Vicar of Leeds from 1837 to 1859, Dean of Chichester from 1859 to 1875, was a scholar and student of the music of the Church. Hook graduated from Oxford in 1821. He was ordained deacon immediately. After further study and the publication of several emphatic statements on the nature of the English Church, he went to Moseley, near Birmingham, where he taught as well as serving as rector. In 1828 he assumed the rectorship of Holy Trinity, Coventry, and revivified the parish. He remained there until his move to Leeds.
Hook was frequently described as a Tractarian, but his views paralleled rather than coincided with those of Tractarianism. He was deeply concerned for the education of the masses, the condition of the working classes, and the role of the Church in the community. He was particularly famous for his sponsorship of the revived choral service. After a spectacularly successful ministry at Leeds he was appointed to Chichester. In his later years he undertook a monumental history of the archbishops of Canterbury. He was made an honorary member of the Cambridge Camden Society in 1843. W. R. W. Stephens' *The Life and Letters of Walter Farquhar Hook, DD., F.R.S.,* in two volumes (London: Richard Bentley and Son, 1880), is the authoritative biography of Hook.

also written hymns, and Hook was particularly interested in the music of the Church. To his countrymen Doane seemed "as complete a specimen of a High Church Bishop as this world has seen."

The Bishop followed his visit to Leeds with an extended tour of the cathedrals, churches, and universities of England, accompanied by Nathan B. Warren of Troy, New York, a layman prominent in Church affairs, and the Reverend Benjamin I. Haight, Rector of All Saints' Church, New York City. For some of the ten months Doane was abroad, Robert Weir, an instructor in painting at the United States Military Academy, was probably also a member of the party. These travelers, who returned to the United States in May, 1842,[6] were in England at an auspicious time and place for architecture. W. F. Hook's new church was destined to be influential in the English Gothic revival, approved by the followers of the young but vigorous discipline of ecclesiology.

St. Peter's replaced an old church which had, in the eighteenth century, been described as "black but comely." In 1837, when Hook became vicar, he found old St. Peter's in a condition which he was forced to describe thus: "Black, I am sorry to say it still is, but comely it has ceased to be."[7] Though large, and in many ways impressive, the church had been repaired frequently, altered incorrectly, and then, in the nineteenth century, neglected. Even a reasonably charitable observer admitted that in the 1830's it was "dark, damp, dirty, and filled with pews."

At first, the new vicar resolved to renovate the old church by rebuilding the walls and piers, moving the tower from above the crossing to a new position above the north transept, increasing the number of seats, removing various unattractive additions made in the eighteenth century, and restoring the original arrangement. He hoped, while repairing the church, to adapt it to the choral service he preferred. When R. Dennis Chantrell, a Yorkshire architect who was experienced in ecclesiastical design,[8] was retained to supervise the

---

[6] G. M. Hills, *History of the Church in Burlington, New Jersey*, 2d ed. (Trenton, N.J.: The W. S. Sharp Printing Company, 1885), p. 473.

[7] E. Kitson Clark, *Leeds Parish Church* (London: S.P.C.K., n.d.), p. 8.

[8] Chantrell (1793–1872), who was trained by Sir John Soane, established himself in practice at Leeds about 1819. Port's *Six Hundred New Churches* contains references to twenty-three churches by Chantrell and illustrates several. H. Colvin (*Biographical Dictionary of English Architects, 1660–1840* [London: John Murray, 1954], pp. 136–37) mentions other works. N. Pevsner (*Yorkshire, the West Riding*, The Buildings of England no. 17 [Harmondsworth: Penguin, 1959]) describes many. In 1843 Chantrell was listed as a member of the Cambridge Camden Society.

extensive work involved, Hook told him that he considered "a handsome church to be a kind of standing sermon, saying to the people, 'See how church-men love and honour God!' "[9] The Vicar must, however, have realized that St. Peter's presented extraordinary problems, for he also directed Chantrell to work within the limits of the site and the money available, even if, in doing so, he was forced to sacrifice "architectural effect."

As soon as work began and it became clear that little of the old building could be salvaged, Hook decided, after consultation with the vestry, to rebuild St. Peter's from the ground up, keeping the lineaments of the original church. The word "rebuild" is important here, for what seemed to the nineteenth century and still seem today forward-looking qualities in the design of the new church were not solely the result of the skill of its architect and the taste of his patron. St. Peter's owes its character and its place as "the first large town church to exemplify the principles of the Cambridge ecclesiologists"[10] to Hook's decision to do his best to reproduce a medieval original. In this attempt Hook and Chantrell created an *avant-garde* example of revivalism.

The church Hook pulled down was a fourteenth-century building which was being added to and altered even in the reigns of Henry VII and Henry VIII. It consisted of four bays, a crossing covered by a square tower one hundred feet high, and a deep chancel of at least three bays (Fig. II–1). It had two aisles on the north and one on the south, which ran beyond the transept parallel to the chancel. The wide transepts crossed this four-part space and emerged on the north and south, where each ended in a large window. There was no west door, the public entrances being through north and south doors under porches. The addition, in the eighteenth century, of the galleries had done serious structural damage to the piers and ruined the appearance of the interior, for they jutted out into the nave. The chancel had been virtually cut off from the nave in 1714, when the organ was placed within the chancel arch. Though a large, impressive, and in many ways extraordinary example of the parish church, St. Peter's had been clumsily adapted to the preaching-hall form preferred in the seventeenth and eighteenth centuries.

New St. Peter's, a wide rectangular building, cruciform in plan, was built

[9] Stephens, *The Life and Letters of Hook*, 1:382.
[10] Addleshaw and Etchells, *The Architectural Setting*, p. 211.

Figure II-1. Old St. Peter's, Leeds, as it appeared in 1837. Southwest view.

upon the foundations of its predecessor.[11] The only major changes in the form dictated by the old church were in the placement of the tower, which in the new church stood on the north side, where its base formed the north transept and contained the major entrance to the nave, and in the addition of one bay to the nave, making it five bays long rather than four (Figs. II–2 and II–3). There were galleries, but they did not protrude into the nave and were heavily, but not successfully, disguised by a decoration of carved wood (Figs. II–4 and II–5). The organ stood in the shallow south transept opposite the north door and tower, an adjustment which must have contributed to Hook's decision to put the tower on the north where it could balance the organ chamber (Fig. II–3). Like the old church, the new St. Peter's had no western door, though the font stood in the orthodox position in the west. Chantrell's design was asymmetrical, a daring departure from the Gothic revival plans which had preceded it and from those contemporary with it.

Hook and Chantrell were determined to restore emphasis to the chancel. Beneath the crossing and slightly to the east of it a large area was reserved for the choir (Fig. II–3). Further east the sanctuary began with a flight of six steps which crossed the full width of the nave. An elevated area before the communion rail separated the public portions of the ceremonial eastern end from the apse and the altar. On the exterior this capacious space appeared as a three-sided mass punctuated by large Perpendicular windows (Fig. II–6). The vestry was arranged around it, its roof well below the sills. In the old church the nave roof had been higher than that of the chancel; Chantrell covered both at the same height. The uniform height of the roof at St. Peter's, as much as its plaster vaults and mixture of late Gothic styles, identify it as a monument of the 1830's.

But a description of the elements of this important church is a meager introduction to its qualities. It was richly embellished, both internally and externally. It was large and expensive: it is said to seat four thousand people, and to have cost £26,000, an enormous sum in the mid-nineteenth century. All this impressed nineteenth-century critics, who were not immune to the effect of

[11] For a description of the church see Addleshaw and Etchells, *The Architectural Setting*, pp. 209–19; Hitchcock, *Early Victorian Architecture*, pp. 103–4; R. W. Moore, *A History of the Parish Church at Leeds* (Leeds: Richard Jackson, 1877), pp. 5–16; Pevsner, *Yorkshire, the West Riding*, pp. 310–11.

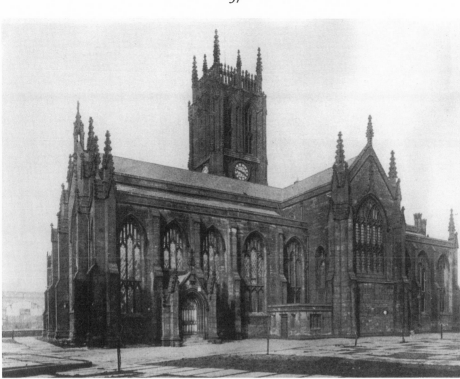

Figure II-2. New St. Peter's, Leeds. Southwest view. R. D. Chantrell. 1837–41.

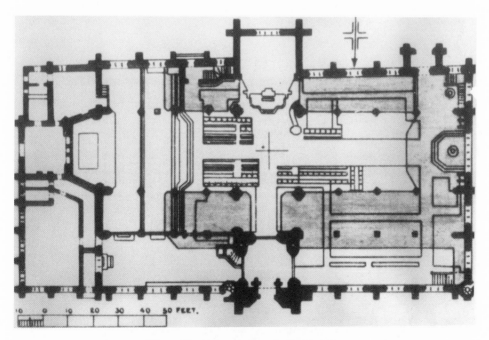

Figure II-3. New St. Peter's, Leeds. Plan.

Figure II-4. New St. Peter's, Leeds. From the east.

Figure II-5. New St. Peter's, Leeds. From the west.

Figure II-6. New St. Peter's, Leeds. Northeast view.

vast expenditure and huge size. The church was, however, admired most at the time it was built and in the decade that followed for the feeling of authenticity it conveyed. Pugin commented favorably on the asymmetrical position of the tower, finding in it evidence that "the present regular system of building both sides of a church exactly alike," which he abhorred, had been rejected by Chantrell.[12] When the ecclesiologists reviewed the church six years after it was built, they admitted grudgingly that, though it antedated the foundation of their society, St. Peter's possessed admirable qualities: "In spite of all its shortcomings, there is an air of rude grandeur about this church; and the east end is striking."[13] They sensed, without quite knowing why, that St. Peter's was close to some medieval model.

It is remarkable that for all the study of medieval building which went on in the nineteenth century no observer knew the old church well enough to recognize the influence it had had on the new. In the twentieth century St. Peter's has been described as "the prototype of the new plan of Anglican church, a plan which in its various forms since the eighteen-forties has been almost universally regarded as the only proper one for an Anglican place of worship."[14]

St. Peter's ushered in a new era. Hook was a man of personal power and marked independence who would not have been pushed by the Cambridge Camden Society into an admiration for old St. Peter's even if it had had the power to do so. However, in 1839, the Society had only just begun its organized existence and was in no position to put pressure on anyone. Hook made his decisions on the size and proportions of the chancel on the basis of his affection for medieval architecture and because he wished to create a setting for the surpliced choir. As much as the Gothic revival in architecture, choirs of this kind were an expression of Victorian taste. Hook was a pioneer in his own right.

Because they were traveling in England under the auspices of Hook, Bishop Doane and his friends encountered the persons most closely connected with advanced thought on church design. For ecclesiology 1841 was a vintage year.

---

[12] *Present State*, p. 22.

[13] "Three Churches in Leeds," *E.*, 8 (December, 1847):129–34.

[14] Addleshaw and Etchells, *The Architectural Setting*, p. 211.

ECCLESIOLOGY IN THE UNITED STATES: 1841–1847

The Cambridge Camden Society published a number of books, including John Mason Neale's axiomatic *A Few Words to Church Builders*; a euphoric atmosphere of achievement and prosperity attended the foundation of the *Ecclesiologist*; the Society was rapidly increasing its membership and its influence on opinion. The Americans, who met a preternaturally united and constructive ecclesiological community, were not sufficiently familiar with architectural or symbolic argument to recognize the prevailing English nuances of taste and conviction about ecclesiastical art. By 1841 theories had not frozen into doctrine. That was to come later. Bishop Doane, because of his High Church proclivities, was sympathetic to the revival of Gothic. He and his companions came home well supplied with artistic ideas.

Shortly after they returned from abroad Doane, Warren, and Weir each built churches which reflected the hazy, pleasant impressions of the old and new buildings the travelers had seen on their tour and indicated that English Gothic, and particularly the smaller English church, had begun to appeal to American churchmen. These buildings did not, however, conform to ecclesiological standards. In the early 1840's, when Doane and his companions were deciding to build in the English style, the Cambridge Camden Society had not yet launched its program to supply information to "colonial" sympathizers. The details of the churches built by Doane and his friends were, therefore, drawn from the illustrations in the voluminous English literature on medieval architecture. As a group these buildings constitute a premature, limited, and specialized Gothic revival which, though it was not directly ecclesiological, was sufficiently related to the ideas of the Cambridge Camden Society to interest the members of the Committee and the editors of the *Ecclesiologist*, who had begun, after 1841, to desire a following in "the Colonies."

Many of the English books about Gothic that Americans such as Doane, Warren, and Weir had at their disposal were historical and topographical. They included accounts of particular buildings, speculations about the origins of Gothic, attempts to date and define the periods of its development, dictionaries of terminology, volumes of careful measured drawings of detail. The reputations of the Pugins, father and son, had been founded upon the excellence of the contributions they had made to this genre before 1837. The numerous and remarkable works of John Britton, which ranged from descriptions and illustrations of specific buildings to treatises on the characteristics of Gothic as a style, also belonged to it.[15] Throughout the 1840's studies of this kind continued to be published though as a result of the wider general interest in and deepened knowledge of Gothic, many of the new books which were appearing were also authoritative. Measured drawings of whole buildings and exact renderings of details were published in increasing numbers; the trilogy produced by the Brandon brothers, for example, still occupies a place among the major accounts of English Gothic.[16] Lewis' book on Kilpeck Church, which has been mentioned, and Ewan Christian's volume on Skelton Church, Yorkshire, demonstrate the specialization of which the writers of the decade were capable. The *Ecclesiologist*, though it admired the scholarship of such books, was troubled by them; the editors correctly observed that with such exact drawings in hand architects might be tempted to copy old churches rather than design new ones.[17]

After 1840, as the enthusiasm for Gothic increased and religious and ethical principles and architectural taste and theory were unified by such authors as Pugin and such groups as the Cambridge Camden Society, another kind of book on architecture made its appearance. Relatively inexpensive, small in format, and without the elaborate illustrations characteristic of the publications described above, these were directed not only to the antiquary and architect but to the consumer of architecture. Though *Contrasts*, which appeared in two editions between 1836 and 1841, was richly illustrated, in his more doctrinaire texts Pugin contributed materially to the tone of books of this new kind.[18] Though his plates stressed the textural richness and emotional evocativeness which the nineteenth century was disposed to admire in Gothic, he enlarged his

[15] In his long and productive life Britton (1771–1857), an author and publisher, established a model for architectural publications of the kind in which he specialized. His major achievement was the *Cathedral Antiquities of England*, in fourteen volumes, published between 1814 and 1835. He followed it with his *Dictionary of the Architecture and Archeology of the Middle Ages*.

[16] Raphael Brandon and J. Arthur Brandon, *An Analysis of Gothic Architecture*, 2 vols. (London: Pelham and Richardson, 1847); *Parish Churches; being Perspective Views of English Ecclesiastical Structures* (London: Bogue, 1848); and *Open Timber Roofs of the Middle Ages*, which first appeared in numbers in 1849 (London: Bogue, 1849), and was published in two volumes in 1852.

[17] In a review of Ewan Christian's *Architectural Illustrations of Skelton Church, Yorkshire* (London: Bell, 1846), published in *E.*, 6 (December, 1846):229.

[18] See *Contrasts*, 1st ed.

written argument to include the social commentary which appealed to his contemporaries. The *Ecclesiologist* and the handbooks published by the Cambridge Camden Society also belong in this category, for in addition to instructing in the correct use, appreciation, understanding, and study of Gothic, they described the buildings being produced in the course of the revival and criticized the architects practicing in the style. A large number of influential books of this sort were produced under the aegis of the Cambridge Camden Society, but independent authors also made contributions. G. A. Poole, whose *Appropriate Character of Church Architecture* (1841) has been mentioned earlier, and J. L. Petit, whose *Remarks on Church Architecture* was also published in 1841,[19] were typical of those who wrote without the direct sponsorship of any group.

Interested Americans were acquainted with all this English literature. The specialized studies of Gothic buildings and details could be found in the library of any well-educated American architect eager to acquire ecclesiastical commissions or to use Gothic in domestic design. The *Ecclesiologist* and the works of Poole, Pugin, and others found their way to America, where they were read both by architects and laymen. It was upon sources such as these that the American Gothic revival was at first based.

In 1842, a few weeks after Doane and his companions left England, an article in the *Ecclesiologist* discussed the benefits to be gained from "the practical study of ancient models" and, as evidence of the correct approach to design, accompanied its advice by a verbatim report of the revised instructions issued in response to ecclesiological pressure by the Incorporated Society for Promoting the Enlargement, Building and Repairing of Churches and Chapels.[20] In a preface the editors of the *Ecclesiologist* admonished those who were working in architecture and the decorative arts to measure, draw, and contemplate actual medieval examples as well as illustrations of them. "We are a reading age," the editors said, "and people expect to learn everything at home from books. We do not undervalue books: there are many of extreme value to the ecclesiologist. . . ."[21] The editors then mentioned the illustrations of medieval churches which the Oxford Architectural Society had begun to pub-

[19] 2 vols. (London: Burns, 1841).
[20] "The Practical Study of Ancient Models," *E.*, 1 (July, 1842):152–56.
[21] *Ibid.*, p. 151.

lish in an attempt to assist the English and colonial builder who had no "ancient models" to study at first hand.

The relationship between the Cambridge and Oxford societies was not easy because the latter sedulously avoided delicate and tense religious issues and so was not harassed by the conflicts which marred the internal affairs of the Cambridge Camden Society. The reasonableness in matters architectural which prevailed at Oxford annoyed the Cambridge men. To the editors of the *Ecclesiologist*, such peace seemed an outcome not of good sense but of failure to face the problems that contemplation of church architecture must induce if conducted properly. A note of asperity entered the discussion in the *Ecclesiologist* when it reported that the Oxford Society had commissioned and published these measured drawings, which, the editors seemed to feel, trespassed upon territory to which the ecclesiologists had prior claim.

The Oxford Society had begun its publication of drawings in 1841, with illustrations of Stanton-Harcourt Church, Oxfordshire, prepared by the architect-draftsman J. M. Derick, and of the church at Littlemore. In 1842 these were followed by a volume on St. Giles's Church, Oxford, prepared by James Park Harrison. Three further numbers appeared in 1844: the Chapel of St. Bartholomew, near Oxford, delineated by J. Cranstoun; J. C. Buckler's drawings of St. Peter's, Wilcote, Oxfordshire; and William Butterfield's presentation of St. John Baptist, Shottesbrook, Berkshire.[22] The text press of Butterfield's volume on Shottesbrook quoted John Rickman's statement that St. John's was "a pure Decorated building, and a beautiful miniature of a Cathedral, having a nave, choir, and transepts. A center tower and a spire, and a north and south porch, all of good design and execution. There are no battlements, but all dripping eaves, and as small a portion of stone as possible is used for the dressings. The tracery of the windows is very good, and the buttresses very good, but plain. This Church will well repay a careful examination."[23] It also included an extensive excerpt from an article by E. J. Carlos, the architectural reviewer for the *Gentleman's Magazine*, who had published in that journal a

---

[22] *Elevations Sections and Details of Saint John Baptist Church at Shottesbroke Berkshire* (Oxford, London, and Cambridge: for the Oxford Architectural Society, by J. B. Parker, Rivington's, and Stevenson, 1846).
[23] *Ibid.*, p. 1.

history, discussion, and description of St. John's in 1840 in which he called the church "an elegant specimen of the workmanship of the fourteenth century, and a beautiful and correct model of a church."[24]

The Bishop of New Jersey had had an interest in architecture and an eye for style and a preference for progressive ideas even before he visited England in 1841. In his years as Bishop, Doane added three notable buildings to the village of Burlington; one, his residence, was built before the English trip and two others, the Chapel of the Holy Innocents and St. Mary's, after he returned. All three were stylistically unusual and challenging. John Notman and Richard Upjohn were his architects. From both men Doane elicited designs which demonstrated their best capacities and developed their tastes.

In 1837 Doane had purchased and reorganized St. Mary's Hall, a school for girls in Burlington, which by 1844 had progressed so satisfactorily that he asked John Notman to design a chapel to stand beside the Georgian house which was the Hall's principal building. Doane and Notman had collaborated before, in 1837 to 1839, when Notman was architect for Riverside, the Italianate villa the Bishop built at Burlington, overlooking the Delaware River. Riverside has been described as "one of the first, if not the first, appearance in America of the new Italianate style. . . . That builder and owner alike conceived [it] as essentially a variant of Gothic was evident both in its elaborate Gothic interiors and Gothic feeling of its bay window and other exterior detail."[25]

On September 25, 1845, the Bishop laid the cornerstone of the Chapel of the Holy Innocents. The religious purpose of the building and Doane's recent contact with English architecture made the choice of Gothic inevitable. Notman was familiar with the style. Between 1837 and 1838 he had participated in the architectural embellishment of Laurel Hill Cemetery in Philadelphia, and

---

[24] *Ibid.*, p. 5.
[25] Alan Gowans, *Architecture in New Jersey, a Record of American Civilization*, The New Jersey Historical Series, vol. 6 (Princeton, N.J.: D. Van Nostrand, n.d.), p. 76. Also see A. J. Downing, *A Treatise on the Theory and Practice of Landscape Gardening Adapted to North America: . . . With Remarks on Rural Architecture* (New York and London: Wiley and Putnam; Boston, Little, 1841), pp. 387, 389–90.

about 1840 he had designed St. Thomas' Episcopal Church in Glassboro, New Jersey, not far from Burlington.[26] These two buildings may be usefully compared with the Chapel of the Holy Innocents.

In the nineteenth century cemetery architecture was flamboyantly eclectic and exotically varied, uniting within one group of buildings styles which reflected both mortuary and religious preoccupations. Since cemeteries of this kind were planned and landscaped in ways inspired by the English natural gardens of the eighteenth century, their buildings were often, as had been the case with garden architecture, stylistically experimental. At Laurel Hill, which resembled other properties of this sort in Europe and elsewhere in America, Egyptian and Gothic mingled with Classical solemnity.

Notman prepared at least two designs for its Gothic chapel; one may be seen in a preliminary drawing (Fig. II–7) and the other, the one actually built, is illustrated in a lithographed view of the cemetery.[27] Notman certainly took the details of the parapet and paneling of the chapel design which can be seen in the drawing from those of Hampton Court and miscellaneous subjects illustrated in Pugin's *Specimens of Gothic Architecture; Selected From Various Antient Edifices in England* (1821–23). As it was finally constructed the chapel seems to have included details taken from King's College Chapel, which were reproduced in *Specimens*. But books were not Notman's only source. Octagonal towers, crenellated parapets, and applied ornaments above pointed windows were features common to other and earlier Gothic revival churches on the American eastern seaboard.[28]

[26] See Historic American Buildings Survey, National Park Service, *Catalog of the Measured Drawings and Photographs of the Survey in the Library of Congress, March 1, 1941* (Washington, D.C.: Government Printing Office, 1941), p. 227. The H.A.B.S. attributes the church to Notman but assigns it no date. *The Inventory of the Church Archives of New Jersey, Protestant Episcopal, Diocese of New Jersey, Diocese of Newark* (Newark, N.J.: The Historical Records Survey, February, 1940), p. 162, states that the laying of the cornerstone and dedication ceremonies occurred in 1846, though the church was built in 1840.

[27] The lithographed view is illustrated in George Tatum, *Penn's Great Town. 250 Years of Philadelphia Architecture Illustrated in Prints and Drawings* (Philadelphia: University of Pennsylvania Press, 1961), Plate 87.

[28] See St. Stephen's Church, Philadelphia (1822–23), by William Strickland; St. Thomas' Church, Broadway, New York (1829), by A. J. Davis; and Grace Church, Temple Street, Boston (1835), by William Washburn. This formula was popular in England in the 1820's. See Holy Trinity, Cloudesley Square, London (1826–28), by Charles Barry; and St. Philip, Stepney, London (1818–19), by Walters and Goodwin.

Figure II-7. Laurel Hill Cemetery Chapel, Philadelphia. John Notman.

St. Thomas', Glassboro, is a parish church in a more mature revival style. The use of stone, the design of the roof, and other details resemble those of the Chapel of the Holy Innocents more than they do the earlier Laurel Hill Chapel. The chancel at Glassboro, which is lower and narrower than the nave, is surprising in so early a church; this elegant feature was surely added to St. Thomas' when the ecclesiological movement had become powerful in America, a decade or more after the church was built.

The Chapel of the Holy Innocents in Burlington (1845–46) was not decorative Gothic. Though far from a polished reproduction of their work, it resembled the designs of the Gothic revival architects of the English generation of the 1840's. It is an unpretentious, rectangular chamber in which the seats for the members of the school are arranged in the choir at the chancel end (Fig. II–8). The longitudinal axis runs north–south; the altar is at the north end. A pair of low steps raises the height of the sanctuary, and within it the altar stands upon a footpace. The door into the school is in the middle of the east wall, and opposite it the organ fills a gabled chamber (Fig. II–9). The seats are set across the nave from the door and the organ to the south end of the room. Originally there was a south door, but when Odenheimer Hall was built in 1868, the chapel was joined to it by an ante-chapel. Now three arches on iron columns span the nave. There is a triplet window above them. Much of this south wall is a result of the modification of 1868, though all early descriptions of the chapel refer to a triplet window over a south door. The window is there, but the entrance is gone. When the chapel was consecrated it was described as 81 feet long, which is the measurement from the north wall to the present arched opening.

The interior woodwork was painted dark brown, and the timber elements of the open timbered and arch-braced roof were stained. There were, in all, three triplet windows: one on the south, which has been mentioned; a second in the organ gablet, which was retained when that part of the building was remodeled; and a third in the north wall over the altar. The tracery in the latter is a copy of the east window of the church at Stanton St. John, Oxfordshire (Fig. II–10). It is an early example, possibly the first, of the exact reproduction of an English medieval detail in an American church. The reredos of the present altar covers the lower portion of the glass. Minton decorative tiles are used

Figure II-8. Chapel of the Holy Innocents, Burlington, N.J. Altar end. John Notman. 1845–46.

Figure II-9. Chapel of the Holy Innocents, Burlington. South view.

Figure II-10. Chapel of the Holy Innocents, Burlington, as it appeared in 1869.

sparingly in the pavement of the sanctuary. The lectern and Bishop's chair are original. The font is in an unorthodox position at the entrance from the school.

The masonry of the chapel is sandstone. There are external buttresses on the east and west walls and single lancet windows from the north wall to the organ chamber; from the organ chamber south there are no buttresses and the windows are double lancets, an arrangement which expresses the distinction between the sanctuary and the general seating (Fig. II–11). In 1900 the organ chamber was enlarged. A bell turret which stood on the roof above the altar is now gone.

The Chapel of the Holy Innocents is a humble descendant of St. Peter's, Leeds, for it is divided by the east door and the organ opposite. The large chancel and the choir, in which the members of the school were seated, also resemble the pattern fashioned at Leeds. The chancel window copied from an Oxfordshire church suggests that Notman and Doane were receiving advice from the Oxford Architectural Society.

Though the Cambridge Camden Society was in the throes of reorganization in 1845 and 1846, the editors of the *Ecclesiologist* kept their eyes on Doane's activities. Late in 1845, when his chapel was well started, the Bishop embarked on another and larger architectural adventure. Word of his plan to build a church at Burlington reached London even before the news arrived that he had already built a chapel. Unwilling to temper their criticism, even out of respect for the eagerness of American church builders and the earnestness and industry of Bishop Doane, the editors of the *Ecclesiologist* pronounced themselves doubtful of his taste. They were alarmed that "the excellent Bishop of New Jersey proposes to build his parish church of S. Mary, Burlington, U.S., taking as his model S. John's Shottesbrooke [*sic*], with a lengthened nave." They went on to say that they had hoped the Bishop's building program might be "a harbinger of good things in the United States," but they were forced to admit that they had always considered Shottesbrook church "a bad model."[29]

---

[29] "New Churches," *E.*, 5 (February, 1846):80. Because of the illustrations by Butterfield, Shottesbrook church was well known in the United States in the 1840's. It was illustrated in S. C. Hall, *The Baronial Halls and Picturesque Edifices of England*, 2 vols. (London: Chapman Hall, 1848), 1:1–4, in a plate dated 1844. In 1849 it appeared in Robert Dale Owen, *Public Architecture* (New York: Putnam. 1849). p. 72.

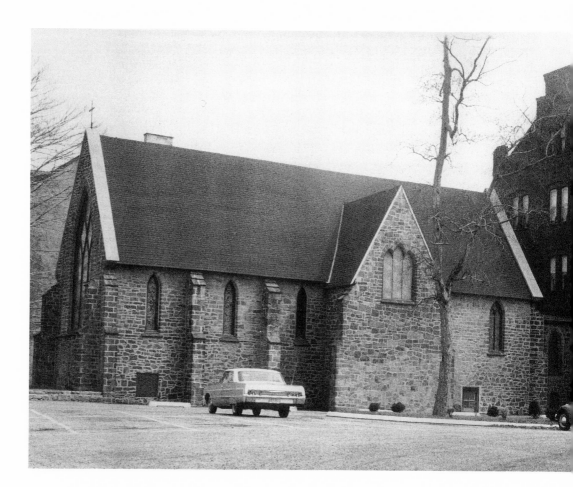

Figure II-11. Chapel of the Holy Innocents, Burlington. West view.

ECCLESIOLOGY IN THE UNITED STATES: 1841–1847

The ecclesiologists were annoyed, probably less by the choice of Shottesbrook than by the fact that Doane had begun his project without consulting
them. His independence was especially galling because he had overlooked the
Cambridge Camden Society's announcement that it, like the Oxford Society,
had in preparation plans for "the Colonies" based upon the finest English
medieval models. G. G. Place had already made complete measured drawings
of St. Mary's, Arnold, Nottinghamshire for the Society, and William Butterfield
was at work on a study of All Saints', Teversham, Cambridgeshire. Both these
churches had been chosen as "good examples for modern imitation, not expensive, nor very large, but well adapted for the wants of country parishes or the
smaller kind of district churches."[30] Though it was proud of these drawings, the
Society had regretfully decided not to recommend them as models for England;
reproduction of old churches, however distinguished, would eliminate the role
of the architect. For the colonies, however, where skilled advice was not always
available, their use was warranted. To satisfy requests from abroad the Society
had actually expanded its program; Le Keux had been set to work on drawings
of All Saints', Hawton, Nottinghamshire, and plans to procure drawings of St.
Andrew's, Heckington, Lincolnshire, were under way. Though assistance of
this kind was available, Doane had turned instead to the Oxford Architectural
Society's publication on Shottesbrook!

As long as they insisted upon Shottesbrook, Doane and his architect could
not receive the approval of the embattled Cambridge men. The rivalry between
the two English societies was too keen. It was particularly unfortunate for
Doane that in June, 1845, the Oxford Society had dealt the Cambridge group
a painful blow by commenting in a lofty and self-righteous tone on the conflicts
in Cambridge, saying that it had "long been anxiously watching the course of
the Camden Society, and, while yielding all merited admiration to the energy
displayed by its directors . . . could not but feel alarmed lest the decidedly
controversial tone of many of its publications should hinder the cause which
both Societies equally desire to promote." In conclusion, the Oxford Society
wished its Cambridge neighbor good fortune in its new existence and suggested
that it should "profit by the experience of the past, and learn, while diminish-
ing nothing of its vigour, to beware lest its good be evil spoken of through lack

[30] "Ancient Models," *E.*, 3 (August, 1844):134–35.

of discretion."[31] Adding insult to injury, the Oxford Society at the same time reported that "various Colonial Bishops" had applied for architectural assistance, and that Mr. Cranstoun had prepared a design "for a church in the diocese of Newfoundland." The editors of the *Ecclesiologist* had every reason to believe that the Bishop of New Jersey was one of the defecting "Colonial Bishops," and were never again more than mildly favorable toward his undertakings.

Throughout this agitation over the plans for a church in Burlington, the *Ecclesiologist* remained unaware of the building of the Chapel of the Holy Innocents. In May, 1847, an account of its consecration and an illustration of the chapel appeared in the *Missionary*, a journal published by Doane. Already disgruntled over Doane's choice of Shottesbrook, the editors of the *Ecclesiologist* reviewed the building in a report entitled "Progress of Ecclesiology in the United States"[32] and expressed surprise and some pleasure at the quality of the design. At the same time they succeeded in conveying their disapproval of Doane. "The idea of a college chapel," said the editors, had been grasped quite effectively. They credited its builder and architect with an attempt to maintain simplicity, dignity, and liturgical correctness. But there were major errors, of which the worst were the multiple use of triplet windows and a dedication different from that of the college. The review was condescending. Because the information at their disposal was scanty, the editors did not discover the most serious of Doane's mistakes: the orientation of the chapel, with its altar at the north, violated a basic tenet of ecclesiology.

The *Missionary* also carried an illustration of the proposed design for St. Mary's, Burlington. The editors of the *Ecclesiologist* were displeased with what they saw:

We are sorry to find from the description and wood-cut in the *Missionary* for April that the plan of copying Shottesbrooke church has been abandoned for a native design by Mr. Upjohn, of New York; a well-meaning architect, we fancy. The church is cruciform, with central tower and spire, and south porch correctly placed, and a well pitched roof, but the style is unfortunately First pointed, with very broad lancets and triplets. The dimensions are, nave 88 feet 5 inches (including tower); chancel 48 feet 5 inches, by 30 feet 10 inches; and the height to the top of the spire

---

[31] Quoted in "Oxford Architectural Society," *E.*, 5 (September, 1845):219.
[32] 8 (October, 1847):68–69.

(a sort of broach) 150 feet. We are sorry to observe in the engraving a door at the end of the south transept. We trust the fittings will be sumptuous and churchlike.[33]

This remark resembled those that had made the Society unpopular among the members of the architectural community in England. To this disagreeable notice, the editors appended a little praise for the sermon delivered by Bishop Ives of North Carolina on the occasion of the laying of the cornerstone at Burlington. The Bishop, who was sympathetic to Tractarianism, had asked for the opening of churches to all and defended expenditure on church building, which views were in agreement with, if not derived from, the *Ecclesiologist*.[34]

Upjohn's drawings for St. Mary's date from September, 1846, to November, 1853, but the church was largely constructed between 1846 and 1848.[35] Since most of the plans must have been complete before the publication of the illustration in the *Missionary* in April, 1847, the general conception of St. Mary's may be dated late 1846 to early 1847. The editors of the *Ecclesiologist* had failed to observe that the design for St. Mary's indicated that Richard Upjohn and Bishop Doane were working, to the best of their ability, to reach the standard set by English architects and architectural theoreticians. Their mistakes were the result of lack of information rather than poor taste.

The significance of St. Mary's, Burlington, and its place in the history of the American Gothic revival and in the career of Richard Upjohn cannot be understood unless the church is related to others of the American revival built before and immediately after it. A decade of serious, well-intentioned revival building had preceded the construction of St. Mary's, and another decade was to follow it. Through all these years Upjohn was a leading figure. St. Mary's was a landmark in his work and among American churches because it was the first attempt to follow a specific English medieval example.

In the early 1840's Philadelphia, Boston, Baltimore, and other cities on the East Coast were graced by buildings of distinction, but New York was the

[33] *Ibid.*, p. 68.
[34] See E. Clowes Chorley, *Men and Movements in the American Episcopal Church* (New York: Charles Scribner's Sons, 1946), pp. 228–34, from whom these details of Bishop Ives's speech are taken.
[35] Everard M. Upjohn, *Richard Upjohn, Architect and Churchman* (New York: Columbia University Press, 1939). All dates of commissions and biographical details on Richard Upjohn are taken from this authoritative study.

growing center of mid-nineteenth-century American architecture. It offered wealth and people of taste. Major architects had their offices there. The influence of European art was strong, its lessons well understood and well received. In the years after 1840 accelerated building activity encouraged experimentation, and the New York churches built between 1840 and 1846 form a revealing group. They were not only large and expensive but they demonstrated the accomplishment of American architects. The Protestant Episcopal churches—St. Peter's, Chelsea, the Church of the Holy Communion, Calvary Church, Trinity Church, and Grace Church—indicate when and how the English Gothic revival arrived and the sources through which it first became known to and admired by Americans.

In 1836 Henry Russell Cleveland could say with considerable justice, in the *North American Review*, that "the Ecclesiastical architecture in our country is in a very unsettled, ill-defined state. It has neither the stern simplicity and unpretending rudeness of the puritanical meeting-houses, nor the grace and richness of form and ornament of European churches. It seems worth while then to inquire, what kind of churches the religion of our country requires, and what points are to be particularly attended to in their construction."[36] If one accepted Cleveland's standards, it was possible to agree with him that, in 1836, "neither New York nor Philadelphia contains a church which has any claim to be called fine architecture, or which is worthy of the wealth and population of those cities."[37] By 1846 this appraisal was no longer valid. At least ten major churches were built in New York City between 1840 and 1845. All but one were in the style Cleveland preferred, for they were "really Gothic edifices, instead of Yankee meeting-houses with Gothic ornaments on them."[38] Nine of the ten belonged to the Protestant Episcopal Church. They make it possible to date the moment at which the English Gothic revival in ecclesiastical architecture appeared in the United States.

St. Peter's, Chelsea (1836–38), marked the beginning of serious revivalism. Designed by Clement C. Moore, architectural amateur, scholar, and poet, St. Peter's was a departure from the late Georgian ecclesiastical style of which St. Luke's was typical (Figs. II–12 and II–13). The size and mass of the

[36] "American Architecture," *North American Review*, 43 (October, 1836):372.
[37] *Ibid.*
[38] *Ibid.*, p. 376.

Figure II-12. St. Peter's, Chelsea, New York City. James W. Smith and Clement C. Moore. 1836–38.

Figure II-13. St. Luke's, New York City. Attributed to John Heath. 1821.

buttresses and the design of their offsets suggest that Moore worked from illustrations of old and new English churches, adopting and adapting some elements and discarding others which were impractical. He must also have known *An Essay on Gothic Architecture*, by the Right Reverend John Henry Hopkins, Bishop of Vermont, which appeared in 1836 and was the first book on Gothic ecclesiastical architecture to be published in the United States.[39] St. Peter's was the typical Gothic revival church of the late 1830's. A square tower stood at the center of the front, just as did the towers of many of the English churches built by the Church Building Commission in the 1820's and 1830's. Though it carried Gothic embellishment on the tower and on the openwork porches which then stood on either side of it, and though it was built of stone, St. Peter's was not "really Gothic." There was no organic relationship between the offsets and the walls adjacent to them, and the moldings were coarse and heavy in profile.

As St. Peter's was being built, Richard Upjohn was at work on St. John's, Bangor, Maine, the first of his long and distinguished succession of ecclesiastical commissions. In the same year St. John's, Cleveland, was begun; Hezekiah Eldredge, its architect and builder, was certainly dependent upon Hopkins' illustrations.[40] It was also in 1836 that H. R. Cleveland, in the *North American Review* article which has been cited, summarized his views on styles for church building by saying that, though he was aware of its complexities, Gothic deserved to be employed. He characterized it as "a style of architecture which belongs peculiarly to Christianity, and owes its existence even to this religion,"[41] a conviction he must have acquired from English literature on the revival.[42]

---

[39] *Essay on Gothic Architecture with Various Plans and Drawings of Churches: Designed Chiefly for the Use of the Clergy* (Burlington, Vt.: Smith and Harrington, 1836).

[40] For the history of St. John's and illustrations, see Sarah E. Rusk, "Hezekiah Eldredge, Architect-Builder of St. John's Church, Cleveland, Ohio," *Journal of the Society of Architectural Historians*, 25 (March, 1966):54.

[41] "American Architecture," p. 379.

[42] See Pugin, *Contrasts*, 1st ed., p. 3. There is a striking resemblance between Pugin's text of the first edition of *Contrasts* (dated 1836) and Cleveland's argument. Pugin had said: "Yes, it was, indeed, the faith, the zeal, and above all, the unity, of our ancestors, that enabled them to conceive and raise these wonderful fabrics that still remain to excite our wonder and admiration. They were erected for the most solemn rites of Christian worship, when the term Christian had but one signification throughout the world; when the glory of the house of God formed an important consideration with mankind, when men were zealous for religion, liberal in their gifts, and devoted to her cause. . . ."

Interest in Gothic was growing. St. John's, Cleveland, represents well a group of churches inspired by Hopkins. Upjohn's practice had moved into its Gothic phase. Cleveland's article revealed that at least some Americans had begun to read the European authorities. The New York churches of the early 40's amplified and enriched but did not modify the basic pattern established by St. John's, Bangor, the illustrations and recommendations presented by Hopkins, and the design of St. Peter's. Upjohn's Church of the Ascension and Christ Church, Brooklyn, built between 1840 and 1843, were rectangular and arranged behind a square tower set squarely on the longitudinal axis. All the conceptions for Upjohn's next project, Trinity Church, followed this formula, though Trinity was planned, from the beginning, to be much larger and more ornamented than the earlier churches had been. Grace Church, built between 1843 and 1846 by James Renwick, Jr., also repeated this pattern, though it was less monumental than Trinity and more elegant in its building material and in its wealth of decorative detail. At the Church of the Holy Apostles (1844–48), Minard Lafever kept this symmetrical plan but rejected Gothic, choosing instead a very early nineteenth-century imaginative Classicism which resembled that used by S. P. Cockerell in St. Anne's, Soho, built in 1802 to 1806.

Trinity Church and Grace Church merit special comment here: they were the largest and most elaborate expressions of this early manner; they were powerful and successful designs; they were each designed by gifted and informed architects destined to be prominent in the later phases of the American Gothic revival; they indicated that the books of A. W. Pugin had acquired an American audience.

Everard Upjohn and others who have considered the career of Richard Upjohn have noted that he was considerably influenced by England. It is possible to specify the sources upon which he drew. In 1836, the year in which St. John's, Bangor, was constructed, Upjohn purchased the fifth volume of John Britton's *Architectural Antiquities*, completing his set. A few days earlier he had acquired *Views of the Most Interesting Collegiate and Parochial Churches in Great Britain*, by J. M. Neale and J. Le Keux.[43] Everard Upjohn also says

---

[43] Upjohn, *Richard Upjohn*, p. 36.

that Richard Upjohn owned the first volume of the *Ecclesiologist,* which included the issues published from November, 1841, to August, 1842.[44] To these English works we can now add two others, Pugin's *True Principles of Pointed or Christian Architecture,* published in 1841,[45] and *The Symbolism of Churches,* by Neale and Webb.

The various plans and drawings which Upjohn prepared for Trinity Church cannot be dated exactly, though it is known that the architect delivered a design which the Corporation accepted on September 9, 1839. These plans either are not now extant or, if they are, cannot be identified as of that date.[46] Since the cornerstone of the church was not laid until June, 1841, it is possible that many changes, even full-scale alterations, were made in the scheme during the months that intervened between the plan of 1839 and the beginning of construction in 1841.

Pugin's *True Principles* contained a beautiful drawing of an imaginary Gothic church, probably one of the series of studies he prepared in connection with his commission to design St. George's, Southwark, London (Fig. II–14). The tower and spire were Perpendicular Gothic, resembling those of St. James, Louth, Lincolnshire. Carried on a tall, dramatic clerestory, the nave roof in the Pugin drawing rose high above the aisles. Battlemented parapets with pinnacles terminated the aisle and nave walls. The chancel, which was as wide as but lower than the nave, was fully visible in the drawing, which presented a southeast elevation. The nave was seven bays long.

As it was ultimately built, Trinity Church resembled the Pugin drawing, though it did not have Pugin's impressive chancel (Fig. II–15), a feature too Catholic for the Corporation, nor did Upjohn reproduce the dramatic pitch Pugin had given his roof. The details of the tracery in the Pugin drawing were not clear, and Upjohn filled the windows to his own taste.

Even as Trinity was being completed, a critic observed the similarities between it and the Pugin drawing. In April, 1844, the *North American Review* published a long and brilliant article on American architecture by the young

[44] *Ibid.,* p. 48.
[45] The Metropolitan Museum owns the manuscript of the *True Principles* and various letters from Pugin to John Weale, who published the book. Pugin sold Weale the manuscript in January, 1841. Publication followed shortly thereafter.
[46] Upjohn, *Richard Upjohn,* chap. 4.

Figure II-14. An ideal church. From A. W. Pugin, True Principles *(1841).*

Figure II-15. Trinity Church, New York City. Richard Upjohn. 1840–46.

architect Arthur D. Gilman,[47] who had a wide understanding of European and especially English building and architectural theory. "The body of Trinity church is now nearly completed," he said, and added that "in size, in the delicacy and propriety of its decoration, and in the beauty of its general effect, we are inclined to think, that it surpasses any church erected in England since the revival of the pointed style."[48] In passing, Gilman mentioned St. Luke's, Chelsea, London, but though he saw similarities between Trinity and St. Luke's, he discounted the latter as Upjohn's primary model. He referred directly to the Pugin drawing in a passage in praise of Trinity:

Governed by simple and consistent principles, the architect has conceived and finished it in the true and delicate spirit of the best and chastest period. It rivals the accurate taste of the best works of the fourteenth century, and is carried out upon a scale which we had deemed it impossible to adopt, in a country where architecture is in so chaotic a state. With the single exception of the guild chapels and private chantries, introduced by Mr. Pugin in his engraving of a perfect church, it very nearly resembles that enthusiastic ideal of an ecclesiastical edifice of the Middle Ages.[49]

In the course of his discussion Gilman indicated that the design for Trinity which had been accepted in 1839 had been heavily or entirely revised before construction began. Describing a design for the spire, no drawings of which are now extant, he noted with pleasure that

the spire has been more highly enriched than in the original design. Had it been erected in so plain a style as was first proposed, it would have been a defect, which in our eyes, would have ruined the whole building. A light and highly decorated tower, surmounted by a plain, naked, heavy spire, without any crocketting, foliated bands, or canopied windows in its sides, would have appeared so distressing a deformity that we should infinitely have preferred, that the first stone of the structure had never been laid.[50]

Pugin's intransigence and pugnaciousness in architectural discourse had been adopted by Gilman.

[47] "Architecture in the United States," *North American Review*, 58 (April, 1844):436–80.
[48] *Ibid.*, p. 477.
[49] *Ibid.*, p.478.
[50] *Ibid.*, pp. 478–79.

ECCLESIOLOGY IN THE UNITED STATES: 1841–1847

Pugin's early buildings and books and the literature on Gothic published before 1840 had emphasized Perpendicular late Gothic. Upjohn followed this leadership between 1836 and 1844. Pugin's ideal church, as presented in *True Principles*, was of cathedral scale; Upjohn also began by using the larger Gothic buildings as models. By 1842, when he designed the Church of St. Oswald, Liverpool, Pugin had moved out of this early, grandiose revival and initiated its second and mature phase, which stressed the parish church (Fig. I–1). But Upjohn, far from England and dependent upon books, in the design of Trinity was still following the instruction Pugin had given in 1841. Henry-Russell Hitchcock has classified Trinity Church as the "analogue" of St. Mary's, Derby, an early Pugin church dedicated in 1839. In the light of the connections between the church illustrated in *True Principles* and Trinity Church, it is possible to date the impact of Pugin upon Upjohn as sometime after 1841, and to relate Trinity not to St. Mary's but to the designs Pugin prepared for St. George's.

The cornerstone of Grace Church, by James Renwick, Jr., was laid on October 30, 1843,[51] only six months before Arthur Gilman had described "the body" of Trinity Church as "nearly completed." The design of Grace Church may thus be dated a year to a year and a half after that of Trinity (Figs. II–16 and II–17). Comparison of the two shows how rapidly competence in the Gothic style developed in the United States, for even if the differences between the tastes and personal styles of Upjohn and Renwick are acknowledged, Grace Church is more tightly knit, less rigorous, and less dry than Trinity. The brownstone of Trinity and the white marble of Grace invite comparison, but the major difference between the two lies in the way in which Renwick developed the ornamental possibilities of the style and reduced the amount of inert masonry in the elevations. It is tempting to link Renwick's design with the drawing in *True Principles*, but, though there are similarities between them, they are not as obvious as in the case of Trinity. That Renwick knew the illustrations in Pugin's works and may have visited his buildings can be asserted because of his close transcription of a typical Pugin formula in his

[51] The Historical Records Survey, *Inventory of the Church Archives of New York City, Protestant Episcopal Church in the United States of America, Diocese of New York, Manhattan, Bronx, Richmond*, 2 vols. (New York: The Historical Records Survey, 1940), 2:65.

Figure II-16. Grace Church, New York City. James Renwick, Jr. Cornerstone laid 1843.

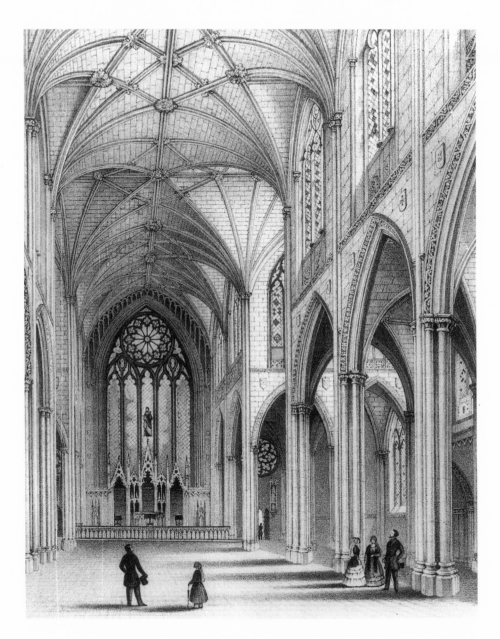

Figure II-17. Grace Church, New York City.

Oak Hill Cemetery Chapel in Washington, built in 1850.[52] Grace Church is, however, too brilliant and too free to derive its character solely from one Pugin illustration. Renwick, though he was only twenty-five when he received the commission for Grace Church, was a gifted architect already well versed in Gothic design.

Suddenly, about 1844, two churches broke the pattern. It is not surprising that each was designed for a parish of High Church inclinations and that Upjohn and Renwick were their architects. In the spring of 1843 the Reverend William Augustus Muhlenberg sailed for Europe, and, while visiting England, he sought out John Henry Newman and Edward Bouverie Pusey, both of whom were impressed and pleased with their American guest.[53] Three years after his return Muhlenberg resolved to establish a new parish in New York City, and, with the financial assistance of his sister, to build a church. He retained Richard Upjohn, who designed the Church of the Holy Communion, which was consecrated in 1846. The Reverend John McVickar, Professor of Moral Philosophy at Columbia College, had organized Calvary parish in New York in 1836, but not until 1844 was there money to build a church. McVickar, an inveterate European traveler and a man of informed and advanced tastes in ecclesiastical art, acquired the services of James Renwick, Jr. The new church was consecrated in 1847.[54]

The Church of the Holy Communion (Fig. II–18) departed abruptly from both the earlier Puginian Gothic revivalism that Upjohn had employed at Trinity Church and the symmetrical plan with the tower on the center of the front. Its tower stood beside rather than in front of the nave. A prominent south transept had an entrance in its façade. The chancel was treated as a separate chamber, though it was the same height as the nave. The plan was

---

[52] H. N. Jacobsen, in his edition of *A Guide to the Architecture of Washington, D.C.* (New York: Frederick A. Praeger, 1965), illustrates the Oak Hill Chapel; see Plate 6b, p. 136.

[53] See James Thayer Addison, *The Episcopal Church in the United States* (New York: Charles Scribner's Sons, 1961), p. 166.

[54] The *Inventory of the Church Archives of New York* does not attribute Calvary Church to Renwick (see p. 84), but in the biography of Renwick in the *American Dictionary of Biography* it is assigned to him. Marked resemblances to Grace Church would indicate that it was his.

asymmetrical. The pitch of the roof was steeper than in the earlier churches. The brownstone masonry was a dominant element in the composition. The grandeur of Pugin's late Gothic manner was replaced by the style of the English parish church.

While Robert Dale Owen described the Church of the Holy Communion as Gothic of the "Decorated" style, he defined that of Calvary (Fig. II–19) as "Early English or Lancet." But whatever the style of its details, Calvary was large and cumbersome, infinitely less poised and elegant than Grace Church. The nave and aisles emerged prominently on the principal front under steep roofs. Two elaborate openwork spires rose above the façade. The transepts, which, like the nave, had aisles, protruded heavily on the sides. Upjohn's inspiration for the Church of the Holy Communion was clear and his choice was cautious, for the parish church was a modest pattern easy to follow and certain to be reasonably successful with or without a specific model. Renwick's idea was more ambitious. Something about the three-part front of Calvary Church and its composition of complex shapes which reveal the equally complex interior spaces suggests that Renwick was still following Pugin. An illustration of St. Barnabas, Nottingham, by Pugin had appeared in *The Present State of Ecclesiastical Architecture in England* in 1843 (Fig. II–20), and Renwick's choice of the "Early English or Lancet" also suggested the cathedral in Nottingham. Calvary and St. Barnabas do not resemble one another, but both are memorable because they emphasize "three-dimensional composition."[55] Though it would be incorrect to pronounce Calvary Church an aesthetic success, it would be equally incorrect to dismiss it. The harsh cubic quality of its composition and the interesting experimentation with lighting suggest that Renwick had begun to move away from careful eclecticism. He was, like his mentor, Pugin, in a brief period of working with, rather than in, the Gothic style.

Thus two English Gothic revival authorities were known in America by 1844. Renwick followed the direction in which Pugin led. Upjohn, in the Church of the Holy Communion, had moved away from Pugin and joined the parish church revival and the Cambridge Camden Society. There is other evidence which establishes the date of Upjohn's departure from the style of

---

[55] Hitchcock employs this term in his description of St. Barnabas, Nottingham (*Early Victorian Architecture*, p. 84).

*Figure II-18. Church of the Holy Communion, New York City. Richard Upjohn.
Consecrated 1846.*

Figure II-19. Calvary Church, New York City. James Renwick, Jr. Consecrated 1847.

THE GOTHIC REVIVAL AND AMERICAN CHURCH ARCHITECTURE

Figure II-20. Cathedral of St. Barnabas, Nottingham. A. W. Pugin. 1841–44.

Trinity and his turn toward ecclesiology. In *The Symbolism of Churches* Neale and Webb had expressed an opinion whose travels can be traced after its arrival in the United States. They said that one "ought to look at least for church-membership from one who ventures to design a church. There cannot be a more painful idea than that a separatist should be allowed to build a House of God, when he himself knows nothing of the ritual and worship of the Church from which he has strayed." With their usual assertiveness they added, "Or, again to think that any churchman should allow himself to build a conventicle, and even sometimes to prostitute the speaking architecture of the Church to the service of Her bitterest enemies!"[56] An earnest man far from the battlefields of English ecclesiology could interpret this statement as an order to do what Richard Upjohn did when, in 1846, he rejected a commission for a Unitarian church in Boston on grounds of his religious conviction.[57] This incident, which occurred just as ecclesiological features began to appear in Upjohn's designs, makes it possible to date his accommodation to ecclesiological doctrine in the period 1844 to 1846—from the time he built the Church of the Holy Communion, to Grace Church, Providence, and finally, to St. Mary's, Burlington.

Grace Church, Providence, was designed by Upjohn in the months that intervened between his Church of the Holy Communion and St. Mary's, Burlington. It conformed to the suggestions the Incorporated Society for Promoting the Enlargement, Building, and Repairing of Churches and Chapels had issued in 1842 and which the *Ecclesiologist* had quoted in full in its first volume, which Upjohn owned.

St. Mary's, Burlington, differs from the New York and Providence churches because when he designed it Upjohn worked not from written directions but from a specific medieval model for which he had measured drawings. When the *Ecclesiologist* condemned St. Mary's and called it the work of a "well-meaning architect," the editors failed to perceive that Upjohn had never given up Shottesbrook (Figs. II–21 and II–22). In their defense it should, of course, be noted that it was not easy to find evidence of the presence of the English church in the south view of St. Mary's which appeared in the *Missionary* (Fig. II–23).

[56] P. xxii.

[57] Upjohn, *Richard Upjohn*, pp. 81–86. The Boston *Christian Register*, on November 28, 1846, reported that "Mr. Upjohn replied, that after having anxiously and prayerfully considered the matter, he had come to the conclusion, that he could not conscientiously furnish a plan for a Unitarian Church, he being an Episcopalian" (quoted in *ibid.*, p. 82).

Figure II-21. St. John Baptist, Shottesbrook, Berkshire. West elevation.
From William Butterfield, Saint John Baptist Shottesbroke, Berkshire *(1846).*

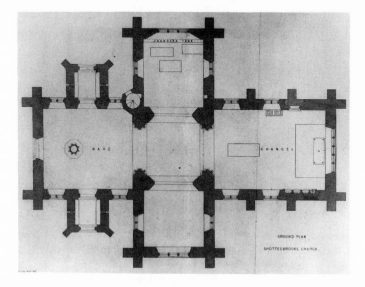

Figure II-22. St. John Baptist, Shottesbrook. Plan. From Butterfield,
Saint John Baptist Shottesbroke, Berkshire.

Figure II-23. St. Mary's, Burlington, N.J. Richard Upjohn. 1846–48.

The resemblance to Shottesbrook could best be seen in a north view. In addition, the ecclesiologists were so angry with Bishop Doane that they would have been unable to praise any design Upjohn prepared for him.

Though St. Mary's was a failure, it was at the same time a success. It did not have the authenticity or the technical accomplishment that English architects could display by 1847. It could not, for example, compare with St. James', Woolsthorpe, Lincolnshire, built in 1847 from a design by G. G. Place (Figs. II–24 and II–25).[58] In building it Place had followed the example of St. Mary's, Arnold, Nottinghamshire, a medieval parish church which he could study at first hand (Fig. II–26). In spite of its shortcomings, St. Mary's, Burlington, was of the utmost importance because the Bishop was unwilling to accept an approximation of an English church and had instead asked his architect to study drawings of an English example, and, second, because the Englishness of St. Mary's appealed to the clergymen and laymen of the United States. With St. James the Less in Philadelphia, which will be discussed in the chapter that follows, St. Mary's initiated the mature parish church revival.

It is sad and at the same time ironic that the editors of the *Ecclesiologist* chose to scold Bishop Doane, who was doing his best to bring to the United States some of the spirit and feeling of the enthusiasm he had encountered on his travels in England, and to assail Richard Upjohn, who was struggling to live up to ecclesiological ideals in design and architectural practice. Jealousy of the Oxford Architectural Society and insecurity bred in the quarrels and disagreements that took place within the Cambridge Camden Society during its transformation into the Ecclesiological Society made it impossible for the ecclesiologists to recognize the first of their "colonial" followers.

St. Mary's is a cruciform church, and, unlike the earlier Chapel of the Holy Innocents, it is correctly oriented. The tower and spire at the crossing impart elegance to the exterior. There are three entrances—an unpretentious west door, a south door covered by a porch, and a door which opens into the south transept, just as at the Church of the Holy Communion. Eight hundred people can be seated in the nave, the transepts, and the three galleries. The chancel is fully expressed externally, and, as at the Church of the Holy Com-

---

[58] See "New Churches," *E.*, 7 (April, 1847):152–53, for a description of St. James'.

munion, it is the same height and width as the nave. The transepts are slightly wider than the nave.

The rectangular masses of which St. Mary's is composed are bound into one by the tower and the grave and graceful spire (Fig. II–27), the latter a modification of a broach. Upjohn used a continuous transition from the rectangle to the polygon upon it, suppressing the pyramidal masses usual at the corners of a broach and using inward-curving surfaces instead. He seems to have found this solution pleasing, for it appears again at Christ Church, Raleigh, North Carolina. The comfortable feeling of authenticity and the charm of the exterior of St. Mary's derive from the stone of which the church is built and the even, unostentatious rhythm of the buttresses and lancets along the walls of nave and transepts. There are but two departures from symmetry; a newel staircase in a turret rises at the northwest corner of the tower, and a chapel stands to the north of the chancel (Fig. II–28). The style of the church, in the terminology of the ecclesiologists, was "modern First Pointed."

The interior of St. Mary's reveals its early date more than the exterior (Fig. II–29). The nave is long in proportion to its width, has no aisles, and is wood-paneled to a height above the backs of the seats. The walls are painted plaster. The small windows, the paneling, and the line formed by the sills compose a series of horizontals which seem to narrow and lengthen the space. A hammer-beam roof of steep pitch looms overhead. At the crossing four chamfered piers intrude at right angles to the walls, reducing the width of the nave by at least a third. They effectively destroy any feeling that nave and transepts unite in a spatial preface to the chancel. Upjohn treated the heavy, almost clumsy, elements at the crossing more freely and in a more personal way than other parts of the design. The piers rise to the base of the spire with a grandeur that owes everything to the preferences of the architect. The crossing is ceiled at the level of the nave roof, where light enters through eight small windows sunk into the masses of the piers (Fig. II–30). The eccentric arrangement of the paired windows in deep embrasures is dramatic. The chancel is large and richly appointed. Its roof is decorated, and the ritual arrangements conform to ecclesiological recommendations, save that the pulpit, with its heavy testor, is out of character with the rest of the furniture, which is done in Upjohn's coarse, emphatic, and effective manner.

One senses in St. Mary's a struggle between the personal style of its architect

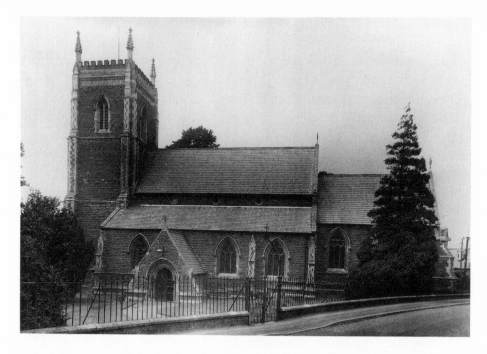

Figure II-24. St. James', Woolsthorpe, Lincolnshire. South view. G. G. Place. 1847.

Figure II-25. St. James', Woolsthorpe. Interior.

Figure II-26. St. Mary's, Arnold, Nottinghamshire. South view.

Figure II-27. St. Mary's, Burlington. North view.

Figure II-28. St. Mary's, Burlington.

ECCLESIOLOGY IN THE UNITED STATES: 1841–1847

Figure II-29. St. Mary's, Burlington.

THE GOTHIC REVIVAL AND AMERICAN CHURCH ARCHITECTURE

Figure II-30. St. Mary's, Burlington.

and his will to employ a model with which he was neither familiar nor entirely sympathetic, no matter how much he wished to be. Both architect and patron had absorbed the lesson that Neale and Webb and the *Ecclesiologist* and hoped to instill: "Gothic architecture is, in the highest sense, the only Christian architecture; that during the period in which it flourished, our Country churches are, in their way, as perfect models as our Cathedrals." The nave of Shottesbrook was shorter than the chancel, an impracticality Upjohn corrected (Fig. II–22). He added galleries and put an unorthodox door in the south transept. The pretty spire was his own. The details are much simpler than those of Shottesbrook, but the piers at the crossing and the turret at the side of the tower are proof that the Butterfield drawings were present in Burlington.

When he was working for Bishop Doane, Upjohn had in hand other important commissions, for by 1847 his practice was established and flourishing. On his visits to Burlington he must have become aware that an unusual and innovating church was under construction in Philadelphia. Knowledge of St. James the Less was to enrich Upjohn's work, change his church style, and sharpen his perceptions of Gothic.

Long before he became Vicar of Leeds, W. F. Hook and an associate, John Jebb, had explored the history of the music of the Church and concluded that the service traditionally sung in the cathedrals of the Anglican Communion was one of the finest expressions of the faith.[59] Nathan Warren, of Troy, New York, had returned from abroad believing that new churches were necessary, that Christian laymen should build them, and that a surpliced choir, such as the one he had seen at St. Peter's, Leeds, had a place in church ceremony.

Some American clergy, particularly those who were closest to the Oxford Movement in the 1840's, had long desired to enrich the Church service. The Reverend William A. Muhlenberg, founder of the Church of the Holy Communion, in the late 1820's and early 1830's had introduced candles, flowers, and surpliced choirs of boys and laymen in services at the chapel of a school of which he was then head.[60] The Reverend John Ireland Tucker, who had been trained by Muhlenberg, assisted Warren in founding and building Holy Cross

[59] See Addleshaw and Etchells, *The Architectural Setting*, pp. 209–19.
[60] See Chorley, *Men and Movements*, pp. 200–1, 362–63; Addison, *The Episcopal Church*, pp. 164–70.

Church in Troy. Together these two men made the church a center of choral service and ceremony of the kind followed at St. Peter's, Leeds, and favored by them both.

Holy Cross Church is now surrounded by urban blight, but something of the charm it once possessed remains. It stands on the slope of a high, steep hill, which, when the church was built, was dotted with the villas of the wealthy, for Troy in the nineteenth century enjoyed a prosperity which is today only suggested by the churches, town houses, and commercial buildings that remain. The Warrens, whose money came from iron foundries, had already built a Gothic mansion, Mount Ida.[61] In 1844 Mrs. Warren and her son established a mission and began to plan the church, which, with its school building, was consecrated in January, 1849. As a full account of the church had been published in the *Missionary* in April, 1847,[62] it is safe to assume that it was completed several years before the consecration ceremony. A large part of the design was attributed to Warren, who, in addition to his gifts as a student of music, was something of an amateur architect.

Holy Cross Church belongs to the same pre-ecclesiological revivalism as the buildings in Burlington. It too was stylistically obsolete even before it was consecrated. The church and school building at Holy Cross, which are constructed of local blue limestone ashlar masonry, are arranged in an L-shaped unit around a natural spring. The west façade of the church is well above the street; the principal entrance to the nave is through a door in the south side of the tower, which dominates the west—a buttressed and battlemented rectangular mass with a newel staircase in a turret at its southwest corner (Fig. II–31). Admirers of the church, and there were many, described it as "First Pointed or Early English," presumably because of the simplicity of its design and the slender lancet windows. The nave—there were no aisles—was paved with stone, and its ornament was simple and dignified. The chancel, the only remarkable part of the interior, which it dominates, is large and is organized precisely as was that of St. Peter's, Leeds: there is seating for the school in the choir, and the altar is raised by a series of low flights of steps. Upjohn de-

[61] Its design has been attributed to A. J. Davis (see Downing, *Theory and Practice*, p. 410).
[62] By far the most complete account of the church is found in the *New York Ecclesiologist* ("New Churches," 1 [January, 1849]:77–79). A report of it in the *Missionary* was quoted extensively in the *Ecclesiologist* ("Progress of Ecclesiology in the United States," 7 [October, 1847]:69).

Figure II-31. Holy Cross Church, Troy, N.Y. Richard Upjohn [?]. Consecrated 1849.

signed this chancel and its furniture in 1847 (Fig. II–32). Warren's church was in no way the equal of St. Mary's, Burlington. From the outset it was a more modest venture, and it followed no English example such as Shottesbrook. But it was important because it was praised when it was built, it was associated with the vogue for the surpliced choir and choral ceremony, and, like the Chapel of the Holy Innocents, it revealed the influence of St. Peter's, Leeds.

The Church of the Holy Innocents, in Highland Falls, New York (Fig. II–33), was built between 1846 and 1847 by Robert Weir, who apparently had for some time been interested in the appearance and mood established by the parish church in the Hudson River Valley (Fig. II–34). He was both donor and architect and expended on it the money he received for his painting in the rotunda of the Capitol in Washington. In àn effort to obtain correct orientation Weir placed the altar of his little church in the northeast, in line with Jerusalem on the great circle of the earth. Otherwise, his building was in no way unusual, extremely plain and utterly without ostentation, a modest rural church in the English style.[63] Extensive and expensive additions made in the twentieth century have so altered the interior that it hardly resembles the original church, but the exterior retains the feeling Weir sought.

When they reviewed the churches at Troy and Highland Falls, American nineteenth-century critics praised their "reality," by which they meant that they evoked a feeling of genuineness and antiquity, that they were in a fresh style, and that they were pretty. Though neither building was an accurate reproduction of a Gothic example, both had a pleasing informality and unity with their environment which was without precedent in the United States. Though today they seem routine examples of a type common in America, they, and the buildings in Burlington, introduced Americans to the potentialities of a basic change in church design and suggested that the more diffuse eighteenth-century spatial arrangement was about to be discarded. But their contribution did not end there. The parish church of the thirteenth and fourteenth century raised aesthetic possibilities and demonstrated architectural refinements which invited a reconsideration of the fundamentals of architectural design. Its interior spaces were legible on the exterior, for the chancel appeared as a separately stated entity, attached to the nave. The function of

[63] See "New Churches," *New York Ecclesiologist*, 2 (March, 1850):89–90, for a full description of the church.

Figure II-32. Holy Cross Church, Troy.

Figure II-33. Church of the Holy Innocents, Highland Falls, N.Y. Robert Weir. 1846–47.

Figure II-34. A parish church in the Hudson River Valley. Painting by Robert Weir.
In the collection of the Corcoran Gallery of Art.

the building was thus expressed in the elevations. Their wholesome emphasis upon building materials appealed strongly to Americans.

These well-intentioned but awkward imitations of the English parish church —the Church of the Holy Communion, St. Mary's Burlington, the churches in Troy and Highland Falls—could only suggest why Pugin and the ecclesiologists had chosen to recommend it for imitation in the nineteenth century. They did, however, provide the Protestant Episcopal Church with a fresh new building form rich in associations with the Church in England and perfectly adjusted to the High Church sympathies which prevailed among the leading American churchmen of the 1840's. Their gift to American architects was of equal importance. Gothic revival building presented an approach to design which challenged Georgian and Greek revival assumptions. Though the revival was not to endure as a revolutionary force, it played that part in America, just as it did in England, long enough to bring about fundamental changes in architectural principles and the character of design.

The churches of Doane and his associates, though they were well received, could not complete the revolution they had begun. Americans required a reasonable facsimile of a Gothic original in order to perceive the full potential of the revival. St. James the Less in Philadelphia was to satisfy that need.

III

Ecclesiology in the United States:
The Second Phase, 1846–1848

St. James the Less, Philadelphia

St. James the Less was the first church in the United States to be erected under the direct supervision of the English ecclesiologists. Built between 1846 and 1848, its history necessarily reflects the confusion and upset of the year and a half from January, 1845, to July, 1846, when the Cambridge Camden Society was held together only because Neale and Webb were determined that it should survive.

In January, 1845, in the midst of the intramural strife and bitterness which attended the departure of the Society from Cambridge and the withdrawal of many of its members, the *Ecclesiologist* published an account of the November, 1844, meeting. The report was virtually a posthumous statement. By the time the journal reached its subscribers, the Society had ceased to have a formal existence. At that last and fateful gathering in November almost the only happy note was an announcement that the project to publish drawings of medieval churches was progressing well. The Committee said it had in hand "full working drawings of three ancient churches, selected to serve as models for the Colonies. The three churches are All Saints', Teversham, Cambridgeshire; St.

Mary's, Arnold, Nottinghamshire; St. Michael's, Longstanton, Cambridge-shire. Tracings of the last have been forwarded to the United States. Tracings of the former are preparing for New South Wales and New Zealand."[1]

The Society had long been interested in and concerned for the welfare of St. Michael's, Long Stanton. (The twentieth-century spelling of this place name was not customary in the nineteenth century.) It and the church in Teversham were near enough to Cambridge to be studied at first hand by the Committee and the members of the Society. In 1843 the *Ecclesiologist* had noted with alarm that St. Michael's was poorly maintained: "The chancel of this very beautiful little Early English Chapel is used for a school, a green curtain being drawn across the chancel-arch, and a common wide, *kitchen-grate* inserted in, and projecting from the north wall, with a huge red brick chimney behind it, for the comfort and accommodation of the teacher (who sits within the Altar rails with his chair against the Holy Table) and his flock, who thus imbibe early principles of irreverence which must be most baneful."[2] The situation at St. Michael's was, unfortunately, typical rather than unusual. Such nine-teenth-century adjustments and additions to medieval churches were common. In many, services were performed in the eastern end of the nave, and the chancel was abandoned or put to secular use.

St. Michael's was, and still is, a remarkable small parish church, one of a stylistic group to which the churches in Manton, Rutland, and Howell, Lincoln-shire, also belong. It is composed of a nave with aisles and chancel. The roof, which covers both nave and aisles, is not broken by a clerestory; it sweeps low on the north and south sides of the nave (Fig. III–1). There are three doors: the one on the north has no porch; the one on the south has a porch and is the principal entry; and there is a door in the south wall of the chancel (Fig. III–2). A pair of heavy buttresses run up the center of the west front, and a double lancet window fills the space between them. Huge diagonal buttresses and a twin bell cote complete the composition of this unpretentious, almost primitive, façade. The nave is but 49 feet by 14 feet, and each aisle is only 5 feet 9 inches wide. St. Michael's is so small it can be described as diminutive. Though the interior is extremely simple, it possesses attributes characteristic of

---

[1] "Report of the Thirty-Ninth Meeting of the Cambridge Camden Society on Thursday, November 7," *E.*, 5 (January, 1845):23.
[2] "Notices," *E.*, 2 (June, 1843):171.

Gothic architecture at its best (Fig. III–3). It is made of stone, massive and undisguised. Arcades of four low piers separate the aisles from the nave space, the westernmost being attached to walls which project from the interior of the west front. The eastern arches are supported on molded brackets upon the chancel wall. The piers are alternately circular and octagonal. The north and south entrances to the nave are opposite one another; they fall between a circular and an octagonal pier.

When the *Ecclesiologist* described St. Michael's in the 1840's, though the chancel had been damaged and was in serious disrepair, it retained some of its thirteenth-century features. The triplet window above the altar contained its original glass, and at the base of each window there was a projecting bracket. The double piscina and a string course, which ran around the chancel beneath the window and over the door, were intact. The seven-sided trussed rafter roof of the nave and the chancel were painted white in the nineteenth century. The aisles were covered by a rafter roof which is a continuation of that over the nave. The roof of St. Michael's was a sufficiently distinguished specimen of its kind to interest the Brandons, who illustrated it in their *Open Timber Roofs of the Middle Ages* in 1849.

The windows of the aisles had been considerably altered by the 1840's. Only one contained its original tracery and glass; all the rest had been renewed in the Decorated style. The two nearest the chancel were each of three lights, and it was these that had been changed most with the passage of time. There was evidence that they had originally been roofed under gables higher than the eaves on the north and south sides.

The salient characteristics of St. Michael's, then, were its small size, its widely sloping roof, the arrangement of the west front with buttresses and diagonal buttresses, and its use of materials. The intimacy and beauty of the interior depended upon the stone interior walls, the simplicity of the arcades, the forms and materials of the roof, and the dignity the church possessed despite its size. St. Michael's was not the most elegant parish church of its period, but, because it was small and of excellent and in many ways remarkable representative design, it was admirable as a model for churches abroad.

After having announced that the Decorated style best revealed the splendors of art and religion in the Middle Ages, the Society decided to recommend St. Michael's and All Saints' (Fig. III–4), which were Early English, because their

Figure III-1. St. Michael's, Long Stanton, Cambridgeshire, ca. 1230, as it appeared in the 1840's.

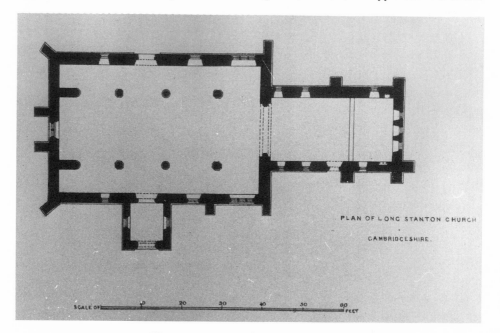

Figure III-2. St. Michael's, Long Stanton.

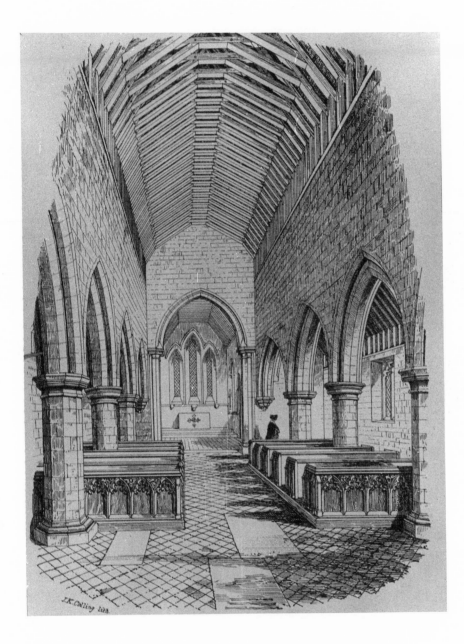

Figure III-3. St. Michael's, Long Stanton.

Figure III-4. All Saints', Teversham, Cambridgeshire, ca. 1250, showing numerous repairs and restorations made in the late nineteenth century.

lack of ostentation made them useful patterns for colonial builders who had neither the funds nor the craftsmen to duplicate more elaborate modes. The reasoning behind the selection of St. Mary's, Arnold, is less clear, for the church is composed of several Gothic styles. The remnant of a fourteenth-century chancel may have attracted the ecclesiologists, or it may have been that the architect G. G. Place, who worked in Nottingham, knew the church and fostered ecclesiological interest in it.[3]

In November, 1846, the *Ecclesiologist* announced with ill-disguised pride that "S. James, the Less, near the Falls of the Schuylkill, U.S.A." was being built under the inspiration of the Society. The note added that "this church is copied from S. Mary Arnold, working drawings of which made by Mr. G. G. Place, had been forwarded to America by The Cambridge Camden Society." The editors were pleased that "the expense in America of building this church is estimated at only 7,500 dollars, or £1520; with all the arches, doorways, window jambs etc. in dressed stone, the interior walls of ashlar and all the wood oak." Their "valued American correspondent" also informed them that "a new church near Newbury, New York, and another near Baltimore have been commenced from the same designs."[4]

Portions of this notice require explanation. First, the new church in Philadelphia was not being built from plans derived from St. Mary's, Arnold, though the error in the *Ecclesiologist* is understandable. Neither Neale nor Webb could remember what plans had been sent, and in the confusion of reorganizing the Society they did not check the announcement that had been made in November, 1844. In late 1846 St. James, Woolsthorpe, enjoyed special prominence (see Figs. II–24 and II–25); patterned after St. Mary's, Arnold, it was being completed under the approving scrutiny of the editors of the *Ecclesiologist*. However, it was the plans of St. Michael's which had been sent to the United States. There was no "Newbury, New York," and the "American correspondent" was not identified. It was perfectly clear, however, that Neale and Webb were prepared to approve St. James the Less, whatever its model, because the Society

---

[3] See "New Churches," *E.,* 6 (November, 1846):193. A notice of the election of G. G. Place to membership in the Society is found in "Report of the Thirty-Sixth Meeting of the Cambridge Camden Society on Tuesday, March 5, 1844," *E.,* 3 (May, 1844):114. See also p. 76, n. 58, above.

[4] "New Churches," *E.,* 6 (November, 1846):193.

had supplied its design and because the church, true to ecclesiological recommendation, was to be open to all.

This outspoken pleasure over St. James the Less was surely related to the difficulties Neale and Webb were having with Bishop Doane's plans for Burlington. Their initial opposition to the design for St. Mary's and their distress over the use of Shottesbrook as a model had been expressed in the *Ecclesiologist* in February, 1846, nine months before the first news of St. James the Less was received. The condescending description of the Chapel of the Holy Innocents and the condemnation of Upjohn's design were contained in an article that appeared in October, 1847, which also reported favorably on the progress of St. James the Less. The editors of the *Ecclesiologist* seem to have regarded St. James the Less as competition for the buildings at Burlington, which they believed to be the work of the Oxford Architectural Society.

The November, 1846, note in the *Ecclesiologist*, though inaccurate and confusing, at least establishes the fact that English plans for a Gothic revival church were available in the United States and that by 1846 one or more churches were being built from them. These plans were to be of decisive importance to American ecclesiastical architecture. How the drawings came to America and found their way to Philadelphia is a fascinating episode in the history of architectural taste. It was also a fortunate accident.

Samuel Farmar Jarvis, son of the second Bishop of Connecticut, was an intellectual leader in the Episcopal Church in the United States.[5] As a young scholar he had assisted in the foundation of the General Theological Seminary in New York, where he was a member of the faculty until 1820. Then, at the age of thirty-four, he left to take up a rectorship in Boston. In 1826 he resigned from that position to travel abroad. He and his family lived in Europe for nine years while Jarvis continued his training in ancient languages and carried on research in the history of the Church. The breadth of his interests and his obvious intellectual gifts led him into friendships with laymen of high rank and Episcopal clergymen in Europe, and he made enduring friends in Italy, France, and England.

---

[5] See Raymond W. Albright, *A History of the Protestant Episcopal Church* (New York: Macmillan, 1964), chap. 5, for the role of Jarvis in the growth of the Church in the mid-nineteenth century.

ECCLESIOLOGY IN THE UNITED STATES: 1846–1848

Upon his return home in 1835 Jarvis entered a period of terrible domestic difficulty, which ended in his separation and divorce from his wife. To recover from these trying events, and, no doubt, to escape from public attention for a time, for the case had been widely publicized and was filled with acrimony, in 1843 Dr. Jarvis went abroad again. This time he was an emissary to Canterbury sent by the American Church.[6] He remained in England until late 1844; in his year there he encountered the Cambridge Camden Society. Religious circles in England were in ferment over the Tracts and the growing Oxford Movement, but Jarvis threaded his way through the turmoil, always in pursuit of knowledge and aware of the advanced ideas within the Church.

Jarvis asked his new friends in the Society to help him obtain plans for a simple church in correct ecclesiological taste which he might take home to be used as a pattern by the small, impecunious parishes which were springing up in the United States. The Venerable Thomas Thorp, President of the Society, advised Jarvis to consult R. C. Carpenter, William Butterfield, and W. Harrison, architects who had, in his view, prepared drawings of the kind Jarvis required. Thorp especially recommended Harrison because he had designed a Gothic revival church for Marston Measey, Wiltshire, which Thorp described as "chaste Christian architecture" which was also cheap. It could be built for £500.[7]

In the end Jarvis settled for drawings which were sent to him in October, 1844, by George Gordon Hall of Nottingham, at the request of S. N. Stokes, a

---

[6] Jarvis had a considerable interest in the arts. While abroad he purchased a large collection of paintings by Italian masters which he brought back to the United States, exhibited, and sold. At the time of his trip to England in 1843 he was historiographer of the Church and a trustee of Trinity College and of the General Theological Seminary.

[7] In T. Bowdler to Jarvis from London, August 10, 1844, Connecticut State Library Collection, Hartford, Conn. See also "Report of the Thirty-Fourth Meeting of the Cambridge Camden Society on Tuesday, December 5, 1843," *E.*, 3 (February, 1844):79. The Reverend T. Bowdler was a member of the Ecclesiological and Oxford Architectural Societies. He joined the latter in April, 1845. Bowdler was a close friend of the architect James Park Harrison, who prepared drawings at the order of the Oxford Society (see p. 44 above). Between 1842 and 1895 Harrison published ten books, of which one was *A Letter to the Reverend T. Bowdler on the Fitness of Gothic Architecture for Modern Churches* (1848). The *Ecclesiologist* took exception to this work, saying that Harrison had been prompted by Lord Lindsay's statement that "a new architecture expressive of the epoch and her Anglican faith" was desirable. The editors were also very much annoyed that Harrison had stated views identical with their own without mentioning the Society's devotion to them ("Harrison's Letter to Rev. T. Bowdler," *E.*, 9 [August, 1848]:45–46).

member of the Committee of the Cambridge Camden Society.[8] The letter
which accompanied the parcel did not specify what church the drawings illustrated. Jarvis only knew that he had plans for "the exact copy of a Church of
early English architecture . . . for a small parish," and that its "chief beauty is
in the proportions of the Chancel which should always be a separate building
from the Nave."[9]

After he returned to America Jarvis kept the drawings until March, 1846,
when he visited a friend, Robert Ralston,[10] at his estate, Mount Peace, in the
outskirts of Philadelphia. In the course of conversation Jarvis referred to his
contact with the Society and the plans he had received through its good offices
when he was in England. Ralston had heard of ecclesiology and the Society and
knew of the reorganization which had recently taken place. Encouraged by Jarvis, he resolved to seek its advice and assistance in the matter of a design for a
church he proposed to build.

The neighborhood surrounding Mount Peace was developing rapidly into a
suburb of villas in ample grounds. The largest new neighbor was Laurel Hill
Cemetery. There were several compelling reasons for the establishment of a
parish, for as Philadelphia grew the gap between the city and Germantown nar-
rowed. A church on the hill overlooking the Schuylkill River would serve the
new residents. Ridge Road, one of the old highroads leading out of Philadelphia, ran below the site Ralston chose. The Laurel Hill Cemetery Company
sold the land to the parish. It was a beautiful tract, so large that, even in the
twentieth century, St. James the Less retains its privacy though the city crowds
about it.

Ralston wrote to the Venerable Thomas Thorp asking for drawings of a
church sanctioned by the Society, and saying that he hoped to build a "proper
church edifice" which would grace the parish and act as a model for the
churches which were much needed in the "coal and iron region" to "humanize

---

[8] Hall to Jarvis from Nottingham, October 18, 1844, Connecticut State Library Collection,
Hartford, Conn.

[9] Jarvis to the Reverend Robert A. Hallam from Middletown, Conn., November 12, 1846,
Yale University Collection, New Haven, Conn.

[10] Ralston operated a family business which had been founded in the eighteenth century.
He was in the China trade. His name disappears from the Philadelphia directories in
1856, and at the same time Mount Peace is no longer listed as the home address for the
Ralston family. The house no longer exists.

ECCLESIOLOGY IN THE UNITED STATES: 1846–1848

the people."[11] Rather than produce new plans, the Society suggested that Jarvis should send those in his possession to Philadelphia.[12] Neither Ralston nor Jarvis knew anything about the plans, though Jarvis persisted in a belief that they were those of Holy Trinity, Roehampton, by Benjamin Ferrey, built in 1841 to 1842, a church of which the ecclesiologists approved.

As soon as Ralston examined the plans, he wrote Jarvis that he was "struck with the thickness of the walls—2½ feet," for he had supposed "that walls only 11 feet high sustained by string buttresses might answer if 18 inches." He added that "it is common here to build walls 30 to 40 feet high 16 inches in thickness of stone." But he was comforted by the fact that the very small windows which accompanied the heavy walls would not be costly to fill with stained glass. This economy would at least in part defray the extra expense occasioned by the heavy masonry.[13]

The project for the church immersed Ralston in ecclesiological research. He was visited by the Reverend W. R. King, an English clergyman and a member of the Ecclesiological Society, who was passing through Philadelphia on his way home from Fredericton, New Brunswick, where he had been chaplain to the Right Reverend John Medley. King promised that when he reached England he would send Ralston further information, and he recommended that Ralston investigate the ecclesiastical tiles which were being manufactured by Minton. The Venerable Thomas Thorp wrote to Ralston expressing pleasure that ecclesiology had found a following in the United States. He suggested that persons interested in the subject might join the Society and receive its publications. Bishops, he said, were entitled to be patrons without cost to themselves.[14] Finally, in the late spring of 1846, Ralston and the vestry voted to use the plans Jarvis had provided stipulating that the final cost of the church should be no more than three thousand dollars.

The vestry of St. James the Less spent the summer of 1846 preparing for construction and raising funds. On Ralston's recommendation, the amount to

[11] See Ralston to Jarvis from Philadelphia, March, 1846, Connecticut State Library Collection, Hartford, Conn., for this account.
[12] "New Churches," *E.*, 5 (March, 1842):77–78.
[13] Ralston to Jarvis from Philadelphia, April 15, 1846, Connecticut State Library Collection, Hartford, Conn.
[14] See Ralston to Jarvis from Philadelphia, June 22, 1846, Connecticut State Library Collection, Hartford, Conn.

be spent was increased to five thousand dollars, a sum to which Ralston contributed heavily. He wrote Jarvis that for the sake of St. James the Less he would gladly sell six Ionic capitals and bases he owned, for he had lost "all further taste for Grecian architecture."[15] Within the vestry, during the months before building began, Ralston had to wage a vigorous campaign to build the church exactly to the English plans, for there were those who wished to raise the walls higher and depress the roof.[16] In the end Ralston acquired an ecclesiological education so rapidly that he was able to express regret that Trinity Church and the Church of the Holy Communion had been built too early to profit from the knowledge the Society had to offer American churchmen and their architects.

In August, 1846, Ralston at last received a letter from the Reverend Benjamin Webb, in response to his request for assistance with details of the design. Webb's letter was warm and friendly. He had dispatched to Ralston plans for a second parish church which could be passed on to others who were eager to build correctly. They were, said Webb, those for "a beautiful church adapted from Teversham" (Fig. III–4). In the parcel with them he had included various publications of the Society. Webb then gave the vestry an astonishing bit of news: he stated categorically that the plans which had been given Jarvis were not those for Holy Trinity, Roehampton, as Jarvis had thought, but were, instead, designs for a church adapted from St. Mary's, Arnold (see Figs. II–24, II–25, and II–26).

When the November, 1846, notice of St. James the Less appeared in the *Ecclesiologist*, then, there were in the United States not only the drawings from which St. James the Less was being constructed but plans based upon the church at Teversham. It seems to have been Benjamin Webb who made the mistake of identifying the Philadelphia plans as those of St. Mary's, Arnold. None of the parties concerned with the venture were aware at this point that St. James the Less was being built from measured drawings of St. Michael's, which had been only slightly revised. It was for this reason that the walls were so thick and the windows so small.

[15] Ralston to Jarvis from Philadelphia, August 12, 1846, Connecticut State Library Collection, Hartford, Conn.
[16] Ralston to Jarvis from Philadelphia, August 22, 1846, Connecticut State Library Collection, Hartford, Conn.

ECCLESIOLOGY IN THE UNITED STATES: 1846–1848

Two further questions raised by the item in the *Ecclesiologist* require explanation. The reference to "Newbury, New York" was a misreading of Ralston's hand; he had surely written "Newburgh." The statement that a church
was being built "near Baltimore" from the plans for St. James the Less admitted
another American diocese to the domain of ecclesiology. St. James the Less
had begun its missionary work; the Right Reverend William Rollinson Whittingham, Bishop of Maryland, visited Mount Peace in the summer of 1846 and
there saw, admired, and discussed the English drawings.

The Ecclesiological Society watched paternally as St. James the Less was
being planned and constructed. In October, 1846, the contract for the church
was signed; it set July, 1847, as the completion date. At the same time the
plans were modified to allow the addition of one more bay to the nave, increasing its length to 61 feet 6 inches, and a vestry was added at the northeast side
of the chancel. The contract also called for the pulpit, chancel rail, lectern, and
all the sash to be brought from England. The cost of the building had now risen
to six thousand dollars.[17]

As the time to lay the cornerstone approached, Ralston, who was still at
work on the details of the project, consulted Major Douglass, past President of
Kenyon College and past professor of architecture and civil engineering at the
University of the City of New York. The unplastered, unpainted interior was
one of the peculiarities of the English design, and Ralston asked Douglass
whether this feature should be kept. Douglass, fortunately, showed good taste,
and responded: "I like very much the idea of leaving the rubble unplastered.
You will need to have the face worked with a little more care than our masons
ordinarily bestow, but with a little caution in this particular you need not fear
for the result. I do not believe a tongue will be found to wag against it, at least
after the novelty of the thing is a little passed off."[18]

[17] Ralston to Jarvis from Philadelphia, October 15, 1846, Connecticut State Library Collection, Hartford, Conn. Ralston wrote: "Our contract and specifications require that the
Church of St. Mary, Arnold, shall be copied to the letter, all the mouldings, Arches,
capitals, bosses, brackets, corbels, etc. The Walls outside and in to be of best possible
work but all the window jams [*sic*] rabbits door hinges etc to be of fine cut stone. All the
woodwork to be of best seasoned oak, no plaster no paint about the church."
[18] Quoted in Ralston to Jarvis from Philadelphia, October 17, 1846, Connecticut State
Library Collection, Hartford, Conn.

In the last six weeks of 1846 Webb and Ralston corresponded frequently. Webb suggested uses to which the second set of plans he had sent—those for All Saints', Teversham—could be put: "You will find it a very beautiful model of simple but excellent detail and accurately recalling the effect of an English rural parish church of the 14th century, the middle pointed period of Ecclesiastical architecture." He also assured Ralston that his request for drawings of a church suitable for a city site would be considered at the next meeting of the Committee. Ralston must have wanted the Society to supply a plan from which to build St. Mark's, Philadelphia, when he wrote the ecclesiologists requesting drawings for "a new stone church to be built in the south-west quarter of Philadelphia, which is intended to have a developed chancel, west tower and spire. It is to hold 800 to 1000 persons."[19] Somewhat perplexed by this request, for it had at hand no plan of the sort Ralston wished, the Committee said, as reported in the *Ecclesiologist*, that "it is not easy for ourselves to forward designs for town-churches to our Transatlantic brethren, because there are not old examples which we can recommend for direct imitation."[20] The ecclesiologists thought of themselves as experts on country parish churches only. In the end, they sent Ralston tracings of the plans of R. C. Carpenter's All Saints', Brighton, as an example of a town church. The reasons for this choice will be discussed below.

In the course of this correspondence in 1846 and early 1847 Benjamin Webb repeatedly suggested that an American ecclesiological society be founded and that the English publications he had sent be circulated widely among those sympathetic to the cause in the United States. Ralston responded enthusiastically to each of these suggestions, and a discussion about the name of such an American society began. Some of the founders felt that the word "ecclesiological" should not be included in its title.

Suddenly, in December, 1846, Webb informed Ralston that he and Neale "had got the names mixed up and that Longstanton church was the model" for St. James the Less.[21] But no one yet realized that the design Webb had provided was not an adaptation but a reproduction of the medieval original.

As soon as building began at St. James the Less, it became apparent that it

[19] Quoted in Ralston to Jarvis from Philadelphia, October 23, 1846, Connecticut State Library Collection, Hartford, Conn.
[20] "Progress of Ecclesiology in the United States," *E.*, 8 (October, 1847) :70.
[21] Quoted in Ralston to Jarvis, December 18–19, 1846, from microfilm, property of the Diocese of Connecticut, in Trinity College Collection, Hartford, Conn.

would be impossible to complete the church in 1847. Stone was hard to obtain, and the complexities of the project increased with each day's work. Ralston sought further advice from the Society, and Webb now referred his letters to William Butterfield, who wrote and sent drawings directly to Ralston. It was Butterfield who arranged that the Communion plate for St. James the Less be made in London from his designs, and it was he who "ordered the tiles for our chancel" and saw to it that "Mr. Minton who is making them is to present to our church Tiles for the reredos as he did for the chapel erected at Fredericton by the Bishop of that See."[22] Ralston was still cheerful, for he felt sure that "the delays which have occurred are all in favor of perfecting the plan and some things have been altered from time to time as we gained knowledge."[23] He had no doubt that St. James the Less would be "considered a very curious church," but he was convinced that its strangeness would be beneficial.

Several times William Butterfield was called upon to prepare actual designs. Ralston discovered, for example, that Jarvis had lost or never had been given the sheet of drawings which included the east and west windows and the external details for the aisle windows. It was Butterfield who made and sent the drawings for the chancel and recommended, Ralston said, that "instead of the steps being placed together to rise to the platform on which stands the altar that they should be spread out more. . . . He [Butterfield] says 'I have left the number of steps as you have shown across the chancel but have added what is called a foot pace, i.e. a step not running across the whole width of the chancel but returning around the altar.' "[24] Finally, Butterfield provided Ralston with a copy of the *Instrumenta Ecclesiastica, A Series of Working Designs for the Furniture, Fittings, and Decorations of Churches and their Precincts*, which he had prepared for the Cambridge Camden Society.[25]

[22] Ralston to Jarvis, July, 1847, from microfilm, property of the Diocese of Connecticut, in Trinity College Collection, Hartford, Conn.

[23] Ralston to Jarvis, December 18–19, 1846, from microfilm, property of the Diocese of Connecticut, preserved in Trinity College Collection, Hartford, Conn.

[24] *Ibid.*

[25] *Instrumenta Ecclesiastica* (London: Van Voorst, 1847) appeared in twelve parts. The designs were by William Butterfield, and the whole was edited by the Ecclesiological Society. Butterfield's position as the official designer for the Society dated from March, 1843, when he agreed to accept orders for the "practical superintendence of the execution of sacred vessels or other ecclesiastical furniture from designs which shall have been approved of by our Society" ("Report of the Thirty-First Meeting of the Cambridge Camden Society, March 13, 1843," *E.*, 2 [April, 1843]:126; and "Report of the Thirty-Sixth Meeting of the Cambridge Camden Society, March 5, 1844," *E.*, 3 [May, 1844]:115).

THE GOTHIC REVIVAL AND AMERICAN CHURCH ARCHITECTURE

By May, 1847, the *Ecclesiologist* could comment comfortably that it was "glad to hear from a correspondent in the United States that the Church of St. James the Less, Schuylkill, is progressing well, and that the chancel has been more correctly arranged in consequence of a communication from our Society. The internal walls of the chancel are to be ashlar; those of the nave are to be ranged but undressed stone. All the splays and moulded parts are to be of well cut stone. There is to be a well-intentioned though unsuccessful rood screen; but the error will, we trust be rectified."[26]

In the end not six thousand but thirty thousand dollars was spent on St. James the Less, for its manifold charms encouraged the vestry to add rich stained glass and elegant appointments of every sort. The stone was gray granite from the Philadelphia area, the glass of the aisle windows was produced by Powell's Whitefriars Glass Works, London, and the designs of the original altar and font and the lectern were taken from the *Instrumenta Ecclesiastica*[27] (Figs. III–5 and III–6). The pews, the stalls, and the Bishop's chair were all richly carved. In 1850 the vestry formally expressed its gratitude to the Reverend Benjamin Webb and the Ecclesiological Society.

By 1849 the church had become so distinguished and so beautiful that the vestry, deciding to enrich it further, commissioned Henry Gerente of Paris to make a new east window to replace the one originally installed.[28] This was a

---

[26] "New Churches," *E.*, 7 (May, 1847):195.

[27] "New Churches," *New York Ecclesiologist*, 1 (October, 1848):39.

[28] In 1849 Gerente also received a contract to fill two windows in Canterbury Cathedral, he was at work at Ely Cathedral, and he was associated closely with A. W. Pugin and his stained glass manufacturer, John Hardman of Birmingham. Pugin admired Gerente's work and considered him his superior in designs in the early medieval styles. When Gerente died of cholera late in 1849, Pugin hastened to Paris to see whether he could purchase the medieval specimens from which Gerente had worked and procure his supply of modern glass. After 1849 the shop of Gerente continued under the direction of his brother Alfred, who gave up his career as a sculptor to administer the firm.

Henry Gerente's fame rested in the main upon his connections with various projects in France. He won his first prize for a design in 1841 and executed glass for Notre Dame de Bon Secours, near Rouen, and Notre Dame de la Couture, at Le Mans. About 1845 he established his own glassworks, and in 1847 he won a competition for the repair and restoration of the glass in the Sainte-Chapelle. In the same year he was sent to England to study the collection of drawings of French architectural and monumental remains which, as a consequence of the French Revolution, had come into the Doucean Collection. After the Revolution of 1848 his business suffered, but Viollet le Duc gave him work at St. Denis.

Gerente was a scholar as well as an artist. Close study of the glass at Canterbury led him to the conclusion that it had been made by the artist who had done the windows at Sens. He published articles in the *Annales Archéologiques* and trained students in the design

singularly fortunate choice, for Gerente was one of the best mid-nineteenth-century artists in stained glass. Though small, the window, a three-lancet group, is of extraordinary quality. It was praised extravagantly when it was dedicated.[29] Some years later the firm of Gerente also filled the two west lancets.

Since the mid-nineteenth century, changes and additions at St. James the Less have followed the *Instrumenta Ecclesiastica*. The lych gate and the designs of the gravestones in the cemetery which surrounds the church were taken from it (Fig. III–7). Through the years men of wealth who have been willing to spend what was needed to maintain its quality and character have been associated with the vestry.[30] St. James the Less retains to an astonishing degree the feeling sought by Ralston and his colleagues.[31]

The success of St. James the Less raises the question of its attribution to an architect. Even a cursory comparison between it and St. Michael's will reveal

---

of glass, its history, and in the history of manuscript illumination (see "Henry Gerente," *E.*, 7 [October, 1849]:97–101, and the manuscript letters of A. W. Pugin).

[29] The *New York Ecclesiologist* said: "He [Gerente] has produced a window which for effective beauty we do not hesitate to say is unsurpassed in this country; it has unity of design and unity of effect together with that sparkling gem-like appearance which is so characteristic of much of the glass of the Middle Ages, especially some in Canterbury and many of the French Cathedrals" (3 [September, 1851]:137–39). The central light is a Jesse window composed of the figures of David, Solomon, the Virgin and Child, and Christ. At the top the Dove descends. The north light contains the four evangelical prophets and the south, the four Evangelists with their symbols. The figures in the north and south lights are seated under canopies. The colors in all three windows are predominantly blue and red.

[30] In 1878 St. James the Less received its most successful enrichment when the roof of the chancel was decorated; a choir of angels was painted above the altar, and plant and abstract ornament was painted over the choir. This decoration was the gift of Moro Phillips; the artist who executed these delightful Pre-Raphaelite figures and the design of palms and lilies is unknown. The light metal rood screen of excellent workmanship and taste was installed at the time the roof was painted and was the gift of the same donor. The altar was enlarged by surrounding, not removing, the original.

[31] The churchyard was walled, and in 1897 a high protective wall along Hunting Park Avenue was constructed, a change which has protected the church and its environs from the vehicular traffic now nearby. The largest single addition to the immediate area of the church is the bell tower and mausoleum, erected in 1908, designed by John T. Windrim in consultation with Henry Vaughan, at the order of Rodman Wanamaker. The Wanamaker Tower stands at the edge of the churchyard on a piece of ground lower than that on which the church is placed. It conflicts in no way with the church and is a careful twentieth-century Gothic revival design. It underscores the artistic precision and richness of the whole complex. Across Clearfield Street a rectory, school, and parish house have been added, but, again, they are in gray stone and of modified and tasteful Gothic revival design.

Figure III-5. St. James the Less, Philadelphia. 1846–49.

Figure III-6. St. James the Less, Philadelphia.

Figure III-7. St. James the Less, Philadelphia.

Figure III-8. St. James the Less, Philadelphia. South porch.

that the measured drawings of St. Michael's brought home by Jarvis had contained only a few changes. Someone had designed a new south porch (Fig. III–8), added the chimney beside it, altered the bell cote, and replaced the Decorated windows with windows of Early English design copied from the single original window which was still in the church in the mid-nineteenth century. Someone had also restored the details which had been damaged or inaccurately replaced as time passed.

When he worked from drawings of St. Mary's, Arnold, G. G. Place, at Woolsthorpe, had replaced a heavy porch with one of his own Early English design (see Fig. II–24). The south porch at St. James the Less and that at Woolsthorpe resemble each other in scale, proportion, and in certain of their details. Either Place or an architect in his office had prepared the measured drawings of St. Michael's and made the minimal changes which seemed required. In his correspondence with Jarvis, Ralston twice referred to "the architect," once in connection with the addition of another bay to the nave, and later in the discussion over the missing sheet of window details. John Notman and Richard Upjohn were both nearby: Notman was in practice in Philadelphia; Upjohn was at work on St. Mary's, Burlington. Neither, however, had anything to do with the design of St. James the Less though recently the church has been erroneously attributed to Notman.[32] The changes made in the Long Stanton pattern were executed in England by G. G. Place. Those made in Philadelphia—the addition to the nave and the added vestry—as well as the excellent craftsmanship displayed in the building, are attributable to a skilled contractor and architect, John E. Carver, who supervised the construction.[33]

St. James the Less solidified the connections between the Ecclesiological

---

[32] See Francis James Dallett, "John Notman, Architect," *The Princeton University Library Chronicle*, 20 (Spring, 1959):137, n. 42. This note refers the reader to J. Thomas Scharf and Thompson Westcott, *History of Philadelphia, 1609–1884* (Philadelphia, 1888), p. 1354, who do not attribute the church to Notman; Dallett does say, however, that Harold Donaldson Eberlein did so.

[33] The Philadelphia directories show that in the late 1830's Carver listed himself as a drawing master. A few years later he appears as a contractor. In 1841, he was calling himself "architect."

ECCLESIOLOGY IN THE UNITED STATES: 1846–1848

Society and the Protestant Episcopal Church in the United States. Because it was a careful and expensive reproduction of a medieval model, it established the authority of the English parish church style which had been tentatively introduced by Doane and his friends. None of the earlier exercises in the mode had been of the quality of Ralston's church. Had Jarvis been given the plans of the church at Roehampton, or even those of St. Mary's, Arnold, as they were adapted for St. James', Woolsthorpe, the church in Philadelphia would have been a mediocre revival example or an overworked copy of a medieval original. Instead, Ralston in his enthusiasm pushed the vestry into building a reproduction of St. Michael's. Many of the Protestant Episcopal churches that followed in the United States were informed with its feeling for materials and for simple but delicate articulation of ornament and scale. At a time when the Protestant Episcopal Church in the United States was about to undergo considerable stylistic renovation with or without a valid model, the importance of St. James the Less is clear. Whether or not one approves the appropriation of a medieval plan for nineteenth-century use and the introduction of the deep chancel as a part of church plans and liturgical practice, one must be grateful for the accident which brought to America a building that demonstrated the aesthetic truths medieval building had to offer the nineteenth-century architect and patron.

The plans Ralston had acquired in his negotiations with Jarvis and the Ecclesiological Society remained available to architects of later American churches. Fortunately, St. James the Less possessed features, such as the west buttresses, the huge diagonal buttresses, and the chimney by the little south porch, which may be recognized when copied in later churches. The widespread use of the deep chancel after 1846 should not be attributed solely to the influence of St. James the Less, however; this feature was much discussed in the literature of the ecclesiological movement, it appeared in Pugin's illustrations, and it was mentioned in almost all the advice to church builders published in England and the United States after 1841. Jarvis understood its importance, and Doane seems to have had Upjohn duplicate the chancel of Shottesbrook at St. Mary's, Burlington, because of this requirement. It was, however, at St. James the Less that the full possibilities of the chancel were revealed for the first time in the United States. Laymen and clergy could see the correct medieval proportions and relationships of the chancel and nave volumes and the way in which the two appeared externally as one and yet separate entities interrelated by their function as parts of a whole. St. James the Less displayed, as well, principles of architectural design, a sense for materials, a feeling for pervasive scale, and an expression of function in design which Americans instinctively understood and enjoyed, and from which they were to profit.

Through Richard Upjohn, the influence of St. James the Less spread in Protestant Episcopal architecture. There were many ways in which he could have come into contact with Ralston's project. Jarvis knew Upjohn and admired his work;[34] in 1846 and 1847 St. Mary's was taking shape, and on his trips to Burlington Upjohn must have visited so new and interesting a building as the one rising on the hill overlooking the Schuylkill. Contact with Ralston would have been immensely stimulating for Upjohn because by November, 1847, at Mount Peace, there were not only the two plans for parish churches but also R. C. Carpenter's drawings for All Saints', Brighton, which had arrived some time before October, 1847, in response to Ralston's request for a scheme for a "town-church."

The parish churches which emerged from Upjohn's office after 1847 provide ample evidence that he knew St. James the Less. The proportions and relationships between the parts of a building and the feeling for materials in his work change abruptly in 1847 and 1848. Calvary Church, Stonington, the prototype of his later small churches, has the bell cote, the pronounced west front, the wide sloping roof, and the over-all feeling of St. James the Less.[35]

Upjohn was only the most prominent of the American architects to reflect the influence of St. James the Less. John Notman was the architect for the vestry of St. Mark's, and Ralston's attempt to acquire a pattern from England establishes a connection which is scarcely needed. With a large and expensive Gothic revival church to design, Notman could hardly have been unaware

---

[34] Jarvis to Hallam from Middletown, Conn., November 12, 1846, Yale University Collection, New Haven, Conn.: "I hear from Mr. Morgan that Mr. Upjohn has so planned the new church at Norwich [with the chancel as a separate building from the nave]. I have great confidence in Mr. Upjohn's taste and trust he will make the chancel deep and have side light in it which adds greatly to the beauty and solemnity of the services."

[35] The cornerstone of Calvary Church, Stonington, Conn., was laid in September, 1847, and the plans are dated January, 1848, and March, 1849 (Upjohn, *Richard Upjohn*, p. 205).

of the singular and exciting potentialities of the building Ralston and his fellow vestrymen were constructing.

St. Mark's, Philadelphia

The leading ecclesiologists had long sought an architect they could call their own, one "equal to building cathedrals." By 1845, when they endorsed R. C. Carpenter, they felt they had found such a man. This alliance both pleased and relieved Thorp and other members of the Committee who, because they feared a possible association of ecclesiology with Roman Catholicism, disliked "the assistance of Pugin."[36] Carpenter was at work on St. Paul's, Brighton, in 1846 and 1847, and the *Ecclesiologist* saw fit to comment extensively on the church, reviewing first the designs, and later the building and its decoration as it neared completion.[37] The editors itemized the errors in taste and in the arrangement of the interior which they observed, but, generally, though it did not spare Carpenter, the *Ecclesiologist* was surprisingly constructive and positive in its criticisms of his work. When Carpenter received the commission to design All Saints', Brighton, the *Ecclesiologist* was quietly jubilant that another "satisfactory" church was to grace that city.

All Saints' was to have aisles of unequal width, a nave of seven bays, a full deep chancel, and a broach spire at its northwest corner. The sacristy was to be south of the chancel. In order that it might accommodate a large congregation without resorting to the use of galleries, All Saints' was to be very large—132 feet long and more than 66 feet wide. The editors described its style as "flowing Middle Pointed." The unusual breadth of the church required an equally unusual treatment of the roof, a problem which Carpenter solved by covering each aisle with a separate gable. The *Ecclesiologist* found this plan "though aesthetically beautiful . . . alien to the spirit of our present rites," and it also questioned the decision to place the tower at the end of an aisle rather than in front of the nave. Though they were puzzled by such major matters,

---

[36] Bowdler to Jarvis from London, May 25, 1846, Connecticut State Library Collection, Hartford, Conn.

[37] "New Churches," *E.*, 5 (February, 1846):154–56; 7 (April, 1847):153; 8 (December, 1847):188.

the editors were content merely to express their "anxiety to behold the actual building." Forsaking the querulous tone they usually assumed when faced with something irregular, they said that they were "conscious that the very high opinion which we have of Mr. Carpenter's talents makes any praise on our part of his works suspicious in some quarters."[38]

It was natural, then, that in October, 1846, when Robert Ralston wrote to the Society requesting a plan for a "town-church," and the Society was puzzled as to what to send, All Saints', Brighton, upon which Carpenter was working, would come to mind. As we have seen, some months later, when drawings were actually sent, it was those for All Saints' that left for Philadelphia. Carpenter's design seemed to answer the American requirements, for it had been prepared for an urban site and it was fresh from the office of the approved ecclesiological architect.[39]

When the plans arrived in Philadelphia, they were handed to John Notman to adapt as he saw fit, but both he and the vestry recognized at once that the three-gabled roof was not at all suitable for the snows of North America. As Notman worked on his design in the late summer of 1847, he had at hand these English tracings, illustrations of English Gothic revival buildings, and the usual manuals on medieval building. By September 18, 1847, he must have determined the general form St. Mark's was to assume because in the collection of the Historical Society of Pennsylvania there is a water color of the south side

---

[38] "New Churches," *E.*, 7 (August, 1847):55–56.

[39] The chronology of this transaction is as follows. When Ralston asked Webb for plans for a "town church," he was told that the Society would consider it. In July, 1847, Ralston reported that he had paid ten pounds for tracings. The *Ecclesiologist* of October, 1847, confirmed that the plans had been sent. In the *Journal of the Society of Architectural Historians* (15 [May, 1956]:19–23), James D. van Trump describes the history of St. Peter's, Pittsburgh, by John Notman. He mentions St. Mark's in passing and states that the Carpenter tracings were in the possession of E. H. Yardley in 1956. He also says that the Minute Book of the vestry of St. Mark's for 1847 to 1863, in the entry for February 8, 1848, states that the vestry applied to the Ecclesiological Society for plans and that those by Carpenter had been sent in 1848. (The Minute Book was not available to me in the preparation of this study.)

This sequence of dates does not seem reasonable. Notman's plans for St. Mark's had reached England and been reviewed by the Society by April, 1848 ("Progress of Ecclesiology in the United States, No. II," *E.*, 8 [April, 1848]:285). The February, 1848, entry could have been occasioned by the dispatch of Notman's plans to London.

ECCLESIOLOGY IN THE UNITED STATES: 1846–1848

of the church signed and dated by Notman[40] (Fig. III–9), which generally resembles St. Mark's as it was ultimately built. There are, however, features in the water color, not present when the church was finally constructed, which indicate that Notman was indeed inspired by an English Gothic revival church which was not All Saints', Brighton. The arrangement of St. Mark's on its long narrow site was derived from St. Stephen's, Rochester Row, Vincent Square, Westminster, which was also begun in the summer of 1847. The 1847 water color is, therefore, a link between Notman's primary source and his final plan.

When the foundation stone of St. Stephen's was laid, the church was much discussed in the press. It was the personal gift of Miss Burdett Coutts, who donated it in the hope that it might improve the religious lot of the poor who lived in the slums of Westminster. The generosity of the donor, her social eminence, and the brilliance of the company of ecclesiastical and lay persons that assembled for the laying of the foundation stone prompted extensive accounts of the new church which was planned. Miss Coutts's architect, Benjamin Ferrey, had been trained by A. C. Pugin and had remained on good terms with A. W. Pugin. In 1852 he was to write a biography of the younger Pugin. Ferrey was a man of peaceable disposition who managed to succeed in staying in the good graces of the ecclesiologists, though they never precisely warmed to him. His capacities were generally acknowledged. On July 24, 1847, as Notman was confronted with the problem of a "town-church," the *Illustrated London News* published an account of St. Stephen's and an illustration.[41] St. Stephen's was to stand with its long axis parallel to Rochester Row; thus the chancel was at the north and the "west door" at the south. The *Illustrated*

---

[40] The library of the Henry Francis du Pont Winterthur Museum, Delaware, also has several water-color renderings which show the church essentially as it was finally built. Dr. Summer has kindly made these drawings available to me and informed me that they were found and purchased in England. They appear to be a portion of the illustrations of St. Mark's which were sent to the Ecclesiological Society in February, 1848. They present a more developed conception of the building than did the water color and plans which are in the collection of the Historical Society of Pennsylvania.

[41] "Miss Burdett Coutts' Church," *Illustrated London News*, 11 (July 24, 1847); see also "S. Barnabas', Pimlico; S. Stephen's, Westminster; and S. Mary's, Crown Street," *E.*, 11 (August, 1850):110–19. There is a slight difference between the measurements given in the *Illustrated London News* and those published in the *Ecclesiologist*. *The Builder* also carried an illustration of St. Stephen's, but Notman's rendering more nearly resembles that in the *Illustrated London News*.

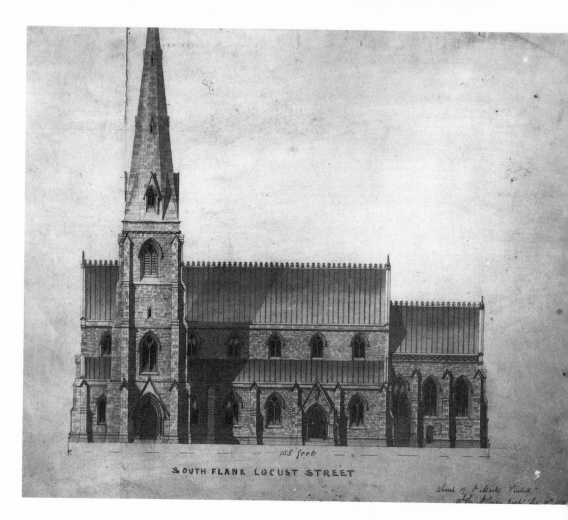

Figure III-9. St. Mark's, Philadelphia. John Notman. 1847–49. Water color,
signed "John Notman, Archt." (September 18, 1847).

ST. STEPHEN'S CHURCH, WESTMINSTER.—FOUNDED BY MISS BURDETT COUTTS.

Figure III-10. St. Stephen's, Westminster, London. West side. B. Ferrey. 1847.

London News view showed the west side, that is, the Rochester Row elevation (Fig. III–10). Measurements and other specifications of the church were given; the design and its details were praised.[42]

St. Mark's, as Notman conceived it in September, 1847, was to have an entrance under the tower and another, with a porch, into its south aisle (see Fig. III–9). The tower entrance did not appear at St. Stephen's, but the porch entrance did. Along the sides of the chancel at St. Stephen's an enriched parapet separated wall from roof. This device appeared both in the water color of St. Mark's and in the church as it was finally constructed. The door into the aisle Notman eliminated before St. Mark's was built. At St. Stephen's the windows of the clerestory were filled with matching tracery. Those in the aisles each had three lights and, as in the clerestory, the curvilinear tracery was all from a single pattern. In Notman's proposal for St. Mark's all the windows had two lights and the tracery was uniform. The 1847 water-color rendering must have revealed that such a scheme would have given a bald and mechanical appearance to the Locust Street façade. In reworking his design Notman corrected this inadequacy by following Ferrey's example, for, though he kept the clerestory tracery as originally designed, he enriched that of the aisles.

Ferrey had raised St. Stephen's from the ground level on a series of ground courses which gave his building a stiff and inorganic feeling, at least so it appeared in the *Illustrated London News* illustration. Notman, by eliminating these courses in favor of an effective and much more simple foundation, related his church well to its site. In his water color Notman had omitted the crockets from the buttresses, though he kept Ferrey's gables; the solution was far from successful, since in the drawing his church appeared spiky and inelegant on the long side. This too was an imperfection which must have been

---

[42] The nave was to be 82 feet by 21 feet with five bays. The aisles were each 13 feet wide. The chancel was large—47 feet long, more than half as long as the nave, and equally wide. A tower 200 feet high was to stand at the west of the chancel. A porch on the west side of the nave would cover a door which opened into the second bay of the aisle. The description mentioned that the church was to be built of "Snenton rag-stone and Anstone stone" similar to that being used for the Houses of Parliament. The buttresses were to be terminated by two stages and to have gables adorned with crockets. The general style was Decorated.

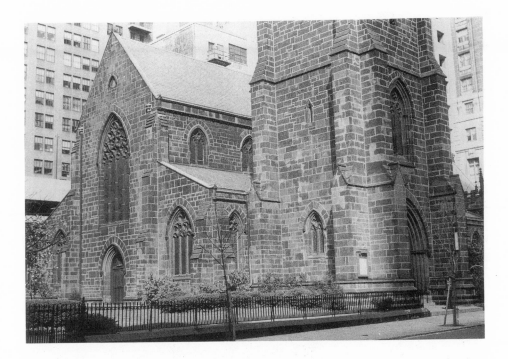

Figure III-11. St. Mark's, Philadelphia.

Figure III-12. St. Mark's, Philadelphia.

Figure III-13. St. Mark's, Philadelphia.

clear to Notman as soon as he prepared his rendering. In St. Mark's as eventually built, Notman used buttresses composed of two stages, the first offset consisting of three elements and the second of five. They, combined with the simple ground course, the pattern of the stone of the walls, the arches of the windows, and the tracery, composed a rich elevation on the Locust Street Side (Fig. III–11).

When he was presented with a site on which the church would expose its long south flank to the street, Notman achieved the solution to his Philadelphia problem by simply reversing the position of the chancel of the Ferrey church. This decision had its advantages, for it put the chancel in the east, where it belonged, and separated it from the tower at the west end.

The spire of St. Mark's was neither a copy of nor inspired by that of St. Stephen's. For Philadelphia Notman used the general form of the spire, which he could study in the tracings of the All Saints' plan. The editors of the *Ecclesiologist* noted the resemblance when they reviewed Notman's proposal.[43]

Between September, 1847, and February, 1848, Notman made not only the changes in the elevations which have been described but also significant revisions in the proportions he had proposed. He shortened the nave from the 155 feet of the water color to 100, while keeping its original width of 56 feet. He did not alter the size of the chancel. These changes tightened and improved the composition. Finally, by removing the south porch at the east end and introducing a west door to the nave, he arranged all public entrances in the west.

In April, 1848, when an approving notice of Notman's church appeared in the *Ecclesiologist*, he hastened to correct an impression it conveyed. The editors had assumed that he had simply adopted and adapted the All Saints' design. Notman clearly felt that this idea was not only untrue but might damage his growing practice and his reputation for originality. Upon receiving his letter the *Ecclesiologist* apologized lavishly, at the same time reporting that as of June, 1848, the walls of St. Mark's were "as high as the cills of the windows; and the architect hopes to roof in the church before the close of the year."[44]

St. Mark's is as successful a "town-church" as St. James the Less is a "rural

---

[43] "Progress of Ecclesiology in the United States," *E.*, 8 (April, 1848):285.
[44] "St. Mark's, Philadelphia," *E.*, 9 (August, 1848):13–14.

parish church." For all the excellence of its balanced and well integrated proportions (Fig. III–12), it is the interior (Fig. III–13) which ultimately distinguishes it. Notman was certainly well aware of St. James the Less when he decided to give St. Mark's unplastered walls of hammer-dressed stone. He skillfully employed only those details of the Decorated style which could be executed properly in the materials with which he was working and by the craftsmen he had at his disposal. He avoided overindulgence in ornament and the arid, academic exactness it would have brought with it. Beneath the dark, open timber roof, in the limited light of the nave, the capitals of the arcades, alternately foliated and molded, assist in the composition of the finest church interior of its period in the United States. In Philadelphia ecclesiology had brought a new church style and a new sophistication to American architecture.

IV

Christ Church Cathedral and the Chapel of St. Anne, Fredericton, New Brunswick

Both the Right Reverend John Medley, First Bishop of New Brunswick, and Frank Wills, the architect who went with the Bishop to Canada when he assumed his see, came from Exeter, Devonshire. It is there that the history of Christ Church Cathedral and the Chapel of St. Anne, in Fredericton, begins. Upon graduating with honors from Wadham College in 1826, Medley had proceeded immediately into the service of the Church. Ordained deacon in 1828, he spent three years as a curate in Devonshire, then was made rector of St. Thomas', Exeter, where, in 1842, he was designated prebendary of the Cathedral. Medley was a likable, energetic man of genuine intellectual attainment. He had assisted John Keble in the preparation of the *Homilies of Saint John Chrysostom* for the *Lives of the Fathers*, and he was one of the most knowledgeable of the English clergymen preoccupied with the history of Gothic architecture and its revival in the nineteenth century. Because he wished to continue in Devonshire the architectural studies he had begun at Oxford, Medley founded the Exeter Diocesan Architectural Society, one of the provincial organizations with which the Cambridge Camden Society kept in touch. Under the auspices of the Exeter Society, of which he was secretary, Medley published a small book entitled *Elementary Remarks on Church Architecture*, in 1841, which the *Ecclesiologist* reported was a work the editors could "safely recommend."[1] They even placed it in a class with John Mason Neale's *A Few Hints on the Practical Study of Ecclesiastical Antiquities* and *A Few Words to Church Builders* and the books of M. H. Bloxam.[2]

The Exeter Society prospered. It promptly acquired more than one hundred and fifty members, sponsored field trips to churches in Devonshire, and exerted pressure upon local church builders to include chancels in their plans. It claimed to have "brought about a thorough restoration of the Chancel of Exminster."[3] The *Ecclesiologist* was delighted when the Exeter Society campaigned "for our national styles in opposition to the fashionable Romanesque."[4] When the Society published a volume of its transactions, in 1843, an essay on Exeter Cathedral by John Medley was included; it was illustrated by Frank Wills and Henry Dudley, architects of Exeter. At the same time Medley was involved in a vigorous personal program of church building; he encouraged and supervised the construction of St. Andrew's in his parish of St. Thomas, Exwick. His architect was Mr. Hayward of Exeter, a "zealous member" of the Diocesan Architectural Society, a member of the Cambridge Camden Society, and the employer of Dudley and Wills.[5] Though St. Andrew's was not expensive, it was designed and fitted out in so scrupulously correct an ecclesiological manner that the *Ecclesiologist* called it "the best specimen of modern church we have yet seen."[6] At his own church, Medley made decorative additions which included a tomb for his wife. These projects also received approving reviews from the *Ecclesiologist*.[7] By the time that Medley left for Canada, he was widely recognized as an authority on ecclesiastical art.

[1] "Ecclesiological Publications," *E.*, 1 (November, 1841):15
[2] "Barr's Church Architecture," *E*, 1 (January, 1842):45, [Neale and John F. Russell], *A Few Hints on the Practical Study of Ecclesiastical Antiquities for the Use of the Cambridge Camden Society* (Cambridge: Cambridge Camden Society, 1841), and [Neale], *A Few Words to Church Builders* (Cambridge: University Press, 1841); for M. H. Bloxam, see p. 25, n. 38, above.
[3] "Exeter Diocesan Architectural Society," *E.*, 1 (July, 1842):178.
[4] *Ibid.*
[5] "New Churches," *E.*, 2 (October, 1842):21–23. For further information on Hayward, see N. Pevsner, *North Devon*, The Buildings of England no. 4 (Harmondsworth: Penguin, 1952), and *South Devon*, The Buildings of England no. 5 (Harmondsworth: Penguin, 1952).
[6] *Ibid.*, p. 23.
[7] "New Churches," *E.*, 2 (November, 1842):58. The *Ecclesiologist* said of the effigy of Mrs. Medley, "Few, in the best ages of Christian art, surpass it."

CHRIST CHURCH CATHEDRAL AND ST. ANNE'S CHAPEL

When he was made Bishop of Fredericton in 1845, Medley immediately announced that he hoped to build a cathedral in New Brunswick which would be patterned after a specific English church. At a farewell celebration on the evening before the new Bishop left to take up his duties, his numerous friends in Exeter and the members of the Diocesan Architectural Society presented him with £1,500 so that he might build a church "after an ancient model of singular beauty and cathedral appropriateness and of dimensions sufficient for solemn rites." Thus when the Bishop set sail for Fredericton with a rector, his five children, their governess, and various servants, he also had with him funds to begin his building program, drawings of the English church he had chosen as a pattern, and a Communion service for his new cathedral.[8]

Medley assumed his arduous tasks with enthusiasm, undaunted by the handicap of a diocese composed of eighty-seven far-flung parishes, forty-seven churches, and only thirty clergymen, as well as the presence of an ardent party among his parishioners that disapproved of his High Church connections and sentiments and watched his every move with grim intensity. He lost no time in beginning his program. He arrived in Fredericton in late spring, 1845, and in October of same year began to build Christ Church Cathedral. The people of the diocese promised to add £4,500 to the money already available. A gentleman of Fredericton presented the beautiful two-and-one-half-acre site on which the Cathedral would stand. A lady generously contributed the stone for the building. Frank Wills had arrived from Exeter and was present on the day of the laying of the cornerstone.[9]

St. Mary's, Snettisham, Norfolk, was the "ancient model" Medley had chosen for his cathedral. The *Ecclesiologist* approved his decision no more than it had Doane's proposal to copy Shottesbrook.[10] The editors were impressed that Medley had, "with a zeal worthy of a Christian Bishop, set sail for his diocese laden with plans for his cathedral" and that his project had been received "nobly," but they were dismayed at his taste, for St. Mary's was, "though magnificent as a parish church," just that, rather than a cathedral. Its chancel and transepts

---

[8] See William Quintard Ketchum, *The Life and Work of Reverend John Medley, D.D.* (Saint John, N.B.: J. and A. McMillan, 1893). All general information on Medley is drawn from this biography and from manuscript materials and the manuscript journal of Medley in the Archives of Christ Church Cathedral, Fredericton, New Brunswick.

[9] Wills was mentioned as present in the description of the ceremony contained in the journal of Bishop Medley (Christ Church Cathedral Archives, Fredericton, New Brunswick).

[10] "New Churches," *E.*, 5 (February, 1846):81.

were lower than the nave, which was a feature of parish churches but not of cathedrals, and the "singular clerestory, in which the alternate windows are circular," was also hardly suitable. The fact that Snettisham had a pretty Galilee porch which Medley proposed to duplicate helped somewhat, but his plan to perform the services in the nave rather than the choir was more than the *Ecclesiologist* could tolerate in silence, though it admired the Bishop and wished him good fortune. The editors could only "grieve that so well-meant, so noble an attempt at better things, should not embody all those characteristic features of an English cathedral, which modern research has already put us in possession of."[11]

The construction of the Cathedral was bound to progress slowly, and until it was complete there would be no church in Fredericton in which the Bishop could officiate. Medley therefore decided to build a chapel in a part of the town some distance from the site of the cathedral. When it was no longer needed as temporary quarters, this small church could serve a parish. The cornerstone of St. Anne's Chapel was laid in May, 1846, and the consecration took place in March, 1847. The Bishop paid for it, and Frank Wills was his architect.[12]

St. Anne's (now Christ Church Parish Church) is, in some ways, more interesting than Christ Church Cathedral, for it is not a close copy of a medieval original but a Gothic revival exercise, devoid of pretension. It reveals Frank Wills's capacity, tastes, and preferences at the moment in his career after he left England as a young, trained, but relatively untried architect, and before he emigrated from Canada to the United States. St. Anne's was consecrated just as St. James the Less was begun, and it may be instructive to compare the two. Wills did not have the money to give his chapel the authenticity possessed by St. James the Less, and such was not his intention. But St. Anne's is the finest small North American parish church of its date in the English Gothic revival style, and Wills was correct when he described it as "the first ecclesiastical building erected in the British provinces on which ancient architecture has been attempted to be honestly carried out."[13] Carefully executed, elegantly ap-

[11] *Ibid.*
[12] Wills, *Ancient English Ecclesiastical Architecture and Its Principles Applied To the Wants of the Church at the Present Day* (New York: Stanford and Swords, 1850), pp. 109–11, contains a full description and illustration of St. Anne's.
[13] *Ibid.*, p. 109.

pointed, it successfully brings together elements derived from an adequate knowledge of Gothic and the originality an architect was able to express within the rigid confines of ecclesiological formulas. St. Anne's reveals characteristics which belong not to the Middle Ages but to the nineteenth-century Gothic revival style, and it shows that when Wills left England he was an accomplished architect.

The little church is gray sandstone, hammer-dressed. In both Fredericton churches the craftsmanship in stone is of high quality (Fig. IV–1). The weatherings of the sills and buttresses and all exterior trim are of a local hard stone which agrees in color with the materials of the walls. The plan consists of a nave without aisles and a chancel, which is separated from the nave by a carved screen. From west to east St. Anne's measures only 74 feet, and of that space the chancel absorbs 20 feet (Fig. IV–2). The nave is 21 feet wide.[14] There is a triplet above the altar, and a large window composed of five stepped lancets filled with white quarries and emblems in the western wall lights the interior splendidly. The only public entrance is through a porch on the south. The font is located immediately inside that door. A tiny sacristy is attached to the north side of the chancel.

The interior furniture and fittings are richer than those of St. James the Less; the seats are carved butternut and the nave and chancel floor and the reredos are of Minton tiles (Figs. IV–3, IV–4, and IV–5). (This was the display that the Reverend Mr. King had described to Robert Ralston when he visited Philadelphia.) Faithful to his Exeter friends and craftsmen, the Bishop obtained the stained glass for the nave from Beer of Exeter. The chancel triplet is, however, a good example of the work of the stained glass artist Warrington, of London, of whom the ecclesiologists still approved in 1846. The screen, eagle lectern, and pulpit are also butternut, enriched with gilded details. There is an open timber roof of dark wood. The original altar service was sent out to St. Anne's from Keith, the London silversmith, and it is copied from one of the designs in the *Instrumenta Ecclesiastica*.

The nave of St. Anne's is 42 feet high, 54 feet long, and 21 feet wide, proportional relationships which at once distinguish it from medieval churches. At

[14] Wills says in *Ancient English Ecclesiastical Architecture* that the church is 54 feet by 21 feet, but Bishop Medley told the Ecclesiological Society it was 57 by 21.

St. Michael's, Long Stanton, the nave had been 49 feet long, 32 feet high, and 25 feet wide and at St. James the Less the addition of a bay to the nave of the plan of St. Michael's flattened the building. Its nave is 61 feet long, 32 feet high, and 26 feet wide. St. Anne's is ten feet taller but not so wide as either. Internally and externally the church seems attenuated, even spindly, when it is compared with the other two, and these qualities are accented by the height of the walls and the choice of the slim lancets. Nowhere is this clearer than in the composition of the western wall, where the grouped lancets with the triple bell cote above are composed into a sharply angular screen of stone held aloft by the great paired buttresses at the corners.

Though its details are, in general, Early English Gothic, the church has none of the sturdiness and solidity of that style. It is, rather, delicate, decorative, even dramatic, pointed and linear. Inside, the glare of the west light contrasts with the shade of the chancel. The dark brown of the furniture, some of it touched with gold, the painted decoration on the walls, and the way in which the room is oriented inward and concentrated upon the chancel are all Victorian. It is as though there were an antipathy between the outside of the building and its interior space, and in the contest between them the forceful, nervous strength of the interior dominates through rich decoration and the power of the painted word. At St. Anne's, and in the English churches of its generation, the many carefully studied and often richly colored details fall into a pattern that is not Gothic, but is preternaturally Gothic. They are an assemblage of perfect parts, united, but never resolved into a whole. Each element exists in and of itself; each is slightly more vertical, more linear, than its Gothic prototype. There are far more details in a characteristic Victorian church than in most medieval examples. They line the interior but disperse attention.

Sometime before May, 1848, Frank Wills left Fredericton to seek his fortune in New York City. The two years in Canada had been personally and professionally rewarding. He had married,[15] worked hard on designs for the Cathedral, superintended the works there, designed and built St. Anne's, and performed other architectural services for the Bishop, who intended to reform church design throughout his see. His reason for leaving Fredericton was that

[15] This information was supplied by Douglas Richardson.

Figure IV-1. St. Anne's Chapel, Fredericton, N.B. Frank Wills. Cornerstone laid 1846.

Figure IV-2. St. Anne's Chapel, Fredericton.

Figure IV-3. St. Anne's Chapel, Fredericton.

THE GOTHIC REVIVAL AND AMERICAN CHURCH ARCHITECTURE

Figure IV-4. Minton tiles of the reredos, St. Anne's Chapel, Fredericton.

CHRIST CHURCH CATHEDRAL AND ST. ANNE'S CHAPEL

Figure IV-5. Minton tiles of the chancel floor, St. Anne's Chapel, Fredericton.

Medley had run out of money to continue building. By 1848 there was every possibility that a young architect skilled in Gothic church design and trained in a good English office could make a place for himself in the United States, where the demand for churches was increasing.

At about the time that Wills left, Medley sailed for England on an expedition which lasted from March to September, 1848. He was in search of money for Christ Church Cathedral, contributions of books for the library he had resolved to establish in Fredericton, candidates for Holy Orders, and missionaries willing to serve in his diocese. Because he was without assistance, his episcopal duties had necessitated his traveling more than two thousand miles a year in the hinterlands of New Brunswick.[16] The Bishop, who was well liked, was much feted upon his return home. He lectured at meetings of the major English church building and architectural societies; his statements at these public appearances make it possible to reconstruct how nearly, by 1848, his plans for Fredericton had become reality.[17]

The Bishop's campaign was a success, and he returned to New Brunswick with £2,000 for the building fund and a good foundation for the impressive library he had planned. As he went about England explaining his aspirations and seeking aid, Medley reported that the nave and aisle walls of his cathedral had been built and that, in the summer of 1848, the nave would be roofed in. The difficult part of the undertaking had arrived, however, for the final decisions about a spire or spires and the design of the transepts and choir still remained to be made. No architect was in residence in Fredericton just when one was most needed. The Bishop had toyed with the idea of two towers "as at Ottery and Exeter," but he said he could be "content with one, if a cathedral-like appearance can be produced at less expense."[18] He called on the Ecclesiological Society for money and architectural aid, saying that he had "really worked for the Church of England under great disadvantages" and that he felt that he had "a claim on the bounty of English churchmen." The Ecclesiological Society gave what he asked: the *Ecclesiologist* endorsed his project and published a plea for subscriptions, and, at the suggestion of the Society, William Butter-

---

[16] See Journal of Bishop Medley, Christ Church Cathedral Archives, Fredericton, New Brunswick.

[17] Quoted in "Colonial Church Architecture," *E.*, 8 (June, 1848):361–63. This article includes illustrations of the church as it was in 1848 and of the Butterfield design.

[18] Quoted in *ibid.*, p. 362.

field produced a scheme for a choir and tower which the Bishop accepted gratefully.

This exchange between the Bishop and the Society proves that Medley had read and been influenced by the *Ecclesiologist's* criticism of Snettisham as a model. An illustration of the "Cathedral in Its Present State" which appeared in the *Ecclesiologist* at the time of Medley's English visit shows that he had substituted a normal arrangement of clerestory windows for the "singular" form at Snettisham, of which the ecclesiologists had disapproved. He had also accepted the idea that in a cathedral the choir roof should be as high as that of the nave. He was even prepared to reopen the whole question of the eastern end and admit the ecclesiologists to his deliberations.

At the end of the summer of 1849 the choir and aisles of the Cathedral were roofed, and the tower arches were to be completed before winter closed in. Upon careful reconsideration Medley had decided that the choir of Butterfield's design was too short for its purpose and had lengthened it. Everyone, including the editors of the *Ecclesiologist*, was in agreement that the alteration was a "great improvement." The Bishop had also modified the design of the tower windows, making them more simple, and he had made the tower batter to obtain greater thickness for the windows. Beer of Exeter was working on the glass for the aisle windows, which, at that point, were planned after those at Merton College Chapel.[19]

In 1851, again in search of money, the Bishop returned to England. Passing through the United States, he paid a ceremonial visit to the Church of the Advent in Boston, with which he sympathized—its rector and parishioners were having difficulties with their Bishop because they persisted in using art and religious services inspired by ecclesiology. From English and American sources Bishop Medley was able to bring back to Fredericton another £1,200. A personal friend, the Reverend R. H. Podmore, rector of Ottery St. Mary, presented two thousand volumes to the growing library at Fredericton and gave the great eagle lectern (Fig. IV–6), the altar service, and the alms dish by Keith (Fig. IV–7), all from the designs of William Butterfield.[20] A lady in Exeter contrib-

[19] "Colonial Church Architecture," *E.*, 10 (November, 1849):192–93, states that the windows in the Cathedral follow those of Merton College Chapel. The plans appear to have been changed, for the windows of the aisles in fact are copies of the Snettisham windows, save for those in the middle of each side, which are from original designs by Wills. In the end the Snettisham patterns predominated throughout the building.
[20] Information from Christ Church Cathedral Archives, Fredericton, New Brunswick.

Figure IV-6. Eagle lectern, Christ Church Cathedral, Fredericton.
Designed by William Butterfield and made in England in 1851.

CHRIST CHURCH CATHEDRAL AND ST. ANNE'S CHAPEL

*Figure IV-7. Silver alms dish, Christ Church Cathedral, Fredericton.
Designed by William Butterfield and made in England.*

uted the marble for the altar, and the Bishop obtained the east window from Wailes of Newcastle, a gift of the artist and the people of the United States. Its tracery was a copy of that at Selby Abbey. The great west window was by Warrington and was a duplicate of the one he had placed in Snettisham in 1846.

The consecration of Christ Church Cathedral in August, 1853, was a religious and personal triumph for the Right Reverend John Medley. In the record time of eight years, in the face of financial difficulties and while at the head of a struggling diocese, he had built two churches in Fredericton, one of cathedral scale. The Cathedral is an exceptional monument, a tribute to the energy of nineteenth-century architectural enthusiasm. It stands alone in its close at the edge of the St. John River, surrounded by the trees the Bishop planted a century ago to keep the ice floes from the building at times of flood. (Figs. IV–8 and IV–9). It is an earnest English building far from home. Fortunately both it and St. Anne's Chapel have survived virtually unchanged because Fredericton has not become a city but has remained a county town.

The determination to duplicate St. Mary's, Snettisham, was, in the end, not carried through because St. Mary's was a challenge. When Medley chose it in the nineteenth century, the church was a meeting house for Methodists and, though a magnificent example of the medieval parish church in the Decorated style, its chancel and transepts had long been in ruins. The spire, much in need of repair, still stood, and the nave was virtually intact. Warrington was at work on the great six-light window in the west. When the Bishop resolved to build a replica of St. Mary's and sent Frank Wills to measure it, therefore, he was committed only to the nave, the spire, and the west front with its porch. A lithograph, signed "Frank Wills, Architect, Exeter" (Fig. IV–10), and a series of detailed drawings (Fig. IV–11) show how the bishop-designate and his architect originally planned to accomplish the difficult feat of restoring the whole east end of Snettisham. Where the evidence at Snettisham was sufficient to permit them to do so, they had decided to use features of the original church, such as the five-light window in the south wall of the south transept. Where parts of St. Mary's were missing, Medley and Wills proposed to substitute desirable features from other churches. This decision accounts for the tracery pattern from Selby Abbey in the east window at Fredericton. The lithographed view and the drawing show a far more accurate copy of Snettisham than was ultimately built. There is no illustration of the interior as planned in 1845, but presumably it too would have been close to Snettisham. The tower of the design at this early stage in its development, though in general taken from that in Norfolk, was considerably, but not gracefully, enriched with tall paneling.

Between 1845 and 1853 several solutions to the problem of the east end were considered and discarded. Though the Bishop had adopted Butterfield's plan, the scheme with two spires which antedated it was published in the *Illustrated London News* in April, 1849. It was Butterfield who raised the choir roof to equal that of the nave roof (Fig. IV–12). The revisions in Butterfield's drawings for spire and choir must have been carried out by the Bishop in consultation with Wills, who was available in New York. Apparently no other architects had a hand in the work, for at the consecration the Bishop mentioned only Wills and Butterfield.

The nave (Figs. IV–13 and IV–14) is attributable to Frank Wills. The roof is not a copy of the one at Snettisham, and the three-light windows on the west aisle end are duplicates of those the Bishop had installed in St. Andrew's, Exwick. The west door is taken from that at Exeter, and the south door is from one in a church in Suffolk. The piers of the nave arcades are not composite as were those at St. Mary's.[21] When it was complete, therefore, the Cathedral, though only an approximate reproduction of Snettisham, was the largest and most carefully ecclesiological church of the North American revival. Clergymen from the United States knew and admired it. The Reverend Benjamin Haight, who had accompanied Doane to England in 1841, was present at the consecration and reported on the church extensively and in detail when he returned. Another American clergyman, the Reverend John Dixon Carder, of Milford, Connecticut, was also present. A few years later he retained Frank Wills to design St. George's, Milford. William Butterfield's connection with the Cathedral added to its importance, not only because of his architectural contribution but because through him the Cathedral came into possession of its dazzling display of ecclesiastical vessels and lectern. What remains of the original furniture for the choir is also from his hand (Figs. IV–15 and IV–16).

The somewhat cumbersome feeling of the Cathedral was not Wills's fault. It

[21] See N. Pevsner, *North-West and South Norfolk*, The Buildings of England no. 24 (Harmondsworth: Penguin, 1962), pp. 316–17: "Perhaps the most exciting Dec[orated] church in Norfolk; and how much more exciting it would be if its chancel—40 feet long—had not been demolished!" Pevsner describes the interior as memorable for "its very tall arcades with piers of composite section, basically four shafts and four thin filleted shafts in the diagonals with five hollows between. Seats round the piers. Nave roof with sweeping arched braces up to the collar beams. The crossing arches of the same type as the arcade."

*Figure IV-8. Christ Church Cathedral, Fredericton.
Frank Wills and William Butterfield. 1845–53.*

Figure IV-9. Christ Church Cathedral, Fredericton.

Figure IV-10. "The Proposed Cathedral Church, Frederickton, New Brunswick, adapted from St. Mary's, Snettisham, Norfolk." Signed "Frank Wills, Architect, Exeter" (1845).

CHRIST CHURCH CATHEDRAL AND ST. ANNE'S CHAPEL

Figure IV-11. "New Brunswick Cathedral." Proposed east elevation.
Signed "Frank Wills, Architect, Exeter."

was, rather, the result of the Bishop's insistence upon following Snettisham which made it necessary to fit together several designs in order to complete the eastern end in a manner appropriate for a cathedral. The preliminary drawings for the Cathedral done in 1845, before he went to Canada, show that Wills was well trained, even gifted. Certainly if Bishop Medley, who was competent to judge him, had not found that Wills was knowledgeable and talented, he would not have invited him to Fredericton. Wills was more competent as a Gothic revival architect in 1845 than John Notman, whose Chapel of the Holy Innocents in Burlington was begun in the year that the cornerstone of Christ Church Cathedral was laid and St. Anne's Chapel begun. Comparisons between Richard Upjohn and Wills are far more difficult, for Wills was almost certainly younger than Upjohn, and his personal taste and style in no way resembled those of Upjohn. Wills had a penchant for light and reasonably authentic decorative detail; Upjohn was inclined to digress into heavy but original enrichment. Wills had been taught to work with and from medieval originals; Upjohn's Gothic was self-taught. The Cathedral in Fredericton and St. Mary's, Burlington, were under construction at the same time. Both were conceived as imitations of specific English parish churches of the Decorated style. When the two are compared, Wills's achievement stands up well, though one must acknowledge that he had the advantage of an educated client and of firsthand study of his model. What does emerge is that Wills and Upjohn were different. When Wills arrived in New York in 1848 with his fresh, aggressive talent and his determination to make a place for himself, he was to influence not only the Gothic revival in the United States but those inside and outside the profession who encountered him.

Even as Christ Church Cathedral was slowly progressing, Bishop Medley carried forward his plan to improve the architecture of the smaller parish churches of his diocese. When he visited England in 1848, he expressed profound discontent with the style, if it could be termed that, of the churches of the New Brunswick countryside.[22] "Throughout the whole of North America," he said, "no correct type of church was formerly to be seen." He gave a vivid description of the "ordinary type" of which he disapproved, saying it was "borrowed from the buildings erected by the Puritans, and from the different religious bodies who sprang up from time to time." Though he found the future

---

[22] Quoted in "Colonial Church Architecture," *E.*, 8 (June, 1848):361.

Figure IV-12. "Choir, Cathedral, Fredericton." Probably drawn by
William Butterfield (1848).

THE GOTHIC REVIVAL AND AMERICAN CHURCH ARCHITECTURE

Figure IV-13. Christ Church Cathedral, Fredericton. West door.

Figure IV-14. Christ Church Cathedral, Fredericton. Nave and choir.

Figure IV-15. Choir stalls, Christ Church Cathedral, Fredericton. William Butterfield.

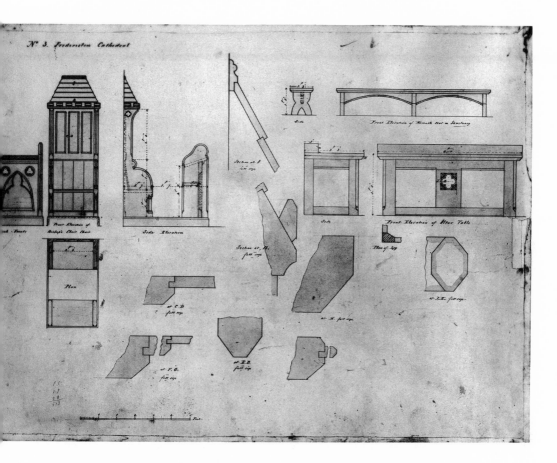

Figure IV-16. Choir furniture, Christ Church Cathedral, Fredericton.
Probably by William Butterfield.

of provincial church architecture not totally black because "the greater part of these edifices were built of wood, and must ere long decay," he was unwilling to wait for nature to take her course. He asked the Ecclesiological Society to supply "small plain wooden models for wooden churches in the country."[23]

Medley was not the only colonial bishop faced with this problem; in the same year the Bishop of Newfoundland wrote that "it would be a great thing to get one perfect pattern (in wood) made in England . . . set up in a crowded suburb of St. John's where . . . the Clergy and others coming from the out ports might see and copy it."[24] Research in architectural history had begun to reveal possible patterns for churches in wood. In 1843 Weale's *Papers on Architecture* had illustrated and discussed the "Primitive Churches of Norway,"[25] but the eccentricities of shape and decoration of these examples did not please traditionalist colonial bishops, who really wanted a transcription in wood of the stone parish churches they admired. The *Ecclesiologist* had also toyed with studies of pisé construction as a possibility for the colonies and had found it inadequate.[26]

Medley was able to rejoice in a new parish church which met his high standards when he went to northern New Brunswick in 1851 to consecrate St. Andrew's at Newcastle (Fig. IV–17), a church which had been constructed with the continuous guidance and assistance of the Ecclesiological Society and "the zealous exertions of the missionary, the Rev. J. Hudson, being the fourth church erected by him in ten years."[27] Other churches nearer Fredericton also show that the Bishop attained the reforms he advocated. The small and extremely pretty wooden church at Burton seems to have been designed by Frank Wills, for its spire was exactly like that at St. George's, Milford, Connecticut.[28]

[23] Quoted in *ibid.*, p. 362.

[24] "On Wooden Churches," *E.*, 9 (August, 1848):22.

[25] John Weale, ed., *Quarterly Papers on Architecture*, 2d ed. improved (London: John Weale, 1844), 1:1–9; pt. 1 of vol. 1 had appeared as a single number in Michaelmas, 1843.

[26] See "Pisé Building," *E.*, 9 (February, 1849):217–20; and "Pisé and Cob Building," *ibid.* (April, 1849): 287–89.

[27] "Colonial Church Architecture. Chapter XVIII Fredericton," *E.*, 12 (February, 1851): 23–24.

[28] Burton Church is illustrated in an article by R. H. Hubbard, "Canadian Gothic," *The Architectural Review*, 116 (August, 1954):110. St. George's, Milford, was illustrated and discussed by Wills (*Ancient English Ecclesiastical Architecture*, p. 112 and plate following). The spire at Burton has been pulled down within the last few years.

Christ Church at Maugerville (Fig. IV–18) remains in excellent condition. It seems possible that this church followed the pattern the Ecclesiological Society supplied the Bishop when he asked for assistance, for the wooden model from which the church was built is still preserved there.[29] Christ Church is an English parish church transcribed in wood. Its interior spaces are succinctly expressed on the exterior. Its only enrichments are the buttresses, which, though ornamental in their wood construction, preserve something of the form of the stone examples which were their inspiration.

Throughout the later 1840's and the early 1850's the *Ecclesiologist* expanded its reports of colonial church building. The editors were pained to discover that many churches in the outposts of the Anglican Communion were being erected along imperfect lines, but they correctly surmised that the Society might have more success abroad than in England, where there were architects and societies with ideas of their own. A series of articles in the *Ecclesiologist* in 1847 and 1848 surveyed the colonial church building movement. One long note was devoted to the Cathedral in St. John's, Newfoundland;[30] in it the editors delivered one of their more spectacular statements. They were at last prepared to acknowledge that differences in climate, building materials and workmanship, and function could, and perhaps should, provoke original rather than eclectic stylistic solutions. G. G. Scott had failed to recognize, said the editors, that at St. John's he was given an opportunity for inventiveness. They lamented that he had "chosen to build by precedent: and the result, though scrupulously correct, appears to us deficient in the indescribable character, the moral feeling, if we may so say—of originality. Under such circumstances, Christian art could afford to be plastic. S. John's Cathedral, as designed by Mr. Scott, reminds us of a first-rate University prize poem. There is authority for every detail and phrase; it is learned and dignified, but perhaps cold: it displays the artist's reading and study more than his genius."[31] The ecclesiologists were truly difficult to please. Only a few years earlier they had said that all the nineteenth century could possibly do was copy devoutly. Colonial building had clarified their ideas, it seemed, and the cathedral at St. John's, in a roundabout way, had been a

---

[29] This information was supplied by Douglas Richardson.
[30] "Colonial Church Architecture. —Newfoundland. Chapter VI. —S. John's Cathedral, Newfoundland," *E.*, 8 (April, 1848):274–79.
[31] *Ibid.*, p. 277.

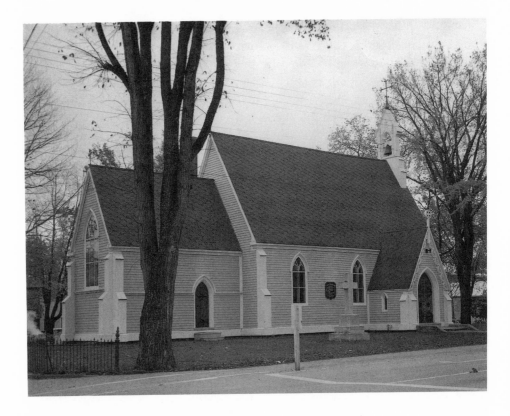

Figure IV-17. St. Andrew's, Newcastle, N.B. Consecrated 1851.

Figure IV-18. Christ Church, Maugerville, N.B.

salutary influence upon the thought of the ecclesiological leaders who discovered what they truly wanted only when confronted by a performance of which they disapproved. The climate and materials in Newfoundland, which they quaintly described as an island that was "the most inhospitable upon which the Caucasian race has permanently settled, and which is so entirely a rock that it is actually difficult to collect sufficient earth to bury the dead," had provoked the editors into facing the implications of their insistence upon revivalism.

It was at this delicate moment in 1848 that the ecclesiologists were asked to reconsider their position. The architects, laymen, and clergy of the Protestant Episcopal Church in the United States had taken the advice of Webb and Thorp and organized a New York Ecclesiological Society which proposed to publish a journal of its own. This Society did not long remain a dutiful offspring of English ecclesiology, for it asked that the editors of the *Ecclesiologist* revise their doctrine and, as they had hinted they might in their discussion of the Cathedral at St. John's, qualify their devotion to medieval models in the interests of necessity in colonial church building. The dispute that took place over this suggestion reveals not only the conservatism of the ecclesiologists but the independence of mind and originality of their American followers.

V

The New York Ecclesiological Society and Its Journal

In 1846 Thorp and Webb had suggested to Ralston that he and other persons interested in ecclesiology should found an American society. By 1848 the time had come to embark upon such a venture. The church was expanding rapidly. Clergymen needed instruction in architecture, for new churches were rising everywhere. Thanks to his intimate experience with St. James the Less, Ralston was a confirmed ecclesiological amateur. When they traveled abroad, faculty members at the General Theological Seminary had encountered art and architecture and ideas inspired by ecclesiology. Frank Wills was in New York and in search of clients.

The first formal meeting of the New York Ecclesiological Society took place on April 2, 1848.[1] Its founders were those clergymen most responsive to the Oxford Movement, architects intent upon and educated in English Gothic revival theories, and laymen of High Church inclinations who possessed an avocational interest in architecture. Robert Ralston, the Society's principal

[1] "Report of the First Stated Meeting of the New York Ecclesiological Society, Monday, April 2, 1848," *New York Ecclesiologist*, 1 (October, 1848):12–14; hereafter abbreviated as *NYE*.

159

organizer, delivered the opening address; he said nothing new, but he presented reasons why the foundation of the association was necessary and timely. There were sixteen thousand Episcopal clergymen in England, and only fifteen hundred in the United States; the Americans, said Ralston, were neither as well trained as their English counterparts nor as informed about architecture, its history, and its proper role in the life of the Church. The phenomenal growth of their denomination and their lack of artistic education had united to produce American Protestant Episcopal church buildings which displayed every sort of "deformity." Where were the clergy to find models for their churches? In order that it might serve as "teacher of the Church" the New York Ecclesiological Society planned to gather information on architectural design and its history and to maintain a library open to all interested persons. The journal which the Society proposed to publish would "throw open columns, concentering rays of light now scattered"; it would educate "by awakening men's thoughts to the reverence due God's house, so often forgotten in this unreverential age, through the special care to be bestowed upon it in all its minutest parts, and through the deep meanings associated with their forms, and speaking forth from their arrangements."[2]

The Right Reverend W. R. Whittingham, Bishop of Maryland, was the only American bishop who extended sympathetic best wishes to the Society upon its foundation. He was promptly elected a patron member. The faculty of the General Theological Seminary was heavily represented in the charter membership, and so were the rectors of the larger New York churches. The presidency of the Society was given to the Reverend John Murray Forbes, a High Churchman who, a year after his election, became a Roman Catholic. The Reverend John McVickar of Calvary Church and the Reverend W. A. Muhlenburg of the Church of the Holy Communion assumed important roles. The Reverend Benjamin I. Haight, Ralston, and the Reverend Mr. McVickar were elected vice-presidents. The ordinary membership read like a roster of the most accomplished, cosmopolitan, and intellectually able men associated with the Church. Caleb S. Henry was a member; he was editor of the *New York Churchman*, rector of St. Clement's Church, and a prolific writer on religious affairs. So was the Reverend George H. Houghton, a student of Muhlenburg's

---

[2] "Address by Mr. Ralston of Philadelphia," *NYE*, 1 (October, 1848):1–4.

who was on the staff of the Church of the Holy Communion. In 1850 Houghton would found the Church of the Transfiguration in New York (the Little Church around the Corner) and sponsor there the construction of one of the prettier examples of the parish church style. Holy Cross Church in Troy was represented by the Reverend John Ireland Tucker, its rector, and by a layman, Captain Edmund Schriver, who was a railroad magnate and retired army officer. The secretary of the Society was Robert Ralston Cox, who was at that time associated with the General Theological Seminary. A few years later, when involved in missionary work in the Middle West, Cox was killed in a steamboat accident on the Ohio River. (His body was one of the first to be buried in the church yard of St. James the Less.)

Even before the first meeting of the Society Frank Wills had been installed as its official architect. The executive committee announced that he was designing a seal for the Society and that he was prepared to answer the queries of clergymen who needed advice on the design and maintainance of churches. If he was to gain a foothold in an architectural community dominated by Richard Upjohn, Wills required affiliations of this sort. He had joined the Ecclesiological Society earlier in 1848.[3] His credentials were becoming more and more impressive.

The Society set great store by its library; the first books presented to it were Pugin's *True Principles*, Barr's *Anglican Architecture*, and Paley's *Manual of Gothic Architecture*. When news of the founding of the New York Society reached London, the ecclesiologists forwarded copies of their publications to New York. By July, 1848, New York members had contributed the works of Rickman, Benjamin Webb, John Britton, and Weale's *Papers on Architecture*.

In October, 1848, the Society began to publish the *New York Ecclesiologist*, which, could have been, but was not, a pallid imitation of the *Ecclesiologist*. Though it survived for only five years, the *New York Ecclesiologist* was a major document on American architectural ideas and on the work and life of the Society.[4] It was the first American journal devoted solely to architecture, and it possessed character, individuality, and independence of mind.

---

[3] "Meeting of the Cambridge Camden Society," *E*, 8 (April, 1848):291.
[4] The journal was published from October, 1848, to December, 1853, at which point the Society decided that the purpose it served could be absorbed by *Transactions*, which it hoped to publish annually. By the time that it was discontinued, it had declined in quality.

The significance of the *New York Ecclesiologist* may be assessed only when it is seen as part of mid-nineteenth-century American critical writing on Gothic revivalism, the arts, and architecture. The journal was not an isolated phenomenon but part of a meaningful pattern in American thought. Before 1840 few books on architecture were published in the United States; those that were fell into two or three categories.[5] There were pattern books and guides to carpenters and builders; of these Asher Benjamin's *The American Builder's Companion, Builder's Guide*, and *Country Builder's Assistant* were typical.[6] A second, and smaller, group consisted of reports on major buildings in progress or recently completed. Thomas U. Walter's *Report of the Architect of the Girard College for Orphans*[7] is a good example of this kind of book, written by men who, like Walter, were professional architects of considerable reputation. The growth of American cities and the development of civic and national pride created a market for volumes of architectural views, but none of the American books of this third group were as sophisticated as their European equivalents.[8] Finally, books were being produced which fell into none of these categories. William Dunlap, moved by the instinct of a chronicler and an enthusiasm for things American, assembled his *History of the Rise and Progress of the Arts of Design in the United States*,[9] which included some comment on architecture.

The first sign that a change was at hand came in 1836 and 1837, when

[5] See Hitchcock, *American Architectural Books* (Minneapolis: University of Minnesota Press, 1962), for the definitive bibliography of architectural books published in the United States before 1895.

[6] *The American Builder's Companion; or, a New System of Architecture Particularly Adapted to the Present Style of Building in the United States of America* appeared in six editions between 1806 and 1827 (Hitchcock, *American Architectural Books*, p. 9). *The Builder's Guide, Illustrated by Sixty-six Engravings, Which Exhibit the Orders of Architecture* was published in six editions between 1839 and 1854 (*ibid.*, p. 10). *The Country Builder's Assistant* appeared in three editions between 1797 and 1805 (*ibid.*, pp. 10–11).

[7] *Report of the Architect of the Girard College for Orphans, to the Building Committee* (Philadelphia, 1834–50). See Hitchcock for other such works by Walter and for similar works by William Strickland.

[8] Theodore S. Fay, *Views in New York and Its Environs* (New York: Peabody and Company, 1831), is a typical book of this kind. American periodicals also carried occasional illustrations of buildings.

[9] (New York: Scott and Company, 1834).

Alexander Jackson Davis published *Rural Residences*[10] and John Henry Hopkins wrote his *Essay on Gothic Architecture.*

In the later 1830's and early 1840's, American architects were aware of what was happening abroad. Well-trained practitioners—men like William Strickland, Ithiel Town,[11] Davis, and Walter—were using European materials. They acquired the books of the leading English authors as soon as they appeared and followed the fluctuations of English taste with curiosity and concern. Informed American opinion on architecture was expressed in articles in periodicals rather than in books; it is for this reason that journals contain the first meaningful and progressive American discussions of Gothic revivalism. Despite its importance as an early work on the Gothic revival, Bishop Hopkins' book, for example, seems conservative and stylistically old-fashioned if it is compared with magazine articles of the same period.

In 1836 an American architectural critic first displayed a literary style and an understanding of aesthetic principles equal to those of his English contemporaries. In the *North American Review* Henry R. Cleveland, historian, Latin scholar, and friend of Longfellow, examined the American architectural scene in a review of *The American Builder's General Price Book* by James Gallier.[12] Cleveland, who said nothing about Gallier but a great deal about American building, felt that Americans possessed a genuine gift for architectural design which, though it was still untutored, would one day mature if obstacles to its progress were removed. He believed that even in the primitive beginnings of the nation a characteristic style had been created. He was obviously predisposed to discover that such was the case because he was convinced that archi-

---

[10] *Rural Residence, etc., Consisting of Designs, Original and Selected, for Cottages, Farmhouses, Villas, and Village Churches.* Hitchcock indicates that publication began in 1837, but he could not determine whether the work, which appeared in numbers, was ever completed (*see American Architectural Books,* p. 29).

[11] See Lydia Sigourney, "The Residence and Library of Ithiel Town, Esq.," *Ladies Companion,* 10 (January, 1839):132. This is a well-known and enlightening article on the house (which is illustrated) and the library and collections of Town. He had eight to ten thousand books.

[12] See p. 56 and n. 36 above. The Index to this journal attributes this article to Cleveland. In 1837, in *Temples, Ancient and Modern* (London: Fraser, 1837), William Bardwell quoted extensively from the article and said it was written by "the editor," a statement which seems unlikely because the Index to the journal lists only a few articles by Cleveland.

tectural styles owed their "origins and perfection to a deep and enthusiastic sentiment, which pervaded society and constituted the spirit of the age." In search of this American national style he described the two "meeting house" types that he felt "the stern spirit of Puritanism" had produced.[13]

Cleveland was not able to recommend that architects pursue this native pattern, however. Instead, he noted, somewhat sadly, that it was being submerged by the "Grecian and Gothic . . . neither of which is discoverable in the earlier architecture of this country." He then considered the "Grecian, including the round arch and the dome, and the Gothic or pointed-arch style." Both were foreign, neither had sprung from "the spirit of the age" to which Cleveland was loyal, but he recognized that they had come to America to stay. He addressed himself to the question of how and where each of these styles should be used and whether American building had lived up to its exciting potentialities. In a fascinating and sometimes vituperative discussion (Cleveland's favorite epithet for a building of which he disapproved was an "abortion"), he appraised the architecture of the major cities on the eastern seaboard.[14]

Having acknowledged that Gothic had a place in America, Cleveland attempted to define its proper role. "The sublime, the glorious Gothic," he asserted, was "the architecture of Christianity." It should be used for funerary and ecclesiastical purposes, but he urged that when Americans employed it they construct "really Gothic edifices," not neoclassical buildings to which flat Gothic ornament had been applied. It is possible to know the kind of Gothic he admired, for he called St. Mary's Chapel, Baltimore, by Maximilian Godefroy, "a little bijou."

The remark about "the spirit of the age" and the definition of Gothic as "the architecture of Christianity" show that Cleveland was familiar with the litera-

[13] *Ibid.*, p. 357; see especially his n. 23 on George Bancroft and Puritanism.
[14] Cleveland felt that the Capitol was "the noblest edifice," though its dome was "very heavy, ill proportioned and out of place." He was not impressed with the architecture of Baltimore in spite of "the tall column" and "the little trophy of marble near Barnum's hotel." Philadelphia had more that he could admire "than any other city in the Union." He held a high opinion of the work of William Strickland. The buildings of New York he found "truly meagre," but he hoped its architecture would improve. He approved of the use of Gothic in secular architecture, proposing it as an antidote for the plain "no known order of architecture" then being built at Harvard. He had little good to say of the architecture and architects of Boston.

ture of the English Gothic revival. The first edition of *Contrasts* had appeared but a few weeks before Cleveland's article.[15] The fact that Pugin's argument, with the exception of his Roman Catholic bias, was repeated by Cleveland shows that, whether or not Cleveland knew Pugin's work, the two men had been reading the same sources. Various allusions in the article made it clear that Cleveland had traveled in Europe,[16] an experience which obviously contributed to the development of his taste and sharpened his judgment.

Knowledge of European buildings in progress and discussion of ideas congenial but not directly applicable to the revival of Gothic also prepared Americans to accept the style and showed them ways in which it could be understood. Extensive quotations from and commentary upon Von Raumer's *England in 1835*,[17] Chateaubriand's *Sketches of English Literature*,[18] and Lockhart's *Memoirs of the Life of Sir Walter Scott* belonged to such peripheral literature. The *Journal of the Franklin Institute* regularly printed excerpts and whole articles from J. C. Loudon's important and creative *Architectural Magazine* and reported on major buildings under construction in England and innovations in structural techniques. The choice of the *Architectural Magazine* for continuing coverage of this kind demonstrated the perceptiveness of American editors, for though Loudon's journal was short-lived, it contained important and progressive architectural opinions and theory. In 1839, for example, interested Americans could read in the *Journal of the Franklin Institute* Loudon's astonishing statement that "the most striking architectural erections that have taken place throughout England in the last two years are, unquestionably, those connected with engineering"; his observation that "the prejudice in favor of ancient architecture, whether classical or Gothic, must be given up, or at all events, diminished; and, while all the forms and details left us by those who have gone before are free to be used, the combinations in which they are employed must depend for their beauty and effect on intrinsic properties, and not on their having been used in the same combinations before, or on associa-

---

[15] See pp. 20, n. 29, and 59, n. 42, above, for full bibliographical information.
[16] "The effect of one large window of stained glass can hardly be conceived by those who have not witnessed it" ("American Architecture," p. 377).
[17] Review, *North American Review*, 43 (October, 1836).
[18] *Ibid.*, 49 (October, 1839).

tions connected with them, whether classical or otherwise, which have no connexion with their present use";[19] and his praise of John Ruskin's essays on *The Poetry of Architecture*.[20]

Quite suddenly the character of American opinion altered, in the late 1830's, when the comfortable estimate of the arts as a secondary and unimportant part of life was replaced by the belief that art revealed the state of society, utilized its highest powers, and should be valued more than material things. English and Continental writing had inspired this change. In 1838 the *United States Magazine and Democratic Review* published a challenging essay entitled "Claims of the Beautiful Arts,"[21] which announced that the aims of American republicanism, "Freedom, Beauty, and Moral elevation," had not been realized in American life. "The golden apples of wealth" had been sought instead of the "inward freedom of the Individual" to which the republic had been dedicated. The nation should encourage, indeed foster, "the luxuriance of genius" through valuing art and the artist. Libraries, public collections of objects of art, and buildings could express the true nature of the American society and its institutions.[22] The author of this essay had acquired his feeling of urgency and obligation from Carlyle, Heeren, and Sismondi,[23] whose works he mentioned and recommended. All three of these authors had shared in the exploration of history and the establishment of patterns for understanding its

[19] "A Summary View of the Progress of Architecture in Britain during the Year 1838," *Journal of the Franklin Institute*, n.s., 24 (July, 1839):57–61.

[20] Kata Phusin [John Ruskin], *The Poetry of Architecture, or The Architecture of the Nations of Europe considered in Its Association with Natural Scenery and National Characteristics* first appeared serially in *The Architectural Magazine* in 1837 and 1838. The edition used here is *The Works of John Ruskin*, ed. E. T. Cook and Alexander Wedderburn (London: George Allen, 1903–12).

[21] 3 (November, 1838):256 (unsigned article).

[22] *Ibid.*, pp. 256–57.

[23] Arnold Hermann Ludwig Heeren (1760–1842); Jean Charles Leonard de Sismondi (1773–1842). On Heeren and Sismondi, see James Westfall Thompson, *A History of Historical Writing*, 2 vols. (New York: Macmillan, 1942), 2; Harry Elmer Barnes, *A History of Historical Writing* (Norman: University of Oklahoma Press, 1937), pp. 167–70; and especially G. P. Gooch, *History and Historians in the Nineteenth Century* (New York: Peter Smith, 1949), pp. 403–8. George Bancroft was influenced by Heeren, whom he encountered in Germany in the 1820's. The first volume of Bancroft's history of America, which appeared in 1834, dealt with the character of Puritanism. It seems entirely possible that his writing and philosophy influenced both H. R. Cleveland and the author of this anonymous article of 1838 in the *United States Magazine and Democratic Review*.

relevance to the nineteenth century. The rebellious and commanding tones of Carlyle's "Characteristics" and "Signs of the Times" could be heard in the American author's assertion that "the spirit of the age is mechanical and utilitarian," and his insistence that a panoramic view of society was possible and instructive was derived from Heeren and Sismondi, whose histories demonstrated sequences of cause and effect and offered explanations of events which encouraged men to believe that by rational means they could control and direct development and change.

After 1840 American preoccupation with architecture developed rapidly, fed by books from abroad and statements by American authors, who were beginning to make public theories tailored to American sensibilities. Travel to Europe had increased, and the travelers visited new, stylistically adventurous buildings as well as the medieval monuments usual in a European itinerary. For example, at about the time that St. Peter's, Leeds, was inspring George Washington Doane and his companions to become patrons of architecture, a lady reported that she had seen King Edward's Grammar School in Birmingham and thought it a "truly beautiful building of the Gothic order."[24]

In American architectural comment of the late 1830's and 1840's three ideas appear and reappear. The notion that "the character of our building" reflects "the state of our society"[25] had taken firm root. Americans also felt sure that "utility" would suggest the forms American architecture would assume. And, finally, they were convinced that there was a special affinity between the American national genius and architecture, for it was "the most popular of the arts."[26] Almost all critics agreed that architecture in America fell short of the excellence it could possess. In Gothic, "ornament . . . is lavished with the most tasteless and unnecessary profusion." In domestic design, "breadth of effect, dignity, and imposing appearance are also most uncommon. . . . the *façades* of most houses are made complete sieves for the admission of light, and it is doubtful in some whether windows or blank wall predominate." Feeling for civic dignity was lacking, with buildings "being crowded one against another, so as to allow no space for the spectator."[27]

[24] Miss M. S. C., "Letters from Europe," *New York Mirror*, 19 (July 10, 1841):222.
[25] [W. Minot], "Art in America," *North American Review*, 52 (April, 1841):313.
[26] *Ibid.*, p. 314.
[27] *Ibid.*, p. 316.

THE GOTHIC REVIVAL AND AMERICAN CHURCH ARCHITECTURE

The traffic in ideas between England and the United States was not one way. At the same time that English writers on Gothic and on architecture in general were beginning to formulate theory with which Americans were in sympathy, they were becoming aware of their American audience and the liveliness of American criticism.[28]

Of the many British theorists Loudon and A. W. Pugin, whose *True Principles* appeared in 1841, were most in accord with American ideals. Pugin's positive, uncomplicated statement of the principles of design suited American propensities, and his argument that in Gothic these principles were fully realized satisfied a group in America which was leaning in the direction of that style. In 1841 a writer in the *New York Review* asserted that churches should not be in the same style as town halls and exchanges. Civic architecture could be Classical; ecclesiastical architecture called for Gothic. A symbol of the growth of Christianity, Gothic could be adapted for churches large and small; it was "susceptible of ornament, chaste in its simplicity—admitting of a great variety of form, so that it does not weary by its sameness—and complete and perfect as a whole."[29] In conclusion the writer recommended Gothic unconditionally as possessing "claims superior to that of any other style," and "preferable for its 'fitness.'" Pugin was perhaps a source for these ideas, but he was not the only one. He was not quoted directly in the article; the argument of "fitness" had appeared in *True Principles*, though the word itself had not. The American author had been reading widely. He included a long and beautiful description of a Gothic church by someone who had been studying Durandus.[30]

[28] See n. 12 above.
[29] "Rural Church Edifices," *New York Review*, 9 (July, 1841):180–88 (unsigned article).
[30] The quotation reads as follows:

The first and chief expression is that of the thoughts raised to God, and, separated from the earth, ascending boldly and straightly to heaven. This is what every one must feel in contemplating the aspiring pillars, arches and vaults, even if he cannot analyze the feeling. All the other parts of the whole are symbolical and significant. The altar was placed opposite the rising sun; the three principal entrances were to receive the crowds of people from the different parts of the world. The three towers express the three persons of the mystery of the Godhead according to the Christian belief. The choir raises itself, like a temple within a temple, with exalted dignity. The figure of the cross was used in the Christain churches from the remotest times; not merely arbitrarily, as it may be supposed, or that it should attract the eye from the other beautiful forms. The rose is the principal feature of all the ornaments of this style of architecture; the peculiar form of the

THE NEW YORK ECCLESIOLOGICAL SOCIETY

This anonymous article is important because it insists that churches should be Gothic and that rural settings are appropriate for them, and because the author demonstrates a level of appreciation and sophistication about medieval architecture not hitherto attained by Americans. The parish church revival in America really begins with this description of the ideal church. His statement that "from a spot where nature has done much, and man can do no more, should go forth the sounds that call the poor to pray; beyond spreads out the rich and teeming valley or the ceaseless ocean, all telling of the majesty of God, yet subservient to man; here the vine creeps over the broad buttress, or in sportive growth stretches its long arms up the moss-covered trunk" suggests, in tone and image, that the author had read Ruskin's *Poetry of Architecture*.[31]

For American architectural publication, 1841 was a productive year. The idea that there were "rural" styles was born, periodical literature increased in quantity and quality, A. J. Downing published his first book, *Theory and Practice of Landscape Gardening*,[32] and English books arrived in America and found a warm welcome. Among these books George Wightwick's *Palace of Architecture*[33] was bound to please a provincial audience. A fascinating work, consciously addressed to "the less-informed, but more susceptible readers," it was fancifully arranged as a guided tour through a garden containing architecture in many styles, which introduced the traveler to the history and varieties of building and the principles of design. One by one Wightwick discussed the attributes of architecture, its monumentality, its capacity to suggest "pictorial romance" and "association," and its "claims as a Material Poetry." Along the way he commented on individual architects and on that constant mid-nine-

---

windows, doors and towers being derived from it, as also the rich decorations of leaves and flowers. The cross and the rose are therefore the chief forms and symbols of this symbolical architecture. The expression of the whole is the solemnity of eternity, the thought of earthly death interwoven with the most enchanting plenitude of a life of perpetual bloom.

James Early, in *Romanticism and American Architecture* (New York and London: A. S. Barnes and Thomas Yoseloff, 1965), p. 135, implies that this quotation is from Pugin. The excerpt is not from *True Principles* or the 1836 or 1841 editions of *Contrasts*, nor is it a quotation from Pugin's "Article the First" from the *Dublin Review*. The literary style is not like that of Pugin. However, identification of the author has not been possible.

[31] See n. 20 above.

[32] See p. 45, n. 25, above.

[33] *The Palace of Architecture: A Romance of Art and History* (London: Fraser, 1841).

teenth-century problem, church design. A. J. Downing enjoyed Wightwick; in 1847 he prepared an American edition of Wightwick's books.[34]

Though English books such as Wightwick's, Pugin's *True Principles*, and Bardwell's *Temples, Ancient and Modern* acquired American readers, in the end it was Downing who focused and gave form to what had been intelligent and perceptive, but diffuse, American opinion. His long chapter on "Landscape or Rural Architecture" in *Theory and Practice of Landscape Gardening* was a masterpiece of comprehensibility. He laid down rules for design which were bound to appeal to his countrymen, and he placed his emphasis exactly where they instinctively wished to find it. Downing had adopted Loudon's "leading principles" in their entirety; architecture should, Downing said, be seen "1st, As a useful art, in FITNESS FOR THE END IN VIEW: 2nd, as an art of design in EXPRESSION OF PURPOSE: 3rd, as an art of taste, in EXPRESSION OF SOME PARTICULAR ARCHITECTURAL STYLE."[35]

Though these were propositions with which Americans were already in agreement, Downing made them even more attractive by demonstrating his willingness to emphasize fitness and purpose more than taste and style. He was no purist; instead he hunted for a kind of building which would be responsive to the needs of American climate, materials, and landscape. Finally, his ideas were appealing because he devoted himself to that great American concern, domestic architecture.

Though he acknowledged that "Grecian architecture is intrinsically beautiful in itself, and highly interesting in point of associations," Downing found that fitness and expression of purpose were not satisfied by it. Public buildings in the style were pleasing, he said, but houses which resembled temples were not. Instead he recommended the Italian and Gothic styles for domestic architecture in the United States, and to prove his point he included illustrations of work in these styles by John Notman and A. J. Davis.[36] When Downing's book appeared, the Classical revival was already under fire. His argument destroyed its last vestiges of authority. Downing's contribution lay, however, not only in the

---

[34] *Hints to Young Architects Calculated to Facilitate Their Practical Operations . . . With Additional Notes and Hints to Persons About Building in This Country by A. J. Downing*, 1st Am. ed. (New York and London: Wiley and Putnam, 1847).
[35] P. 371.
[36] See pp. 45, n. 25, and 84, n. 61, above.

content of his assertions and judgments but in the comment his principles provoked from those who read them. One reviewer was so stimulated by his ideas that he announced he was "inclined to believe that there is great room open for the genius of native architects, to devise and to combine new forms particularly adapted to manners in America, which will unite external beauty of proportion with internal convenience and economy."[37]

In 1842, in his second book, *Cottage Residences*,[38] Downing defined "fitness" as "the *beauty of utility*," expanded "purpose" to include "the *beauty of propriety*," and said that "expression of Style" was derived from "the *beauty of form and sentiment,* which is the highest in the scale." Though it is tempting to relate these ideas to those Pugin had expressed in 1841 in *True Principles* (for Downing could well have known the book[39]), it should be noted that in his argument Pugin was more preoccupied with architectural structure than Downing ever was, nor does Pugin's use of the word "propriety" resemble Downing's meaning.

Such philosophical and aesthetic ideas as there are in *Theory and Practice* and *Cottage Residences* were largely extracted from Loudon, Ruskin, and Wightwick; Downing was surely familiar with Loudon's *Architectural Magazine,* in which Ruskin's *Poetry of Architecture* had appeared.[40] Ruskin's pronouncement that "the house must NOT be a noun substantive, it must not stand by itself, it must be part and parcel of a proportioned whole: it must not

---

[37] "Downing on Landscape Gardening," *North American Review*, 53 (July, 1841):261. The authorship of this article is uncertain. The *Index to the North American Review, vols. I–CXXV, 1815–1877* (Cambridge, Mass.: Wilson, 1878) does not attribute it, but this listing seems inaccurate, for A. Gilman appears to have written the discussion of Downing that appeared in the later volumes (56 and 59). The *Index* attributes the volume 56 article to W. B. O. Peabody. The article cited above should be assigned to Peabody. Another article on Downing (59 [October, 1844]) is certainly by Gilman, and in it he alludes to that in volume 56, saying, "Of Mr. Downing's treatises we have spoken in a former article." This could have been an editorial "we," but that seems unlikely.

[38] *Cottage Residences; or, A Series of Designs for Rural Cottages and Cottage Villas. And Their Gardens and Grounds. Adapted to North America* (New York and London: Wiley and Putnam, 1842).

[39] See Vincent Scully, "Romantic Rationalism and the Expression of Structure in Wood: Downing, Wheeler, Gardner, and the 'Stick Style,' 1840–1876," *Art Bulletin*, 35 (March, 1953):125, for an enlightening discussion of Downing and the suggestion of Pugin as a source.

[40] In an article in *The Horticulturist*, 1 (January, 1847):300, Downing referred to Loudon's *Horticultural Magazine*.

even be seen all at once; and he who sees one end should feel that, from the given data, he can arrive at no conclusion respecting the other, yet be impressed with a feeling of a universal energy, pervading with its beauty of unanimity all life and all inanimation, all forms of stillness or motion, all presence of silence or of sound"[41] describes Downing's preferences exactly. Downing must have known immediately what Ruskin meant when he said that "no man can be an architect, who is not a metaphysician."[42]

George Wightwick's *Palace of Architecture* ended with an essay on the "Anglo-Italian Villa," which he recommended for high, open landscape situations where its masses could be seen from below.[43] Though Wightwick was certainly not the only source for Downing's proposal of the Italian style—it was obviously suited to the American climate and to building in wood, and there was much favorable discussion of Italianate building in the English literature on villa design—his approval of it must have been at least partially responsible for Downing's choice.

Examination of and debate on architectural questions and the merits of the styles increased in 1842 and 1843. A brilliant article, "Principles of Gothic Architecture," which appeared in the London *Quarterly Review*,[44] was discussed intelligently and at length in America, and it introduced those Americans who were still uninformed about ecclesiology to the Cambridge Camden Society and the Oxford Society for Promoting the Study of Gothic Architecture. Their publications, along with those of Pugin, Hope, Whewell, Rickman, and Willis, were described by the English author.

New commentary on Downing's books contributed to the conflict between the Gothic and Classical styles. Some Protestant writers showed alarm at the growing preference for the medieval.[45] It was, however, the appearance of two

---

[41] *Poetry of Architecture*, p. 187.

[42] *Ibid.*, p. 5.

[43] P. 202.

[44] William Sewell, "Principles of Gothic Architecture," *Quarterly Review*, 69 (December, 1841). Attribution of authorship is by W. E. Houghton (ed.), *Wellesley Index to Victorian Periodicals, 1824–1900* (Toronto and London: University of Toronto Press and Routledge and Paul, 1966), p. 724. A review of this article appeared in the *American Eclectic Magazine*, 3 (March, 1842).

[45] Early, *Romanticism and American Architecture*, chaps. 3 and 4, covers this period and includes material not discussed here. Mr. Early's book appeared as research was being completed for this one, and this chapter on American architectural taste and theory was reorganized to avoid duplication of material contained in his essay.

new critics which finally distinguished these years. Horatio Greenough began to publish his observations on American art and architecture, and Arthur Gilman wrote in defense of Gothic and lectured on architecture to packed houses at the Lowell Institute. Though Greenough lived in Italy, he was regarded as the hope of American sculpture. His friends and patrons included discriminating persons of his generation. The arrival in Washington of his sculpture of George Washington was so eagerly awaited that in 1841, after discussing the short-comings of American art, W. Minot ended on a cheerful note by saying that his hopes for the future would be fulfilled when Greenough's portrait, which he called "the marble personified image of Washington," landed "on the shores of the Potomac."[46] In 1843 the sculpture arrived, and Greenough began to write for the *United States Magazine and Democratic Review*. His first article was entitled "Remarks on American Art"; a month later a second, "American Architecture," appeared.[47] With them the traits of taste and mind which had made earlier American writing on architecture spirited and meaningful attained maturity.

National pride and dislike of the "European Academies" with their "stupefy-ing discipline" were the themes of Greenough's first essay. Though the United States had been engaged in "pioneer efforts" and some European critics had assumed that susceptibility and taste were denied her people, Greenough felt she had, in fact, evolved "institutions . . . more favorable to a natural, healthful growth of art than any hotbed culture whatever." The second article elaborated these ideas, illustrating them by a comparison between European and Ameri-can performances in architecture. Greenough believed that eclecticism had run its course and that European tastes were destined to fail in a country like America, whose people were constitutionally unwilling to invest money and effort to replicate styles and buildings meaningless outside of their original social and artistic environment. American instinct in the matter was correct. European architecture, Greenough felt, had abandoned the "great principles of Architecture. . . . correctness gave way to novelty, economy and vainglory

---

[46] "Art in America," p. 320.
[47] 13 (July, 1843):45–48, and *ibid.* (August, 1843):206–10. The literature on Greenough is large. Typical examples of analyses which relate his writing to the subsequent develop-ment of American architectural ideas and styles are Richard P. Adams, "Architecture and the Romantic Tradition: Coleridge to Wright," *American Quarterly*, 9 (Spring, 1961):46–63, and Harold A. Small, ed., *Form and Function: Remarks on Art by Horatio Greenough* (Berkeley and Los Angeles: University of California Press, 1947).

associated produced meanness and pretension." He believed that Europe had had her great architectural moments—he paused in his discourse to describe the beauties of the genuine Gothic cathedral and the Greek temple—but he concluded that the source of distortion and decadence lay, in the nineteenth century, in "the adoption of admired forms and models for purposes not contemplated in their invention."[48]

Greenough then asked rhetorically whether order could be brought out of this chaos, and whether "the absurdities that have successively usurped the name and functions of architecture" could be eradicated. His response to these questions has been widely discussed and described, its sources sought and variously explained, but it continues to astonish us, for Greenough proposed that "the law of adaptation," as he observed it at work in nature, should be the model for an experimental architecture. He found this law in the functional beauty of ships, an example which "from its nature and uses commands us to reject authority" and to replace it with "the manly use of plain good sense so like that of taste and genius too, as scarce to require a distinctive title."[49]

Greenough despaired of eclecticism because it constricted the expression of function and, more often than not, limited the usefulness of buildings. He recognized that knowledge of the architecture of the past had its place as an inspiration for the future, and he described two great categories of "edifice" which could be set up by the contemplation of earlier building. The first category, he said, contained structures "in whose construction the principles of architecture are developed"; these he termed "organic" and called "machines." Some architecture, which he entitled "monumental," was "addressed to the sympathies, the faith or the taste of a people"; this second category fulfilled its purpose and performed its function by suggesting the "sentiments" and "sympathies" it was created to satisfy. The "organic" and the "monumental" did not exclude one another; they could exist side by side. While he asserted his admiration for the genius of Greece, Greenough concluded that reproduction of Greek architecture for any but proper and suitable "monumental" reasons was pointless. He believed "firmly and fully that they can teach us; but let us learn principles, not copy shapes; let us imitate them like men, and not ape them like monkeys. Remembering what a school of art it was that perfected

[48] "American Architecture," pp. 206–7.
[49] *Ibid.*, p. 208.

their system of ornament, let us rather adhere to that system in enriching what we invent than substitute novelty for propriety."

The writing of Greenough, of which these two articles constitute but an early and small part, has justly been held in high esteem, but to appraise his importance it is necessary to note that certain of his ideas had been formulated by architectural theorists some time earlier. Loudon had asserted that while "forms and details left to us . . . are free to be used, the combinations in which they are employed must depend for their beauty and effect on intrinsic properties, and not on their having been used in the same combinations before."[50] E. B. Lamb had said very much the same thing in his "Observations on the Classification and Details of the Architecture of the Middle Ages," in 1836:

I do not mean that ancient architecture should be exactly copied in modern buildings, as this ought never to be the case, I merely recommend close study, that the spirit and feeling of the ancient artist may be understood, that a modern design may be in the spirit of the ancient style, though not in the actual style. . . . the Architect should always bear in mind, that it is his duty . . . to invent forms, and improve upon the architecture of by-gone days; yet still to follow the same general feeling, and to create a style perfectly distinct from any other known specimen, which shall be yet perfectly characteristic of the times and purposes for which it is intended.[51]

Wightwick had said, "He, however, who would rival the Greek Temple, must imitate—not the temple—but the Greek."[52] Alfred Bartholomew had asserted that "PURE TASTE IN ARCHITECTURE HAS IN ALL PAST AGES BEEN PURELY STRUCTURAL; *and that a departure from this wisdom is the true cause of the* TASTE (*or so to speak more properly the* WANT OF TASTE) *in modern architecture being so* VARIABLE, SO CAPRICIOUS, SO MUCH QUARRELLED ABOUT, SO MUCH QUESTIONED, AND SO SHORT-LIVED."[53] A. W. Pugin, too, had participated in the search for "principles" and in the end accepted those of Georg Moller.[54]

---

[50] "A Summary View of the Progress of Architecture," p. 61.
[51] "Progress of Civil Engineering. Observations on the Classification and Details of the Architecture of the Middle Ages," *Journal of the Franklin Institute*, 18 (August, 1836):135.
[52] *Palace of Architecture*, p. 70.
[53] *Specifications for Practical Architecture* (London: Weale, 1841), p. 14.
[54] The sources of Pugin's principles have been much discussed. Some critics have suggested that he drew upon the ideas of Francesco Milizia and Laugier. Georg Moller's *Denkmäler deutscher Baukunst* (1815–51), *Beiträge zu der Lehre von den Construcktionen* (1833–

Arthur Gilman has been mentioned in connection with his observations on Trinity Church and Upjohn's use of the Pugin illustration in *True Principles.* There is less to be said about Gilman than about Greenough, for after a brief excursion into architectural discourse in 1843 and 1844 Gilman entered active architectural practice and stopped writing. His few articles are, however, important. It is regrettable that there is no record of the contents of the twelve lectures on architecture which he gave before the Lowell Institute in 1844 and 1845.[55] Gilman's first article appeared in the *North American Review* in January, 1843;[56] it was a review of Downing's *Theory and Practice of Landscape Gardening* and *Cottage Residences.* Gilman was then twenty-two years old and neither a Greek nor a Goth. He was "weary of the eternal Grecian" because the roofs were too flat for the climate, windows contradicted the style, chimneys were hidden; but he hoped that "Gothic, too, as far as cottages are concerned, had nearly had its day." He wanted "a kind of rural architecture suited to this country," and he said that "there may be appropriate forms, not slavishly borrowed from any other, nor yet fastidiously rejecting any of their advantages, which shall be characteristic of life in this country, making the exterior expressive of what is within." On the whole he rather liked Downing's "bracketted" style.

Ten months later Gilman entered a controversy in defense of Gothic for ecclesiastical buildings,[57] and in April, 1844, he published the brilliant article,

---

41), and *Essay on the Origin and Progress of Gothic Architecture Traced in and Deduced from the Ancient Edifices of Germany with References to Those of England* (London: Priestley and Weale, 1824) seem on the face of things more likely; Pugin did not own the books of either Milizia or Laugier, but he did own a fine copy of Moller's *Denkmäler deutscher Baukunst.* Moller's *Essay* was translated into English and appeared in two editions, one in 1824 and another in 1836. Bartholomew recognized the exceptional character of Moller's books, for he said, "*Moller's Memorials of German-Gothic Architecture,* by W. H. Leeds, London, A.D. 1836 is a most valuable work, as it develops principles in the formulation of buildings, never before treated of: the embellishments of it, though destitute of the force and elegance of our own beautiful modern English engravings, are, from their accuracy, much to be admired" (*Specifications for Practical Architecture,* pt. 1, chap. 23, item 187).

[55] Harriette Knight Smith, *The History of the Lowell Institute* (Boston: Lamson, Wolfe, 1898), p. 51.

[56] The *Index to the North American Review* attributes this article to W. B. O. Peabody, which seems to be inaccurate (see n. 37 above for a discussion of this attribution).

[57] See Early, *Romanticism and American Architecture,* p. 122, for a description of this controversy, which took place in the pages of the *Boston Daily Advertiser* in 1843.

mentioned earlier,[58] in which he discussed Upjohn's use of the ideal church in Pugin's *True Principles*. Gilman read and was convinced. For the first time Pugin was quoted forthrightly in America as an authority: Gilman found Pugin's architectural principles attractively enumerated in his book. The article showed Gilman's tastes to be catholic, his reading wide; he had, it seemed, traveled extensively in Europe. Now he intensified his attack on the Greek revival, announcing that "whatever may be thought or said of it, *in the abstract*, we only see that it has, so far, failed to produce among us a single example that does not contradict and stultify itself repeatedly, upon the most cursory reference to the principles of its ancient prototypes." For one thing, the style was grossly inflexible.

The form of the Italian Renaissance palace held possibilities, Gilman thought, for urban situations and for substantial villas. King's Chapel, Tremont Street, Boston, was, he said, an American prototype of good design, for it was characterized by "an utter absence of clap-trap and pretension, —a stern disclaimer of wishing to appear any thing more than it really is, —a plain rejection of extraneous and adscititious fictions." He had made his choice among the styles and confessed that he held "the strongest predilection" for Gothic, which was connected "with the origin and progress of our faith" and was certainly *"the Christian style."* This was no novel conclusion: Cleveland had said very much the same thing in 1836, Pugin had pronounced it as doctrine, and other English authorities had been making similar statements for more than two decades. As early as 1822 one of them had announced that "in a Gothic church no idea can possibly arise, save that of Christianity and of the rites of Christianity."[59]

Gilman was exceptional because for the first time in American writing the statements of Loudon, Pugin, Leeds, Bloxam, Britton, and Gwilt were united into a system of criticism which was applied to architecture in the United States.

---

[58] "Architecture in the United States"; see p. 56 above. The following quotations from Gilman are taken from this article.

[59] "Application and Intent of the Various Styles of Architecture," *Quarterly Review*, 27 (July, 1822):315. This extraordinary article was mentioned in Chapter I above, in the course of the discussion of the importance of Durandus. The article is so brilliant that it makes almost all writing on Gothic which followed in the next two decades seem derivative. Included in a brilliant description of Gothic is the statement that "Gothic architecture is an organized whole, bearing within it a living vegetating germ."

Though he publicized the arguments for Gothic revivalism, he disagreed with Pugin and the other English authorities. He acknowledged that the Decorated style had "with great propriety, been generally considered by the critics as the most beautiful style of English architecture, not exhibiting the daring flights of constructive talent so much as the next period, but certainly reaching the *acme* of beauty in design," but he chose instead, for American revival, "the style of the thirteenth century," which he found "best fitted for our imitation." He recommended Salisbury, Wells, and Lincoln as examples. His apology for this choice was clearly directed to Pugin, who had espoused the cause of Decorated in *True Principles*.

Gilman was harsh and yet amusing in his remarks upon American buildings of which he disapproved; he demolished Edward Shaw's *Rural Architecture*, the nominal subject of his article, saying that "for originality in the invention of ugliness, it may safely stand without a parallel." A few months later he renewed his attack on the Greek revival, this time in a review of Loudon, Downing, and Colman.[60] He stressed his objection to the "Greek temple house, painted a staring white, and ornamented with Venetian blinds of the most intense shade of greenness" which, he said, conflicted with the "undulating features of external nature."[61] Loudon's intelligent arguments dominated Gilman's thought. They perfectly suited his pleas for the preservation of the American landscape. To the native American belief in function as a source of design, Downing and Gilman added the conviction that architecture and its landscape setting should be woven into one—that "the outline of the house and its offices should blend agreeably with the surrounding scenery, and harmonize with the character of the situation in which they are placed."

The main lines of American taste and architectural theory had been defined by 1845. Reviews of Downing's books provoked outright rebellion against "the imitation of the forms of antiquity," along with admonitions to use correct taste. One reviewer went so far as to say that "whoever builds an illproportioned, unsightly house, insults the community, wrongs his neighbors, perhaps lowers the standard of taste and detracts from the common weal."[62] The prin-

---

[60] "Landscape Gardening," *North American Review*, 59 (October, 1844).
[61] *Ibid.*, p. 309.
[62] "Landscape Gardening and Rural Architecture in America," *United States Magazine and Democratic Review*, 16 (April, 1845):350.

ciples of architectural design, the place of architecture in relation to the other arts, and the meaning of ecclesiastical building became popular subjects for elegant essays.[63] Expanded reading in English writers even brought Kenelm Digby's theories about the meaning and practice of chivalry into the public domain.[64] Gothic was victorious by 1847, and even as its place among the styles was being assured, some writers began to distinguish good Gothic from bad.

In 1847 an American recently returned from travel abroad found New York filled with new churches which he disliked. They were "small copies of large models," he said, and the cathedral style, transplanted to America, was but "a forced and feeble plant" used by every known denomination, though it was properly a product of "Catholic" worship. This commentator was willing to accept Trinity Church, in spite of its manifold limitations, but Calvary and Grace Churches he found impossible in every way. Only one of the New York churches of the 1840's really pleased him; the Church of the Holy Communion, he said, was "no would-be metropolitan, but an unpretending, simply beautiful parish church—such as you find by dozens yet in the 'rural districts' of England."[65] The parish church revival had acquired a following.

St. James the Less, St. Mark's, and St. Mary's, Burlington, were being completed when the *New York Ecclesiologist* was founded in 1848. Behind lay the intelligent, sometimes brilliant, and often original American writing on architecture which has been described here. The *New York Ecclesiologist* was to identify itself as much with native ideas as with those of its titular leaders, the ecclesiologists. About a quarter of the contents of the *New York Ecclesiologist* consisted of items republished from the *Ecclesiologist*—extensive reports of the meetings of the Ecclesiological Society, the Oxford Architectural Society, the Exeter, and other local architectural societies. Though it was borrowed, this material performed a service for American readers, since it made available theories current in a limited but influential and well-educated group

[63] The *Yale Literary Magazine* carried four such essays in 1845 and 1846. They add nothing to the content of ideas on Gothic but merely show the extent of preoccupation with it.
[64] "Chivalry," *Yale Literary Magazine*, 11 (June, 1846):291–98.
[65] "S," "Church Architecture in New York," *United States Magazine and Democratic Review*, 20 (February, 1847):144.

in England, it broadened popular knowledge of English principles, and it provided authorities for the kind of design the American Society had been founded to promote. Though a specialized form of Gothic was its major concern, the *New York Ecclesiologist* explored other new developments in the history of architecture and deliberated upon the endlessly fascinating topics which had been evolved in architectural circles within and without the Gothic revival in England.

The *New York Ecclesiologist* was significant, however, as much for the ways in which it did not resemble the *Ecclesiologist* as for the ways in which it did. It was, first of all, outspoken in its admiration for A. W. Pugin and his books; unlike the English ecclesiologists, the Americans did not feel compelled to disown Pugin and decry his theories and his buildings out of fear that praise of him would attract accusations of Roman Catholic sympathy. Second, though the involved, esoteric, and often far from reasonable ideas of the English ecclesiologists were known and studied by Americans, they simply overlooked, chose not to acknowledge, or disagreed with the contents of such turgid masterpieces as the long Neale and Webb introduction to the translation of Durandus. The reasoning in these works was hard to follow, and detailed knowledge of the history and symbolism of Gothic architecture and the methods for its study were irrelevant to American revivalism. Finally, the *New York Ecclesiologist* was never stylistically conservative. Though the *Ecclesiologist* was not willing to regard contemplation of Gothic as a way to develop general and stylistically abstract principles of architectural design, the *New York Ecclesiologist* was. It was prepared from the outset to assume what was by English standards an unorthodox position on how, in the nineteenth century, revival of Gothic architecture could be of service to "the Age."

As soon as it was founded in New York, the Society was inundated with requests for assistance. Wills was called upon to answer queries from puzzled clergymen as far away as St. Louis and North Carolina. He even presented one Maryland parish with a complete church design. A questionnaire was prepared so that rectors could forward systematic descriptions of their churches and obtain in return useful, realistic, and practical suggestions on rehabilitation of old buildings and design of new ones. To satisfy these inquiries and at the same time help the patrons of church architecture to acquire proper taste, the *New York Ecclesiologist* published illustrations and a descriptive account of a pattern church suitable for impecunious parishes. From its inception the Society had known that its activities would differ from those of the parent organization in England. At the first meeting, the executive committee said, with admirable practicality, "We have no churches to restore from sacrilege and spoil, but we have many churches to build."

In October, 1849, the *New York Ecclesiologist* published an illustration of the small church it could recommend (Fig. V–1). Its plan and a discussion of the proper way to enlarge it were also included.[66] The architect of this model church was Frank Wills, the style was "First Pointed," and the building showed the influence of St. James the Less and the drawings of St. Michael's, Long Stanton. The west front with its buttresses and the exterior of the nave were derived from those sturdy examples, and the porch resembled the one G. G. Place had added before the drawings for St. Michael's left England. This church also contrasts interestingly with St. Anne's, Fredericton, which Wills had earlier designed, for he had adopted some of the "reality" of St. James the Less and thus had modified his personal style. The church proposed by the *New York Ecclesiologist* sat lower on the ground than had St. Anne's, the angle of its roof was less acute, and the roof itself came down further on the north and south sides. The proportions were also different; the model church was three feet wider and two feet longer than St. Anne's, and, if one can judge from the view, it was considerably lower. Either Ralston had contributed his plans or Wills had visited Philadelphia and seen St. James the Less in the course of the year and a half that intervened between his arrival in New York and the publication of the pattern church in 1849. He could also have studied St. Michael's in Brandon's *Parish Churches* after his attention had been called to it by Ralston's project.[67]

The text which accompanied the illustrations of the pattern church specified relationships which should prevail between the parts of churches. The nave, said the *New York Ecclesiologist*, should be twice as long as it was wide and the chancel at least half as long as the nave, divided into choir and sanctuary

---

[66] "A First Pointed Church," *NYE*, 2 (October, 1849):18–19.

[67] It appears that the New York Ecclesiological Society did not own a copy of Brandon in 1849, but Wills did, for in October, 1848, he wrote in the *New York Ecclesiologist* that he perceived similarities between St. James the Less and St. Michael's, as it was figured in Brandon. For bibliographical data on Brandon, see p. 42, n. 16, above.

THE GOTHIC REVIVAL AND AMERICAN CHURCH ARCHITECTURE

Figure V-1. "A First Pointed Church."

by three steps. The south porch should be no further east than the second bay from the west front. The Society urged that transepts, if they were present, be fully developed, not ugly, ill-expressed extensions on the sides. The New York Society did not advocate the cruciform plan, probably because the *Ecclesiologist* had ceased to do so and because parishes that could afford so large and complex a building would be likely to use an architect rather than the pattern it proposed. Instead, the article said that when money was available churches should be enlarged by adding aisles rather than by the costly and uncertain expedient of attaching transepts and a spire. St. James the Less and St. Mark's were mentioned as demonstrations of the ways in which roofing in of aisles might be carried out.[68] Thus by 1849 St. James the Less was firmly established as the example for Episcopal parish churches in the United States. Even its eccentricities were recommended. Wills had accepted it as authoritative and found a compromise between it and his earlier personal manner.

In imitation of the *Ecclesiologist*, the *New York Ecclesiologist* resolved to review church building candidly. As might have been expected, its first discussion was an extended commentary on Trinity Church,[69] with which the critic, who was probably Wills, found much fault. The article was patronizing. It described Trinity as a monument from an "era well worthy to be commemorated by American Ecclesiologists," and it congratulated Upjohn upon his achievement "amid many difficulties arising from the scanty knowledge of the principles of Christian Architecture, and still greater ones arising from the prejudices and parsimony of the age." Like other writers before him, the reviewer was distressed by the plaster vaults and walls dressed to look like stone. He suggested that an open timber roof would have expressed "truth and reality" better. Though he implied that he had read Pugin—he spoke of "principles of Christian Architecture" and repeated Pugin's statement that Perpendicular Gothic showed "symptoms of decline"[70]—the author strangely failed to note the resemblance between Trinity Church and the ideal church Pugin had illustrated. He either did not recognize or chose to overlook the similarity.

The conflict between Upjohn and the *New York Ecclesiologist* continued

68 "A First Pointed Church," p. 19.
69 "New Churches," *NYE*, 1 (October, 1848):34–38
70 *Ibid.*, p. 35.

when, a few months later, the magazine reviewed his Grace Church, Newark. Though the discussion began sympathetically enough, it quickly degenerated when the reviewer said, "We must not judge this edifice by the standard of Ancient Church Architecture, since scarcely a feature in its general plan is correspondent thereunto" and added that the tower, being too small in relation to the nave, looked like nothing so much as a chimney and had "a consumptive appearance." The painting on the interior was described as "paltry and insipid."[71] Upjohn's Grace Church, Brooklyn, was to fare no better. The church was much in need of its tower, said the review, for the effect of the exterior was "from what ever side you view it somewhat unsatisfactory."[72] But this time Upjohn was tendered an apology of sorts, for the author said that he was compelled, as a practicing ecclesiologist, to make these points, though he had enjoyed studying the church and had found much to praise in it.

Upjohn had many friends and admirers, and, as the most distinguished architect of Protestant Episcopal churches he was defended by members of the Society and outsiders as soon as these hypercritical remarks began to assume a pattern of denigration. By October, 1849, however, when Upjohn was finally invited to become an honorary member of the New York Ecclesiological Society, Wills had already established a reputation through his position of official architect to the Society, which he had held for a year and a half. He had advised those who appealed to the Society for architectural assistance, and he had been responsible for the editorial policy of the journal. Commissions for churches in Texas and California, as well as on the East Coast, had come his way. His name was fixed in the minds of everyone as an architect from whom satisfactory and ecclesiologically correct designs could be procured. Articles in the *New York Ecclesiologist* identified him with the churches in Fredericton. He was able to demonstrate his expertness and knowledge of the English architectural scene in his signed articles and the lectures he delivered before the membership.

In July, 1850, Upjohn's friends came to his assistance when a truly damaging review of his small wooden parish church of All Angels', Yorkville, New York, appeared. The *New York Ecclesiologist* apologized promptly, saying that its comments "had been the cause of some unpleasant feeling on the part

[71] *Ibid.* (April, 1849) :127.
[72] *Ibid.* (June, 1849) :146.

of the friends of the architect." It insisted, however, that if architects wished their distant churches properly discussed they should submit plans directly to the editors. Otherwise, they should be willing to suffer reviews based on the reports of untrained persons. The tone assumed by the editor was distinctly testy; he said that the journal did not propose to "become the mere flatterer of any man or set of men" and that it would not "willingly be a respecter of persons to the detriment of that good cause of church restoration, in which we are engaged."[73] After this preamble the article went on to disapprove of the western door of All Angels', and took particular exception to the practice of furring out walls to give an appearance of thickness. The attacks on Upjohn continued. In July, 1851, the roof of St. James, New London, was condemned as resembling Moorish more than Gothic.[74] In September, 1851, Holy Trinity, Watertown, and Zion Church, Rome, both in New York State, received tepid praise. At the same time St. Peter's Church, Milford, Connecticut, by Wills (Fig. V–2), was enthusiastically praised.[75]

By January, 1852, the Society was prepared to name the architects whom it approved. Its first list consisted of Richard Upjohn and Company, Frank Wills, and Henry Dudley, who were in partnership, Dudley having arrived from England in 1851,[76] and John W. Priest, whose offices were in Brooklyn and in Newburgh, New York. The scale of prices charged by Wills and Dudley was published: a full set of designs and supervision of construction cost 5 per cent of the total expenditure on the structure; plans, which included all details, cost 3 per cent; on designs for furniture, internal fittings, and glass, the fee was 10 per cent. Plans for a small church could be had for one hundred dollars. In July, 1853, the Society added John Notman to its list of approved architects.

Wills, Dudley, Upjohn, and Notman were Englishmen settled in the United

---

[73] *Ibid.*, 2 (July, 1850):152–53.
[74] *Ibid.*, 3 (July, 1851):100–1.
[75] *Ibid.* (September, 1851):159–67.
[76] Originally from Exeter, Dudley joined Wills in New York in 1851. The first report of a design by him appeared in the *New York Ecclesiologist* in September, 1851 (3:141). It was a plan to rebuild St. Peter's, Morristown, New Jersey. The comment on his work was reasonably favorable, though the editor added: "We will venture one word of advice, though there is nothing in the plan before us which particularly calls for it: we want not here the exact reproduction of the English parish church. There is a difference, both in the character of our country, and of our people; and our architecture should show that difference. Let Mr. Dudley, therefore, identify himself with our church and country, if he wishes to be a great *American* architect." (See also p. 128 above.)

Figure V-2. St. Peter's, Milford, Conn. Frank Wills. 1851.

THE NEW YORK ECCLESIOLOGICAL SOCIETY

States. Priest was a more mysterious figure. His country house, at Balmville, was near Newburgh, where he was associated in some way with A. J. Downing. Priest was a teacher of architectural students.[77] It was certainly he who in 1846 had planned to build a church at Newburgh from the drawings used for St. James the Less.[78] He is most important, however, for his articles on the English literature on architecture and its aesthetics that appeared in the *New York Ecclesiologist*, for they show him to have had a literate, discriminating, and able mind. Curiously, no church of his design was ever reviewed.

The New York Ecclesiological Society had a mind of its own. It approved the Gothic parish church as a model. It condemned galleries. It considered correct orientation essential. It dubbed the sale of pews bad form. But beyond these essentials the Americans parted company with their English brethren. Avoiding the endless complexities of ecclesiology, they devoted their energies to abstract aesthetic problems and to the practical question of how the principles of good design might be realized in building. Rather than follow English ecclesiology, they continued the dialogue on architecture which had been in progress in America since the mid-1830's.

The *New York Ecclesiologist* believed that the nature of building materials should never be disguised. An article in the first issue, "Cheap Churches,"[79]

[77] Henry M. Congdon was apprenticed to Priest, and E. K. Shaw of Newburgh also studied with him. In September, 1859, *The Crayon* published Priest's obituary, from which the following facts are taken. His interest in architecture began early. He was born in 1825, and so was but twenty-four when he wrote the remarkable articles which are considered here. He graduated with honors from Washington College (now Trinity College) in Hartford, which accounts for the "M.A." which usually appears after his name. Priest was known for following his profession—"ardently and successfully" in spite of the fact that he was seriously handicapped by poor health all his life (it was for this reason that he lived in Newburgh rather than in New York City).

"A friend" who contributed to the information in the obituary mentioned in particular Priest's "frankness, his respect for knowledge," and "his wise application of the fruits of experience," and added that "the studies of ecclesiology and architecture were ever combined with him." Priest was, he said, primarily a designer of churches: "Baltimore, especially, has several monuments of his skill and good taste while New York, New Jersey, Maryland, North Carolina and Alabama, all show enduring mementoes of his genius." In addition he built "cottages, country-houses, parsonages, and schools, in many of our States, and was well-known for his rigidity in carrying out to the utmost extent his principles of thoroughness and good-taste, seldom failing to call forth sentiments of perfect satisfaction from his constituents."

[78] See p. 97 above.

[79] 1 (October, 1848) :6.

declared that the Gothic church of the fourteenth century most nearly expressed "Christian truth and temper" and then launched into a denunciation of attempts to make materials appear more valuable than they were. The author deplored the fact that "one-quarter or one-third the expense of many of our modern Churches, has arisen from the attempt to make the worse material appear the better," and he equated such dishonesty with unethical practices—attempts to deceive not only man but God. Builders were told that if they followed "true principles," beauty and economy would result. Churches should first be sound and proper structures; ornament could follow. Ecclesiology offered ways to avoid "that false economy [and] real prodigality which teaches how to make the greatest display with the smallest means."[80]

The *New York Ecclesiologist* borrowed not only the ideas but the language of Pugin. To the struggling parishes of the United States, his pronouncement that "architectural propriety as regards ecclesiastical buildings requires that they should be as good, as spacious, as rich and beautiful, as the *means and numbers of those who are erecting them will permit*"[81] was comforting. Pugin never knew that his principles inspired the design of Protestant Episcopal churches in the United States, but the validity and the abstract nature of his observations allowed them to survive and thrive when so transplanted. Though it had inspiration to offer, English ecclesiology had, in fact, few practical solutions for churchmen in the colonies. St. James the Less was a modest work of art, but it was also exceedingly costly. Already aware of English architectural theories, Americans explored the ecclesiological system, and when they had set aside its extravagant demands and rigid requirements that Gothic be accurately reproduced, they were led back to Pugin and his principles. Henry-Russell Hitchcock has pointed out that English ecclesiology failed to solve or face problems because of its devotion to a special form of eclecticism. American ecclesiology did not make this mistake.

The second article in the first issue of the *New York Ecclesiologist*, a paper read by Frank Wills at the first general meeting of the Society in April, 1848, reveals that it was Wills who was the follower of Pugin and the probable author of the essay on "Cheap Churches." His opening statement, "the age in

[80] *Ibid.*, p. 7.
[81] *True Principles*, p. 43.

which we live is essentially that of great show: it requires no deep penetration, no acute reasoning, no elaborate argument to prove this: we need only open our eyes, and in everything around us this truth is evident," was an echo of the last paragraph of the text of the 1836 edition of *Contrasts*, in which Pugin had joined the chorus of complaints about "the Age." One by one Wills presented and argued Pugin's ideas, until he declared his indebtedness by saying that "the great and true principle of Gothic architecture is, as Pugin expresses it, 'the ornamenting construction and not constructing ornament.' "[82] He then set up a realistic standard that American parishes could meet; "No church should be pretty: it should be simple, or modest, or dignified, or rich or gorgeous; but there should be never anything puerile about it, to lower its tone or degrade its character."[83]

Wills was forced to consider the thorny problem of building materials, for stone, a Gothic necessity, was often either costly or unattainable in the United States, while wood and brick were available. Armed with Pugin's principles, Wills ventured forth on his own to conclude that "the interior of a brick Church can be finished precisely the same in manner as the interior of rough stone walls. If it be a large structure there can be no objection to brick pillars, and arches with moulding wrought in cement; but they should be left in their integrity, and not scored and stained to produce delusive stone."[84] No part of his paper is more progressive or more intelligently comprehending of Pugin's theories than Wills's trenchant observations on the intemperate eclecticism of his times, for he said with regret that if one sought a "style to characterize the 19th century" all one would find would be "one grand motley—from a Mausoleum built like the Pyramids of Cheops, to a Villa finished after the model of 'the house that Jack built.' " The past possessed perseverance, said Wills, while the nineteenth century was all "excitement": "They had *weight*, we have *velocity*." In a prophetic and perceptive aside Wills declared that in the nineteenth century there was "no selection of any one style, nor an attempt to fully develop it through a series of years, and, by its development, probably produce a new system of architecture." Wills felt that the imitation of a great historical style (and he was not dogmatic about which style but was sure that

---

[82] "Reality in Church Architecture," *NYE*, 1 (October, 1848):11.
[83] *Ibid.*
[84] *Ibid.*

THE GOTHIC REVIVAL AND AMERICAN CHURCH ARCHITECTURE

churches should be Gothic), if properly understood, would lead architecture out of eclecticism into originality.

A point of view such as this was neither new nor unusual in England, yet it was far from commonplace. As early as 1842 the *Christian Remembrancer* had challenged the Cambridge Camden Society's rigorous recommendation of the parish church as the sole model for revival.[85] It had flirted with all the points later raised by Wills. For the purposes of its attack on architectural bigots, the *Remembrancer* had lumped Pugin in with the Society, though in the end it had been forced to admit that Pugin, not the Society, had logic on his side. Only in Greek and Gothic buildings, said the author, was the inner consistency of great architecture observable: "In them only do we find their different ideas perfectly brought out—in them only does each member take up a position which is at once its own, and yet absolutely required for it by all the rest, —in them only is nothing meaningless —nothing, the real use of which must be ignored or forgotten before we can avoid regarding it as a disfigurement." This was, of course, a roundabout way of saying what Pugin had put clearly in *True Principles* a year earlier, but it was also a preamble to the *Remembrancer*'s central point. The author questioned whether one style, and one style only, was indeed the answer to England's architectural problem, for he felt that there was evidence that "with the whole modern character of England, with her enlarged commerce, and her enlarged knowledge, with the genius of her literature and her language, . . . she should be capable of adopting everything really excellent in architecture, which suits her aim and can answer her purpose." Though his opposition to architectural orthodoxy and the imprisonment of a single style led him to create this flurry of progressive ideas, the author ventured no further in pursuit of them.

By 1847 English critics had grown to accept the idea that the nineteenth century would and should produce an architecture of its own. Professor Thomas Leverton Donaldson was asking, "Are we to have an architecture of our period, a distinct, individual, palpable style of the 19th century?"[86] and Lord Lindsay, Earl of Crawford (of whom more will be said in connection with the writing of J. W. Priest), also held that the nineteenth century offered

[85] "Styles of Church Architecture," *Christian Remembrancer*, 4 (1842). The quotes which follow are from p. 260.

[86] Quoted in Sir John Summerson, *Heavenly Mansions* (New York: Charles Scribner, 1948), p. 194.

"the Pledge, as it may be hoped, of a distinctly new style of architecture, expressive of the epoch in human progression of which Great Britain is the representative, as well as of a sculpture and Painting founded, not on servile imitation, but on sound principles and the inspirations of genius."[87]

Frank Wills was, of course, in no way as important as Donaldson and Lord Lindsay. His ideas never had a large following; his convictions and conclusions were not entirely original, for they had grown out of his English training and developed in the experience of architectural practice in the United States. But Wills did recognize that if one did what Pugin instructed one to do, a style based upon the principles could emerge. He predicted for the experience of eclecticism a destiny which differed from that proposed by the ecclesiologists. They began and ended with Gothic. For Wills the revival was a step in an evolving process; its end was not to be Gothic, but Lord Lindsay's "new style." The ecclesiologists had feared Pugin's theories as much for this possible interpretation of them as for their author's Roman Catholicism.[88]

In subsequent articles on form and arrangement of churches Wills was instructive but not startling. He insisted that all architecture begins with the plan and that if it is misconceived, the building will fail. He alluded to the fact that churches should express "Catholic Faith, and Order, and Truth," by which he meant Neale and Webb's "sacramentality," but dropped this idea almost at once to return to abstract analysis. The parts and uses of buildings should be "marked externally and internally," he said, but he warned that "circumstances," not "morbid love of the picturesque," should control such arrangements. By "circumstances" he meant function and utility, and he distinctly implied that he would consider it "morbid" to insist upon ecclesiologically accurate revivalism if every practical problem militated against it.

In 1850 Wills published *Ancient English Ecclesiastical Architecture*,[89] which

---

[87] Alexander W. C. Lindsay, 25th Earl of Crawford, *Sketches of the History of Christian Art*, 3 vols. (London: John Murray, 1847), 1:cclvii.
[88] See p. 20 above.
[89] The *Ecclesiologist* (11 [October, 1850]:168–69) gave this book a generally favorable review. It ignored all the issues Wills raised concerning the creation of a new style, criticized Wills's tendency to hyperbole, and mentioned peculiarly American problems discussed by Wills. In the same issue, under "New Churches," Wills's churches were reviewed favorably. The *New York Ecclesiologist* (2 [June, 1850]:107–9) was generally pleased, but it, too, expressed astonishment at the tone of the writing. It laid special emphasis upon Wills's statement on "the much disputed point of free or close copy in our following of ancient models."

once again demonstrated his debt to Pugin. Even the binding and design of the book resembled those of *True Principles.* Bishop John Henry Hopkins' *Essay on Gothic Architecture* of 1836[90] had been the first work on Gothic to be published in the United States. Wills's *Ancient English Ecclesiastical Architecture* was the second.

Wills had read *The Seven Lamps of Architecture* by John Ruskin and been sincerely puzzled by it, for "among the great many very good things" Ruskin had said were others which Wills could only describe as "absurd." *Seven Lamps* was a disappointment: "Ruskin is a clever writer, but a poor architect; the high moral tone he takes cannot be sufficiently lauded, the Lamp of Sacrifice is worth many volumes of sermons, but when he descends to detail, and endeavors to give reasons why this is beautiful and that is not, we think his fancies get the better of his judgement, and in carrying out an undisguised crude theory he often sacrifices his common sense."[91]

In spite of Wills's obvious attempt to make his book an advertisement for himself, his use of the language of English architectural controversy must have been astonishing—if not actually alarming—to his readers. Americans were accustomed to writers who said that some churches were "wretched Gothic abortions," but they were hardly prepared for feelings about architecture as intense as those expressed by Wills, who thought nothing of saying that "the most beautiful creations of mediaeval Architecture" had in the nineteenth century been "bedaubed with layer upon layer, generation upon generation, stratum upon stratum of abominable whitewash; but with even this accumulation of conglomerated barbarism and unhallowed taste, they are most beautiful." Greenough's literary style, for all that he expressed ideas which were revolutionary, had been Augustan, rational. Gilman had been dry, critical, sardonic. Downing had been gently assertive, sometimes bland. Through the *New York Ecclesiologist* and his book, Wills managed to intensify the emotional tone of architectural writing.

Frank Wills united the best of English mid-nineteenth-century thought on Gothic with American practicality and optimism about the future of architecture. He remained convinced that "when the principles of ancient Architecture are fully comprehended and practised, a healthy development may be expected

---

[90] See p. 59, n. 39, above.
[91] Wills, *Ancient English Ecclesiastical Architecture*, p. 81; see also p. 89.

and a style of superior beauty will arise from it." Though he was a disciple of Pugin, Wills also joined his American contemporaries such as Greenough in saying that "in the vegetable, animal or mineral kingdom, it is not the beauty of form alone which the most enchants us . . . but it is the combination of utility with beauty which impresses us with wonder and awe"[92] and that in the imitation of ancient work Americans should not follow "a slavish literal copying of any particular building, but rather adopt the spirit which actuated its builder: we should endeavor to get *that* by a comprehensive imitation which realises the deep and holy poetry pervading the structure rather than by a narrow-minded combination of its minute portions."[93] He called for what he termed "reality."

In three declarative articles published in the *New York Ecclesiologist* in 1849 and 1850, J. W. Priest joined Wills in establishing the policy of the New York Ecclesiological Society. Priest organized his essays around reviews and discussions of five books, a poem by Robert Browning, and volumes 1 to 8 of the *Ecclesiologist*.[94] Though his choice of works to review was, to say the least, odd if not idiosyncratic, it revealed the breadth, depth, and character of Priest's interests and knowledge and the direction in which he hoped to lead American ecclesiology.

One of the books Priest chose to review was *A History of Architecture*, published in 1849, the first major work by Edward Augustus Freeman. Freeman (1823–1892) was destined to be "one of England's greatest scholars."[95] He entered Trinity College, Oxford, in 1841, and because of his brilliance promptly became prominent. In 1846 he published a pamphlet entitled *Principles of Church Restoration*,[96] which intrigued the ecclesiologists, and he was an active

[92] *Ibid.*, p. 45.
[93] *Ibid.*, p. 91.
[94] "Church Architecture," *NYE*, 1 (August, 1849):179–85; *ibid.*, 2 (October, 1849):9–17; *ibid.* (March, 1850):73–77. These articles discuss Edward A. Freeman, *A History of Architecture* (London: Masters, 1849); J. Fergusson, *An Historical Inquiry into the True Principles of Beauty in Art, more especially with reference to Architecture*, pt. 1 (London: Longman, 1849); Lord Lindsay, *Sketches of the History of Christian Art; Ecclesiologist*, vols. 1–8, for 1841 to 1849; Ruskin, *The Seven Lamps of Architecture* (New York: Wiley, 1849), and *Modern Painters* 2 vols. (New York: Wiley, 1848); and Robert Browning, *Paracelsus, a Poem.*
[95] Thompson, *History of Historical Writing*, 2:318.
[96] (London: Masters, 1846); reviewed in the *Ecclesiologist*, 7 (May, 1847):161–68.

and contributing member of the Oxford Architectural Society, and its secretary for some time. In 1844 Freeman was a founding member of the Brotherhood of St. Mary at Oxford, a society designed "to study ecclesiastical art upon true and Catholic principles." In his undergraduate years, though he had seriously considered the possibility of becoming an architect, he had rejected the idea because "he doubted whether the profession ranked high enough to be worth following, owing to the miserable pretenders who crowded into it." He was acquainted with the Cambridge ecclesiologists and was their host on a visit they paid to Oxford. On this occasion he enjoyed his contact with Thorp and Webb but found Neale "the gravest and most reserved man" he had ever seen. In his lifetime, though he wrote at least a dozen books on medieval architecture, Freeman attained enduring fame as an historian. He was made professor of modern history at Oxford and ultimately published prodigiously in his chosen field.

The *Ecclesiologist* behaved toward Freeman as it did toward anyone so bold as to disagree or question. A. J. B. Hope reviewed a paper Freeman had read in 1845, challenged his theories, and refuted his attacks on ecclesiology. Hope's anger was caused by Freeman's pugnaciousness and his derogatory remarks about the *Ecclesiologist*; Freeman had said, among other things, that no matter what the ecclesiologists believed, Perpendicular Gothic surpassed all other styles and that the Cambridge men did not regard the "awful naves of Peterborough and Ely as fit temples for Christian worship."[97]

Priest's second choice, James Fergusson's *An Historical Inquiry into the True Principles of Beauty in Art*, was another book of which the ecclesiolo-

---

[97] Quoted in Hope, "Development of Roman and Gothic Architecture, and their Moral and Symbolical Teaching, A paper read before the Oxford Architectural Society by E. A. Freeman, Esq., B.A., Fellow of Trinity College, on November, 12, 1845," *E.*, 5 (February, 1846):53–55. The attribution of this article to Hope is based upon a letter from Freeman to Miss Eleanor Gutch, of February 1, 1846, in which he said: "I should recommend you to get the *Ecclesiologist* for this month, which, as I believe I told you, is to contain a review of my Development Paper by Hope. I am most anxious to see it—I suppose it will be out to-morrow" (W. R. W. Stephens, *The Life and Letters of Edward A. Freeman*, 2 vols. (London: Macmillan, 1895), 1:88.

Freeman was an adversary worthy of the *Ecclesiologist*. J. W. Thompson describes his "blustering ways" and says that his reviews in the *Saturday Review* did "as much as any man's to earn this severe journal the nickname of the 'Reviler'" (*History of Historical Writing*, pp. 316–17).

gists ardently disapproved.[98] No mildly controversial scholarly history, as Freeman's book had been, it was a landmark in nineteenth-century architectural thought, brimming with ideas that brought the rigid patterns of ecclesiological medievalism into serious question. Early in life Fergusson (1808–1886) had entered a family business in Calcutta, but by 1835, having made a small fortune, he retired from the enterprise and returned to London to pursue his major interests, archeology and architecture. As an expert on the buildings of India, he had no difficulty in finding a suitable audience.[99] In 1840 he was elected a member of the Royal Asiatic Society, and he was frequently invited to read papers before the Royal Institute of British Architects. There seems some doubt as to whether Fergusson was, in fact, trained as an architect. The *Ecclesiologist* called him "an amateur genius," but since "Architect" follows Fergusson's name on the title page of *Historical Inquiry*, and he was made a member of the Royal Institute of British Architects in 1859 and received its gold medal in 1871, it appears safe to assume that the editors were merely expressing one of their more disagreeable moods when they made this remark.

In 1850 the *Ecclesiologist* attacked Fergusson, called his plan for the rebuilding of the National Gallery *outré*, and said he had "amused everybody with a volume to prove, with the utmost seriousness, that the so-called Mosque of Omar, which as all the world knows stands on the site of the Temple, is the veritable Church of the Holy Sepulchre."[100] At the time of this onslaught Fergusson was forty-two: as well as the offending book, he had published *Ancient Topography of Jerusalem*, a treatise on fortifications, *Picturesque*

[98] The *Dictionary of National Biography* account of Fergusson is helpful. This summary of his activities is also founded upon study of the *Catalogue of the Architectural and Miscellaneous Library of the Late James Fergusson, Esq. C.S.I., D.C.L., F.R.S., etc.*; the library was sold by Sotheby, Wilkinson and Hodge after Fergusson's death in 1886 (document in the collections of the British Museum). John Steegman, *Consort of Taste, 1830–1870* (London: Sedgwick and Jackson, 1950), contains much information on the period and matters under consideration here.

[99] Fergusson's books were reviewed in *The Builder*, which also published reports of his lectures and articles: see "The Lighting of Greek Temples," *The Builder*, 8 (January 13, 1849):19, for diagrams and comment on his theory; *"The Royal Institute of British Architects," ibid.*, 7 (February 10, 1849):65; "On the Topography and Antiquities of the City of Jerusalem," *ibid.* (March 3, 1849):99–100; "On the History of the Pointed Arch," *ibid.* (June 23, 1849):290–91; and "Architecture of India," *ibid.*, 8 (January 12, 1850):14–15, for examples of the comment on him and his work.

[100] "Architectural Room of the Royal Academy," *E.*, 8 (June, 1850):43.

Illustrations of Ancient Architecture in Hindostan, and admirable articles on the rock cut temples of India. The *Ecclesiologist* was biased and incorrect in its estimate: Fergusson was destined for even greater achievements. In the years that followed he was to establish a firm place for himself among English and Continental scholars of architectural history. Some of his many books were translated into French. He wrote extensively not only on India but on Persia and the archeology of ancient Greece. He collaborated with H. Schliemann, who dedicated his volume on Tiryns to him. He published works on the Erechtheum, the Temple of Diana at Ephesus, and the Mausoleum at Halicarnassus and wrote a monograph on his theories of the original lighting of the Parthenon. Fergusson was one of the first, if not the first, scholar to photograph architecture and use the photographs as an aid to his research.[101] He was also known as an expert draftsman.

The quality of Fergusson's contribution to architectural history and criticism was, at least in part, a result of his knowledge of Asiatic and ancient Greek building and his intelligent interest in primitive art and architecture. Among his late books were an essay on *Tree and Serpent Worship* (1868) and another on Stonehenge and other megalithic remains. Even early in his career he had been unwilling to restrict his consideration of the history of building to squabbles over the relative merits of the Decorated and Perpendicular Gothic styles. As Viollet le Duc would later do, he brought to his work genuine understanding of the architecture and arts of cultures foreign both in time and place. The details of Fergusson's biography are not definite, but the character, subjects, and number of his publications indicate that he spent considerable time in Greece and Persia as well as in India. His close association with Schliemann, who described him as "the historian of architecture, eminent alike for his knowledge of art and for the original genius which he has applied to the solution of its most difficult problems," dated from his months and perhaps even years of study in Greece. The two men could well have been drawn to one another by similarities of personal history; both had left careers in commerce to pursue archeological research.

[101] In the sale of Fergusson's library and household effects there was an entire section devoted to his collection of photographs on Indian architecture and scenery. The photographers were D. H. Sykes, Lindley and Warren, and J. van Kinsberger. The sale also included a collection of twelve hundred photographs of Indian buildings, which Sotheby described as equal in quality to the only other known collection, that of the South Kensington Museum.

THE NEW YORK ECCLESIOLOGICAL SOCIETY

For all the quantity, quality, and variety of his achievements Fergusson is best known for his *Historical Inquiry*, his *Handbook of Architecture*, which first appeared in 1855, and *A History of Modern Architecture*, published in 1862. The last two were republished together from 1865 to 1867 as *A History of Architecture in All Countries from the Earliest Time to the Present Day*.[102]

It is known that Ralph Waldo Emerson was acquainted with Fergusson's theories, and the significance of this important encounter has been evaluated and discussed elsewhere.[103] But the contact between Emerson and Fergusson's books seems to have come after 1868 and to have involved only the *Handbook of Architecture*. Priest's choice of the *Historical Inquiry* for his review and commentary in 1849 and 1850 places the appearance of Fergusson on the American scene earlier and in a quite different context than has previously been recognized.

The *Historical Inquiry* is a fascinating, important,[104] and eccentric book. It consists of two parts, an Introduction of 174 pages and a history of architecture and the arts from Egypt through Rome. In his Introduction Fergusson said that he had hoped to cover the entire history of architecture but that the plan proved too great for his funds and capabilities. The Introduction established the principles upon which his history was founded. Art for Fergusson was *"all those modifications that man works on nature's productions,"* and beauty was perfection, for "whatever is perfect is beautiful in the eyes of those who understand it."[105] The breadth of these definitions and Fergusson's insistence "that all of the fine arts are based on and grow out of useful ones"

[102] *The Illustrated Handbook of Architecture, being a concise and popular account of the Different Styles of Architecture Prevailing in All Ages and All Countries* (London: John Murray, 1859) is the version in which this work is best known and most readily available. The 1859 edition was the second, the first having appeared in 1855.

[103] Robert W. Winter, "Fergusson and Garbett in American Architectural Theory," *Journal of the Society of Architectural Historians*, 17 (Winter, 1958):25–29.

[104] The *Quarterly Review* paid considerable and respectful attention to Fergusson and his works. A. H. Layard reviewed the *Handbook of Architecture* and *Historical Inquiry* in a joint review in vol. 106 (October, 1859):285–330, and Whitwell Elwin reviewed *A History of Architecture in All Countries from the Earliest Times to the Present Day* in vol. 120 (October, 1866):425–61. Edward D. De Zurko, *Origins of Functionalist Theory* (New York: Columbia University Press, 1957), pp. 143 and 148, includes a discussion of Fergusson. Ronald Bradbury, *The Romantic Theories of Architecture in Germany, England, and France* (New York: The Dorothy Press, 1934), is also helpful on the background of Fergusson's ideas.

[105] P. 23.

led him to consider such mundane achievements as heating, ventilating, and carpentry. His was a singularly nineteenth-century idea, similar to the assumptions of Quatremère de Quincy,[106] who preceded him, and Gottfried Semper,[107] who came after him.

Fergusson believed all art consisted of the "technic," the "aesthetic," and the "phonetic" elements, and he ranked the technic the lowest on the scale. He recognized that some of the arts would contain no part of the highest, or phonetic, and that others, though they were properly arts by his definition, would contain none of the qualities he termed technic. He illustrated his theory with diagrams and charts, which make it infinitely easier to understand. Architecture, Fergusson felt, contained equal parts of his three elements, but his study of the architecture of primitive peoples and foreign cultures had shown him that this balance could be and had been varied. He noted that the "Pyramids of Egypt—though technically magnificent beyond all the buildings of the world—have very little aesthetic, and scarcely 1 of phonetic value" (Fergusson worked out a system of values expressed in numbers[108]).

[106] A. C. Quatremère de Quincy, *Essay on the Nature, the End, and the Means of Imitation in the Fine Arts*, trans. J. C. Kent (London: Smith, Elder, 1837).
[107] *Der Stil in den technischen und tektonischen Künsten oder praktische Ästhetik*, 2 vols. (Frankfurt am Main, Stuttgart, 1860–63).
[108] Pp. 140 and 143. One of his charts and a diagram are reproduced here. Fergusson has selected a variety of arts at random, which explains the omission of sculpture. He says that one should multiply the figures in the first column of the chart by 1, those in the second column by 2, and those in the third by 3 to obtain a product which, he says, will "very nearly express the relative value of any class of works of art."

Art Form		Element	
	Technic	*Aesthetic*	*Phonetic*
Heating, Ventilation, etc.	11	1	0 = 13
Joinery	9	3	0 = 15
Gastronomy	7	5	0 = 17
Jewellery	7	4	1 = 18
Furnishing	6	5	1 = 19
Clothing	5	6	1 = 20
Céramique	5	5	2 = 21
Gardening	4	6	2 = 22
Architecture	4	4	4 = 24
Music	2	6	4 = 26
Painting	3	3	6 = 27
Drama	2	2	8 = 30
Poetry	—	2	10 = 34
Eloquence	—	1	11 = 35

THE NEW YORK ECCLESIOLOGICAL SOCIETY

Since it was immediately apparent to Fergusson and to his contemporaries that there was in this system no room for beauty derived from association, Fergusson discarded it as "a form of phonetic utterance which throws a veil of beauty over some objects in the minds of particular persons, which to others appear only commonplace, or even ugly." He perceived to his sorrow that architecture and the other arts were, in his times, "cursed by the influence of this lowest and most unreasoning source of beauty." Sculpture was "entirely enslaved" by it, and even the decorative arts suffered its "slavish and retrograde" influence. Fergusson was opposed to eclecticism, which he termed a "strange mania." No amount of ability, integrity, or inspiration would help "in an age cursed with a false system of art." Art in the nineteenth century was "retrograde," and "its highest aim is to copy as correctly as is possible, without making it an entire sham." He was sorry for architects, for they seemed to him "like men fishing for stars whose reflexion they see in the stagnant waters of a former world." There was hope for the future only if art was willing to return to "its progressive vitality . . . to give up all imitation of past styles"; if "a higher order of minds" would participate in its practice and patronage; if it would serve "some higher aim than merely to please the dilettante or the connoisseur."

Fergusson felt there was evidence that England might reverse her downward course and correct her artistic errors, for the arts she had "cultivated on the most commonsense principles" had yielded spectacularly successful results. And it is at this point that he embarks upon his well-known and often quoted praise of the achievements of civil engineering, which he said resembled the anonymous, communal brilliance of medieval art. Fergusson refused to predict whether all borrowing from past styles would cease. He would only say that the history of architecture had taught him that "the only path by which any nation, at any age or in any country, ever accomplished any thing that was

---

Fergusson represented these ideas diagrammatically in the following fashion:

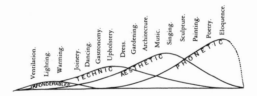

great or good either in science or in art, was by steady progressive aggregation of experience, without ever looking back or attempting to copy."

The tone and the import of remarks such as these made the ecclesiologists lie in wait for Fergusson. Since he was outspoken and frank, he gave them their opportunity in 1850, when he commented in *The Builder* on the "Effect of the Want of Reality on the Works of Modern Architects."[109] His subject was churches, his inspiration a bitter lament by Pugin on the shameful shams employed in much Gothic revival building. Fergusson agreed that there was a problem, but his solution was hardly what Pugin, who responded to his article,[110] or the ecclesiologists wanted to hear, for he suggested that everyone stop using the style:

It is proposed to erect a building, say a parish church, to accommodate a certain congregation. This can be done in a common-sense modern edifice, with a sufficient amount of ornament and character, for say 5,000£. No, say all the ecclesiologists, archaeologists, and amateurs of mediaeval antiquities, this can never do; and the architect is made to ask 5,000£ more, to put the church into a mediaeval dress, —in other words, to crowd the floor with pillars, which prevent people from seeing and hearing, —to abolish galleries, which accommodate crowds at a small expense; to deepen the chancel, so that the clergyman's voice cannot be heard, etc, etc.[111]

Pugin, who was truly a conservative, felt that abuses such as those he mentioned would disappear when people were sufficiently educated to demand genuine Gothic. Fergusson disagreed, assuring Pugin, the ecclesiologists, and the rest of the enemy camp that "once the public are as familiar with the modes in which Gothic buildings were produced as they are with the forms, I am very much mistaken if they do not adopt the spirit, and reject the form; and the moment they do, there is an end of all Gothic or pagan reproduction. Architecture will resume her progressive and creative course, and servile copying and retrocession become impossible."[112]

[109] Fergusson's comments in *The Builder* were prompted by the editorial in the issue of April 14, 1849, p. 169, and by an article entitled "Arguments in Favour of Internal Ecclesiastical Decoration," which immediately followed it. Fergusson's statement, "Effect of the Want of Reality on the Works of Modern Architects," appeared in the issue for March 16, 1850, p. 122.
[110] Pugin answered Fergusson in "How Shall We Build our Churches?," *The Builder*, 8 (March 23, 1850):134–35.
[111] P. 122.
[112] *Ibid.*

Priest was attracted to Fergusson precisely because he opposed the ecclesiological system, because he expressed ideas Americans had been struggling to formulate for themselves, and because he offered a view of the arts acceptable to a nation proud that it had no aristocracy and firm in the belief that its people constituted a progressive and intelligent government by the majority. Fergusson insisted that some of the greatest building of the past had been the product of a hundred commonplace minds, working with gifted men. English constitutional government, he said, was itself such a work of art. Architectural excellence would emerge from a similar union of high aims and practical needs, and when it came it would bear no resemblance to a historical style.

The third book Priest discussed was *Sketches on the History of Christian Art* (1847) by Lord Lindsay (1812–1880), 25th Earl of Crawford, which Lord Lindsay had preceded by a small but important work, *Progression by Antagonism: A Theory Involving Considerations Touching the Present Position, Duties and Destiny of Great Britain*, published in 1846.[113] The earlier treatise had described his philosophy of historical development and his explanation of the causes of philosophical, artistic, and political change. The development of human nature "in the aggregate," said Lord Lindsay, followed a pattern of "progressive development of Sense, Intellect and Spirit, strictly analogous to that of the Individual Man." The energy for this evolution came from

the mutual antagonism of the two classes of Sensual and Spiritual men, in their successive generations, . . . from the unequal predominance assigned to Imagination and Reason in the intellectual character of the Individual Man, whereby God has provided in every nation, as it rises in civilization, two vast political and ecclesiastical parties, each discerning half the truth and supposing it whole—each struggling to maintain it—and neither perceiving that it is from the collision of partial truths that Truth in the abstract, disencumbered from the alloy of earthly prejudice soars aloft and darts onward to her goal.[114]

In his *Sketches* Lord Lindsay presented the history of art in five periods, which began with Roman and Byzantine art and ended with the French Revolution and what he called "the Second Regeneration of Catholic Christianity . . . to a period as yet undetermined." The transitions from one period to another occurred as the "Sensual" or the "Spiritual" became dominant. The Middle

[113] (London: Murray, 1846).
[114] *Ibid.*, p. 12.

Ages were controlled by Spirit (Lord Lindsay's Period I), but they were displaced in the fifteenth century by the development of intellect (his Period II), and so on until the nineteenth century, a time he found more difficult to define but about which he was genuinely optimistic. It was at this point in his treatise that he expressed his belief that "a distinctly new style of architecture" devoid of "servile imitation" would be forthcoming. In the first of the three volumes which compose the *Sketches* Lindsay's pattern is set forth in outline form. The remaining two volumes are devoted to exposition of the arts, their development and their meaning, through the fifteenth century. At this point Lindsay stopped, promising that more was to follow, but the treatise was never continued.

All this is deeply significant to the history of taste and the growth of knowledge of the history of art in the nineteenth century,[115] but one may feel quite sure that John Priest, American architect and literary connoisseur, did not read this complex book to acquire an understanding of the painting of the fourteenth and fifteenth centuries in Italy (a subject on which Lord Lindsay was especially interesting). Priest was, instead, attracted by the discussion of architecture contained in the *Sketches* and by the conviction that a "new style" would emerge.

It is fortunate that Priest explained his next choice, *Paracelsus*, by Robert Browning;[116] otherwise, one would find it hard to understand how the poem could be relevant to architectural discourse. Priest admitted that the reasons for this selection were somewhat obscure and said that he would find it "a pleasing task to analyze this noble Poem," but because to do so was impossible in his context, he announced that he understood Browning's message to be that *"God had made it a duty to all men to give 'expression' to what He has given them, each in his own way."*

Two books, Ruskin's *Modern Painters* (1848) and *The Seven Lamps of Architecture* (1849), and volumes 1 to 8 of the *Ecclesiologist* completed Priest's list. His response to Ruskin was mixed, for he found him sometimes confusing but often inspiring. It was to the *Ecclesiologist*, however, that these

---

[115] For a general comment on the content of the *Sketches* and Lord Lindsay's place as a member of the critical and art historical circle in England, see John Steegman, "Lord Lindsay's *History of Christian Art*," *Journal of the Warburg and Courtauld Institutes*, 10 (1947):123–31.

[116] *The Works of Robert Browning*, 10 vols. (London: Smith, Elder, 1912), 1:39–168. *Paracelsus* was published in 1835.

articles were in fact addressed, for Priest had set out to disagree with its policies in every fundamental way. He challenged the premises of ecclesiology more boldly than any English critic had dared or cared to do.

Priest stalked his quarry cleverly. He began his first article by saying that he proposed merely to present the lessons he had learned from the books he was reviewing. When he said that he would arrange his materials "for a practical end," however, he revealed his real plan. Freeman, Lord Lindsay, and Fergusson had shown him that architectural change was an evolutionary process, with styles coming out of styles, forms combining and recombining. Early in his remarks Priest reported his preference among the various Gothic styles, and explained his choice. He had three recommendations to consider: Freeman championed the cause of Perpendicular and the ecclesiologists chose "Middle Pointed," while Ruskin said that "early Middle Pointed" was best because it did not show the signs of decline, the "substitution of the line for the mass, as the element of decoration," which came later. Priest weighed all three and took a position midway between Ruskin and the ecclesiologists, saying that "the highest development of Christian Architecture which the world has ever seen, was exhibited in the early days of flowing Middle Pointed."

Quite suddenly Priest then shifted his ground to ask whether there could be a "yet more perfect style" and, if so, whether it was not the duty of ecclesiology to create it. At this point the influence of Fergusson appears, for from him Priest had learned that "the nations of antiquity were only great in Art when they attempted to fill the wants, and give 'expression' to the principles, the feelings, and the aspirations of their own age." The early building cultures of Egypt, India, and Greece had been content to develop "their primal types of building," but the later Byzantines, Lombards, and Goths, though they had borrowed from foreign and earlier architecture, had "fused" these materials in the "crucible of their own genius," making it "the exponent of their own vitality in Art."

There were, said Priest, two ways to attain the "more perfect style" that he believed possible. From the productions of the past the best might be selected, or the nineteenth century could "originate" by its own genius and "fuse both what we gather and what we invent into harmony with our own thoughts, and thus attain . . . the expression of our own life." Priest preferred the second solution. In passing, he noted that for three centuries there had not been a "living" style and that modern man, who was without a loyalty to any antecedent style, was therefore free to exercise his originality. Gothic, lovely though it was, was "capable of being carried forward."

Pride and insolence did not inspire these aspirations. The message of *Paracelsus*, the history of architecture as it was presented by Fergusson, showed that "the Artist must 'express himself' in his work." And so, Priest said, the aim should be "the development of early flowing Middle Pointed, and at the same time the expression of our taste, our power, and our aspirations as well as the exponent of our love and adoration of Him whose glory we seek to advance." The creation of a new style was nothing less than a moral and spiritual obligation.

In the second article of his series Priest disclosed the ideas for which the first had been but a preface. He said flatly that the nineteenth century would never express its own life in its architecture *"so long as we are content to copy existing examples, or blindly to follow ancient precedent,"* and added insult to injury by citing the *Ecclesiologist* in his footnotes as an example of the point of view he deplored. From Lord Lindsay, Browning, and Ruskin he extracted and compiled further evidence that to follow the *Ecclesiologist* was to contradict divine law. He even showed that there were statements in the Neale and Webb introduction to Durandus which supported his position.

To copy the most beautiful examples would yield only a building "as dead as leaves in December." The ecclesiologists, he said, "who are foremost in demanding 'truthfulness, devotion and self-sacrifice' in church building, yet reject the only principle upon which these can be embodied in Art, —the fulfilment of the duty of 'expression.' " Having dissolved the ties by which he was bound to the ecclesiologists, Priest declared, with a firmness equaled only by theirs, that *"all Art must have rigid laws, but they must rest on propriety, not precedent.* Propriety may be *learned from precedent*, but cannot be *determined by it*, even . . . in a phase of Art which is not an original development." He respected the ecclesiologists for their earnestness but regretted that they had "tried to blind the artist with other laws than the universal ones to which he already owes obedience."[117]

Actually, Priest was thoroughly annoyed by an unsigned article which ap-

[117] "Church Architecture II," *NYE*, 2 (October, 1849):14.

peared in the *Ecclesiologist* in January, 1846, in which the author said that the nineteenth century was hardly the time to indulge in creativity, for "we have not learned our alphabet, and it is absurd to attempt to compose: we do not know the names of our tools, and it is insane to attempt to model. All that we can expect to do is to copy carefully in hopes of realizing at the last, through numberless copyings, some first principles which we may store up for our children to make use of." In his conclusion Priest devoted himself to this statement and destroyed it by fragmenting its analogy between architecture and language.

In long notes appended to this article Priest severed every remaining link with the English ecclesiologists. They were set in very small type, but they were legible all the same. Note A itemized the matters in which the ecclesiologists had contradicted themselves, including the fact that they had been forced to "admit new developments in colonial Churches and under a tropical sun." Note C was the most disastrous for future transatlantic amity, for in it Priest pledged his allegiance to Fergusson and accepted his idea that the notion of "symbolism" was but a "beautiful relic of *past* superstition."

By the time they had read Priest's second article and decided to publish it, the editorial committee of the New York Ecclesiological Society, although aware that a storm was brewing, was prepared to accept the consequences, for it agreed with Priest. The editor added a note to Priest's second article saying that "we agree in the main with our correspondent; yet (with him) we do not wish it to be supposed that we are embarking in a crusade against Ecclesiology in England—far from it. We are too deeply sensible of the debt of gratitude which we, in common with the whole Christian world, owe them, and too well aware of their superiority to ourselves to profess ourselves other than humble, though, we trust not *blind,* imitators of them." The important word here was, of course, "blind."

His declaration of independence demanded that Priest establish a positive program to replace what he had forsaken, and this was what he proposed to do in his third article, which was published in March, 1850. But there was another authority to be considered and refuted, for Priest had read Ruskin's *Seven Lamps of Architecture* carefully and found in it an argument which contradicted his own. Like the ecclesiologists, Ruskin had used an analogy between language and architecture. In the course of his discussion he said: "We must determine what buildings are to be considered Augustan in their authority; their modes of construction and laws of proportion, are to be studied with the most penetrating care; then the different forms and uses of their decorations are to be classed and catalogued, as a German grammarian classes the powers of prepositions; and under this absolute, irrefragable authority, we are to begin to work; admitting not so much as an alteration in the depth of a cavetto, or the breadth of a fillet." Priest perceived what he called "an unfairness" (by which he meant inconsistency) in Ruskin's reasoning, and he expressed dismay that the author of *Modern Painters* and the *Seven Lamps* should have failed to relate one of his statements to another. Undaunted by Ruskin's confusions, Priest concluded his article by reiterating his deep belief that unless the forms borrowed from the past were "brought into harmony with our own ideas of beauty" they would be not only meaningless but pernicious. He could not predict the form that architecture would assume, but he was sure that the mid-nineteenth century should begin at once "to follow the principles we have learned, and to obey the laws we have acknowledged; to express the ideas that we possess, and to embody in the works of our art, the yearning of our souls for that unearthly beauty, of which, the loveliness of things material is but the shadow and the type."

Exactly one month after the second of Priest's articles appeared, the *Ecclesiologist* responded. The editors were very annoyed:

We cannot understand the writer's drift. He praises our spirit of development, and yet he blames us for statements of some years back. Did he mean that we should have sprung into existence all-perfect? or would he desire a formal heading of retractions each number? In one respect he quite misunderstands us. He blames us for our advice to architects to learn principles by copying old models. We never meant by this to order the bodily reproduction of ancient churches, which if his argument is to hold water must have been the case.[118]

Then, for several paragraphs of their report on events in the New York Society, they avoided the matter of Priest and his opinions, only to return to them, this time conspicuously omitting mention of the offending author and his works. "American ecclesiology has, as it was right and likely that it should do, looked to England to learn its first lesson," a phenomenon which the *Ecclesiologist*

---

[118] "The New York Ecclesiologist," *E.*, 7 (November, 1849) :202.

accepted as a compliment. However, it would be best if the Americans could remember that with their diversity of climate and materials styles other than English might best suit their purposes. In a final angry flourish the *Ecclesiologist* added that what America needed most of all was "a staff of indigenous architects and church-artists. The demand is very pressing and we are very much at fault about the character of our brethren of the New World if they do not speedily meet it by a sufficient supply. All we say to them is, prosper, worthy descendants of the old Anglo-Saxon stock!" Since both Wills and Priest were architects, the Society's implication was hardly flattering. On only one subsequent occasion did the *Ecclesiologist* ever again allude to its New York descendant.

Priest and Wills had succeeded; by 1850, less than two years after its foundation, the New York Ecclesiological Society had wandered far from orthodoxy. In a formal address to the membership the President reviewed the whole question of models for American churches and attempted to solve the problem of originality. He agreed that the English parish church was the "type" suitable for the parochial church, but he was careful to make clear that by "type" he did not mean anything more than the "principles" which "lay within it." He understood that "what those principles are which constitute the *Ideal* . . . are more easily felt than defined," but he was positive that "dogmatic rules" were no substitute for them: "He who is thoroughly imbued with their spirit and use may work freely in Church design, providing it be in love and reverence; *he* is not tied to the letter." The Society was not ready to go as far as Wills and Priest, but it accompanied them part way in their rejection of what Priest had called "servile imitation."[119]

This movement to the left in architecture was definite and final. In 1851 George L. Duyckinck (1823–1863), editor of the *Literary World*,[120] read a paper entitled "Originality in Church Architecture" before the Society. It was

[119] "Church Architecture II," *NYE*, 2 (October, 1849) :17.
[120] Duyckinck, a graduate of Hobart College and the University of the City of New York, studied law but did not practice. His literary career began in 1843. He traveled abroad with his brother Evert in 1847 and 1848 and edited the *Literary World* from 1848 to 1853. When he was editor a number of articles on architecture appeared in the journal. Duyckinck was concerned with religious matters and Christian education for children. He was the author of various biographies, including one of Jeremy Taylor.

reprinted in full in the *New York Ecclesiologist*.[121] Duyckinck had the intellectual poise and assurance of a man of good education and the enthusiasm and insights of a new generation. His message was stirring rather than conservative. He opened his discussion with a tribute to Gothic, which he said was the product of men of "originality," training, and steadfast purpose. While lamenting that "no Winckelmann has yet arisen for Christian sculpture," he recognized the contributions of Lord Lindsay's "noble book," and he hazarded the opinion that a thorough study of medieval sculpture "would change the present style of sculpture as effectually as Overbeck has influenced the Art of Painting in our day." Within recent times, he said, Gothic art and architecture had come to be understood as great art rather than the "works of demi-savages," and Europe had passed through a "transition period of attempts at the beauties of Gothic architecture" and entered a phase in which building followed not Gothic models but the "true principles" they illustrated. Copying had been disastrous; eclecticism had always been "unfavorable to art . . . a mushroom growth, fostering insincerity and entailing dull and stupid formalism."

One of the most remarkable characteristics of Gothic architecture, Duyckinck said, was its variety—its national styles—and for this reason, if for no other, attempts to reproduce English churches in America were doomed to fail. He declared that he wished "every work, and especially every work of the importance and solemnity of a church, to show to some extent that it is the work of an American, or produced under American influences." Accordingly, he suggested that American plants be represented in decorative sculpture and that portraits of actual persons connected with parish work be introduced. In a short digression on the subject of memorials such as those in Westminster Abbey, his outspoken disdain was the equal of Pugin's similar attack in *Contrasts*: "no monuments at all," Duyckinck said, "would be preferable to such an heterogeneous collection of puffy Cherubs and scantily clad Virtues, blatant Fames and blubbering Britannias."

Satisfaction of functional needs and experimentation with building materials were the points at which to begin the creation of a national style. Because seating for large numbers of people was a necessity, Duyckinck suggested that galleries be used. He was, however, opposed to attempts to disguise them. He

[121] 3 (July, 1851):71–80.

said that instead, since "galleries were a temporary expedient," they should be installed so that they could be removed without weakening the structure and that their "means of support [should] be decided and apparent." They should be made of iron, a material with many advantages not the least of which was that it was "an indigenous product of our own soil, and as a representative of the vast mineral kingdom, and as one of the sources of national wealth, is well worthy of being a component of our Christian temples."

In conclusion, Duyckinck said that, like the Church, architecture would have its share of great men, "but when they come they will not be perpetually conning over Mr. Pugin's books, they will seek and find a development of their own, an architecture which built on the past shall embody the forces of the present. . . . Had not the same process taken place in the past, we should not look back over so many buried ages to admire its innovations and improvements on its predecessors." He asked for "daring originality."

By 1851 the New York Ecclesiological Society had settled into a routine existence. Periodically the *New York Ecclesiologist* published laudatory reviews of Pugin's books. A body of articles on special aspects and problems of American church design was being built up. The Society made an arrangement to sponsor the manufacture of altar plate from patterns by William Butterfield. Finally, just as publication of the *New York Ecclesiologist* was to cease, a long article on "Stone and Iron" showed that the journal had not altered its progressive and thoughtful theories on building materials and architectural aesthetics. The Crystal Palaces of London and New York were described as "triumphs of art," but the author of the article was disturbed by the fact that some people were so attached to tradition that they could not perceive the brilliant possibilities of this new building material. With the usual openmindedness of American ecclesiology, the Society said that it had earlier advocated the use of stone because it was durable but that it was willing to change its mind on this essential point. The question of iron for church buildings should be considered. A gracefully phrased exposition of the formal problems raised by the use of iron shows with what care it was being studied:

Now iron and stone are so different in their nature, that when used, even for the same purpose of building, they still require an entirely different mode of construction; stone requiring, of necessity, a construction which impresses strongly upon the mind the ideas of firmness and durability, whereas, on the other hand, iron, by a like necessity, requires a construction which as strongly impresses upon the mind the ideas of lightness and temporary use; nor can iron free itself from this, its essential character, except by an unreality, which, the moment the deception is discovered, at once destroys its power over the mind; we refer to its employment in the shape of hollow blocks which indeed look solid, but which, from our knowledge of the material, we are certain cannot be so.[122]

For parishes too poor to build more extravagantly, iron was the perfect answer. In 1844 an iron church was shipped from England for assembly in Jamaica, and by 1854 a firm in Bristol was offering for sale a variety of iron buildings.[123] In the United States the use of iron was new but by 1853 not unusual. Acceptance of the material by Duyckinck in 1851 and the Society's endorsement of it in 1853 were in accord with progressive architectural opinion and practice. When it described the iron church it was considering, the Society did not, however, give any indication that it was prepared to modify the normal parish church plan because of the use of iron as the building material. Iron churches, it concluded, should have expressed chancels. The use to which the building would be put, not the nature of its materials, was to dictate the form and shape of its plan and parts.

In the years between 1835 and 1853 many books on architecture were published in England, and at least two major journals, *The Architectural Magazine* and *The Builder*, were devoted to the subject. As the profession of architecture grew in self-consciousness and independence of expression, so did research in the history of building. Architects began to collect earlier treatises as well as recent literature on their art. Travel and books were the two major resources of the designer. It is significant that the Americans should have chosen as they did from among the many books that had been and were being written in England. They obviously preferred theoretical works, were not greatly interested in the detailed drawings, and did not collect early and foreign books such as Seroux d'Agincourt's *Histoire de l'art par les Monuments* (Paris,

---

[122] "Stone and Iron," *NYE*, 5 (October, 1853):142. By 1843 the Ecclesiological Society had decided to take part in the design of iron churches.
[123] *Illustrated London News*, 5 (September, 1844):208. Also see Hitchcock, *Early Victorian Architecture*, chaps. 15 and 16.

1823) and F. Milizia's *Memorie degli Architetti Antichi e Moderni*. In all of the American writing on architecture there were only one or two references to Joseph Gwilt, Whewell, and Willis, and none to the young but very promising Owen Jones. And when the list of "Literary and Graphic Works, which a Practical Architect, may possess and consult with advantage to himself," provided by Alfred Bartholomew in 1841 in his *Specifications for Practical Architecture*, is compared with the books discussed by Americans, it is apparent that, for all the resources that were available to them, American readers found only some books useful. It can, of course, be argued that American articles on architecture did not reflect the presence of the many books owned and used by architects. At any rate, it is obvious that architects and critics in America knew and read Pugin's *True Principles* (though there are few references to his other books) and the books and journal articles of Fergusson, Ruskin, and Loudon, all of whom had raised questions relevant to the architecture of the future, though Ruskin's contribution was in some ways more negative than positive.

The *New York Ecclesiologist* was dedicated to a special type of building, churches, on which subject much was being written in England, but in spite of this English interest its ideas were closer to earlier American architectural thought than to orthodox ecclesiology. Americans accepted Gothic tentatively because it was involved with Christianity and because they had nothing as good to substitute for it. They were not unquestioningly loyal to a single Gothic period, and they did not propose to reproduce the style accurately. The characteristic Victorian arrangement and proportions of the chancel and the nave pleased them because it worked well. They kept an open mind on the matter of building materials. So long as function was satisfied, style could be experimental. "Reality" came to mean expression of purpose, and if references to Gothic helped, they were tolerated.

VI

*Some Buildings and
Architects of the American Gothic and
Parish Church Revivals*

The place of St. James the Less in the history of American architecture may now be reconsidered. If, as was the case with the Americans, the nineteenth-century student of architecture was not deeply involved with the belief that revival of Gothic was an ethical or religious obligation, he could learn much about the nature of architecture from close acquaintance with St. James the Less. The church illustrated well the qualities in medieval building which had moved Pugin to formulate his abstract principles of design, with which Americans instinctively agreed. Its interior and exterior demonstrated the aesthetic possibilities of building materials handled directly and without disguise and the potential power and beauty of unornamented structure. St. Michael's, Long Stanton, and its American replica were, in other words, buildings which encouraged the development of "progressive" architectural observations and showed the truth of those already formulated.

The modesty, simplicity, and understated qualities of the English parish church, and of St. Michael's and St. James the Less in particular, made them

213

especially suitable for the role they were to play in America. Pugin and the other English and Continental theorists knew well the larger and much more complex medieval monuments. They understood the intricate relationships which bound Gothic architecture and the other arts into a symbolic and aesthetic whole. They were able to reproduce at least some of the qualities of medieval building in their revival. The American designers could not study European and English Gothic so closely, and they had neither the will nor the capacity to reproduce it. In any event, their reasoning about architectural values differed from that of their English contemporaries. They began where Pugin, Ruskin, Fergusson, and Lord Lindsay had ended, with the principles of design and the belief that a new style would emerge in response to new re-quirements and a new "Age." They were free to accept or reject Gothic as such, to learn principles of design from it, to let it displace the style which had preceded it, and to make use of it in the interval between the disappearance of the earlier manner and the appearance of the promised "new style" which they felt sure, and were assured, was coming.

The English parish church was not bewildering, complex, and overwhelming; it was small enough and simple enough to be copied exactly, and it had few features which were so elaborate as to encourage the use of shams and inade-quate substitutes such as Upjohn's plaster vaults and flying buttresses at Trinity Church. Had there been no St. James the Less, American church builders would not have produced as much simple, functional architecture and the revival would not have been as fruitful of ideas.

The following comparison between a sample of the churches built in the United States before 1846 and others built between 1846 and 1855 will show how widely St. James the Less and English architectural ideas influenced American ecclesiastical design.

The history of a number of these churches is also significant in other ways. Churches compose an identifiable and representative category within the body of nineteenth-century architecture in the United States. Many of them survive, for in the passage of time they have been less likely to be pulled down or allowed to fall into disrepair than secular buildings. Since the best energies and tastes of the period were often expended on them and leading architects de-signed them, these churches offer a meaningful reflection of the time from which they come. Finally, it should be remembered that the parish church and

SOME BUILDINGS AND ARCHITECTS

Gothic revival did not end in 1855, though at about that time they ceased to be an innovating stylistic preference. In the later nineteenth century and into the twentieth many parishes have continued to follow this pattern, sanctioned by tradition and familiarity. The churches described here are, therefore, not only representative monuments of their own time but the forerunners of a building type and style which has not yet entirely disappeared.

The mid-nineteenth-century parish church revival in the United States was fostered by the generation of churchmen within the administrative and intellectual structure of the Protestant Episcopal community who had inherited the ideas of the Right Reverend John Henry Hobart, Bishop of New York from 1816 to 1830. The enthusiastic acceptance of the English church form with its deep chancel is the expression in architecture of the sympathy with the Oxford Movement and High Church practices which Hobart shared with the brilliant men who followed him.[1]

Hobart, who knew and was respected by John Henry Newman and others of his circle at Oxford,[2] was personally involved in the training of many of the American clergy who attained prominence between 1840 and 1850. He had founded the institutions in which they were educated and had established the church periodicals in which they expressed their views. By 1835, though Hobart had passed from the scene, William Rollinson Whittingham, Benjamin T. Onderdonk, William Delancey, Henry U. Onderdonk, George Washington Doane, Levi Sillimen Ives, John Henry Hopkins, Nicholas Hammer Cobbs, Alonzo Potter, William Crosswell, William A. Muhlenburg, and Samuel Farmar Jarvis were rising to positions of power as bishops or senior clergymen. Many of them had been trained at the General Theological Seminary, some were members of its faculty, and all understood and sympathized with its objectives. These men took the parish church revival into their dioceses and parishes, where they would become influential; by 1844 among the members of this group were the bishops of Alabama, North Carolina, Vermont, New Jersey,[3]

[1] Albright, *History of the Protestant Episcopal Church*, chap. 5, contains the best and most recent account of this period and the men who were involved in these developments. See also Chorley, *Men and Movements*, chap. 6.
[2] See Chorley, *Men and Movements*, pp. 140–59.
[3] See Chapter II above.

Maryland, Western New York, Pennsylvania,[4] and New York. Numerous clergy and laymen in Connecticut and Massachusetts were friendly to the High Church position and to the new architectural style. By 1845 all along the eastern seaboard a sympathy for the parish church revival had been established and, like the Church and the nation itself, these new ideas were expanding into the South and Middle West.[5]

William Rollinson Whittingham was in many ways typical of the new group of clerics. He became Bishop of Maryland in 1840, after a prolonged and difficult election, for a number of clergymen and laymen in the diocese were dismayed by his High Church affinities and his rumored interest in the Oxford Movement. Despite this opposition and the tension which it inevitably engendered, Whittingham was to make a notable record as bishop; he was brilliant and personally assertive, an able administrator, and a vigorous representative of his generation.[6]

Younger than many others in Hobart's circle, Whittingham entered the General Theological Seminary in 1822; immediately upon graduating, he was appointed its librarian. He was made deacon by Hobart in 1827, served briefly as rector of St. Mark's, West Orange, New Jersey, and then was rector of St. Luke's, New York City, where Dr. L. S. Ives, a close friend of Doane, had preceded him.[7]

Whittingham quickly established himself in the educational, academic, and journalistic branches of the High Church party because of his obvious scholarly capacities and literary gifts. After acting as publisher-editor of several smaller Church magazines, he became editor of the *Churchman*, a post he held from 1831 to 1836. In 1834 he traveled for a year and a half in the Mediterranean

---

[4] Sixty-two churches were consecrated in the Diocese of Pennsylvania between 1840 and 1854. This figure is based upon information contained in the *Journals of the Conventions of the Protestant Episcopal Church in the State of Pennsylvania* from 1840 (the fifty-seventh convention) through 1854 (the seventieth).

[5] See Chorley, *Men and Movements,* p. 167.

[6] William Francis Brand, *Life of William Rollinson Whittingham, Fourth Bishop of Maryland,* 2 vols., 2d ed. (New York: E. and J. B. Young and Co., 1886), is the definitive biography. Additional data have been added to the discussion here from the papers of Bishop Whittingham, now in the collections of the Diocese of Maryland and the library of Duke University.

[7] See The Historical Records Survey, *Inventory of the Church Archives of New Jersey,* p. 319, and Chorley, *Men and Movements,* p. 238.

countries, France, and Switzerland. Upon his return he was appointed Professor of Ecclesiastical History at the General Theological Seminary and, once again, became its librarian. It was from the Seminary that he was called to be Bishop of Maryland, in which position he remained until his death in 1879.

Having become head of a diocese in dire need of new churches, Whittingham resolved to emphasize the missionary aspects of his duties. He set out to improve the physical condition of existing churches, reform and dignify ceremonial practice in the diocese, and increase the number of parishes and church buildings, but the antipathy of those opposed to High Churchmanship remained. Whittingham's tendency to rule the clergy of the diocese rigidly, his insistence upon "full episcopal prerogatives during his visitations," and his appropriation of collections "for diocesan use" ultimately involved him in conflicts and charges of "tyranny and persecution of his presbyters." In 1850, however, when the General Convention defined the duties and role of bishops, it generally supported Whittingham's conception of the tasks of the episcopacy.[8] External circumstances also added to the trials of his long administration. Though there were many in Maryland who sympathized with the Southern cause in the Civil War, the Bishop insisted that the Church remain politically neutral.

In addition to all his routine duties (and Whittingham was unusually diligent), he found time to pursue his interest in ecclesiastical architecture and its history. His library contained an impressive and representative collection of the English books and periodicals on architecture which the ecclesiologists and others had written for the enlightenment of amateurs rather than architects.[9] He acquired the works of Poole, Bloxam, and Freeman as soon as they appeared and he read them carefully; they bear his annotations. In the summer of 1846 he visited the vestry of St. James the Less and studied its building plans. When the New York Ecclesiological Society was established, he founded an architectural society in Maryland, an event which the *Ecclesiologist* noted with pleasure. Whittingham was a patron member of both the Ecclesiological Society and the Oxford Architectural Society.

In 1853, because he was beset by ill health, Whittingham visited Europe to

[8] See Albright, *History of the Protestant Episcopal Church*, p. 242.
[9] The library of Bishop Whittingham is now part of the Diocesan Library of the Diocese of Maryland.

rest and recover. This time he went to England. Dr. W. F. Hook of Leeds entertained him, and in London he attended services in St. Barnabas', Pimlico, a church which had been described in glowing terms by the *Ecclesiologist*.[10] He spent his last day abroad in the company of John Keble, an experience which was the climax of his ecclesiastical and ecclesiological tour. Later in the year he went abroad for his health once again, and, while touring Germany, he filled his notebooks with observations on church architecture and the care of church buildings. The Bishop of Maryland was thus a confirmed and well-informed architectural connoisseur.

Though the population of Baltimore had increased in the 1830's, the number of its Protestant Episcopal churches had not. Throughout the diocese new churches had to be built and old ones needed repairs. This situation was not unique to Baltimore, however, but prevailed almost everywhere on the East Coast in 1840. Whittingham made his stylistic preferences known in personal conversation and through his annual reports, which were published in the *Journal of the . . . Annual Convention of the Diocese of Maryland of the Protestant Episcopal Church in Maryland*.[11] He mentioned the design and, where applicable, the architect of the churches he consecrated. He praised those parishes with building aspirations and encouraged others to acquire them. By the end of his first ten years of tenure, he was beginning to achieve his objective:

---

[10] "S. Barnabas, Pimlico; S. Stephen's, Westminster, and S. Mary's, Crown Street," *E.*, 11 (August, 1850):112. St. Barnabas' was designed by Thomas Cundy, II, assisted by William Butterfield, who did the interior decoration. The editors of the *Ecclesiologist* called it "the most complete, and, with completeness, most sumptuous church which has been dedicated to the use of the Anglican Communion since the revival: and this fact, gratifying to record, and most honourable to the presiding spirit who raised its walls, would far more than compensate for even greater shortcomings than those which we have felt it our duty to touch upon."

[11] The annual "Report of the Bishop to the Diocese" contained in these journals was written each year during his tenure by the Bishop. In the mid-nineteenth century the geographical boundaries of the Protestant Episcopal dioceses in America were not as they are today. When Whittingham became Bishop of Maryland, his diocese was an unwieldy area which was later broken into several bishoprics. The Diocese of Easton was formed to include all the state east of the Chesapeake Bay and the Susquehanna River, and when further growth at the end of the nineteenth century prompted another division in 1894, the Diocese of Washington was created. The same thing happened in Pennsylvania. This discussion will be concerned, therefore, with the various dioceses—Pennsylvania, Georgia, New Jersey, Maryland, etc.—not as they are now but as they were at the time of the revival.

in 1850 every Protestant Episcopal church under construction in Maryland was in the parish church style. Although Whittingham's convictions and enthusiasms were typical of American High Churchmen, he was, rather more than others, personally preoccupied with architecture and ecclesiological theory.

As this discussion and description of the churches of New York City has shown, the revival of the parish church, which took shape in America with the building of St. James the Less, did not mark the beginning of Gothic revivalism in American ecclesiastical architecture. The endeavors of John Henry Hopkins had met with considerable success after the publication of his *Essay* in 1836. The widened appreciation of medieval building and knowledge of the English Gothic revival and its literature had been reflected in intelligent commentary in American periodicals. By 1840 there were a number of churches in a primitive, half-Georgian, half-Gothic style in many Protestant Episcopal dioceses on the eastern seaboard.

When in search of architectural advice, Maryland and New Jersey parishes had been able to turn to architects in Philadelphia; it was from William Strickland that the Reverend Henry M. Mason obtained plans for a new church for Salem, New Jersey, in 1836. The Salem church, St. John's, was dedicated in February, 1838. Having completed this project, Mason moved to Easton, Maryland, where Christ Church was a sturdy and growing parish with a vestry which included many leading Talbot County gentlemen. Since the old church was small and in desperate need of repair, Mason convinced the vestry to build a new one from the plans which had worked out well at Salem. In August, 1840, the second church was begun from the Strickland design, with the vestry and rector of Christ Church cooperating with Mr. Reynolds, a local builder.[12] Even while it was under construction, Christ Church was praised by Bishop Whittingham; it was consecrated in 1848 and generally regarded, quite justly, as

---

[12] Information from manuscript material in the vestry records of Christ Church, Easton, and St. John's Church, Salem, New Jersey, the latter provided by the Reverend Fred B. Schultz. Information on Strickland other than that on the Salem and Easton churches is drawn from A. A. Gilchrist, *William Strickland, Architect and Engineer, 1788–1854* (Philadelphia: University of Pennsylvania Press, 1950), and "Additions to *William Strickland, Architect and Engineer, 1788–1854*," *Journal of the Society of Architectural Historians*, 13 (October, 1954), which together constitute a monograph on Strickland.

a jewel in the crown of the Church in the eastern counties. In 1852–53 Richard Upjohn designed its rectory.[13]

Both the Salem and Easton churches are built of Port Deposit granite. Originally, each consisted of a spacious nave without aisles and a square tower supporting a tall wood spire with four Gothic pinnacles of wood at the base (Figs. VI–1 and VI–2). In 1878 and 1880 the churches were renovated and chancels were added to make them conform to the ecclesiological pattern which was by then common. The façade at Easton was also altered, not for the better, in 1878; the central window was shortened and the three-part door was replaced by a single opening. Though there is no record that the roof at Easton has been replaced, it is so much heavier and more expert than the roof at Salem that it can hardly be the original. At Salem the original arrangement of the front is intact. Loss of the pinnacles at both churches has weakened their design. In both churches the shape of the windows is unchanged, though much of the original glass has been replaced. Where the old glass survives, the tall lancets are filled with quarries in abstract patterns, the central portion opaque white patterned in black and the borders green, red, and blue. The windows are large in proportion to the walls. The naves compose into bright and pretty spaces, as un-Gothic as are the churches themselves, which, in spite of their buttresses, spires, and pinnacles, are crisp essays in neoclassicism Gothicized. They possess balance, solidity, and independence from their setting, products of their deliberately symmetrical design, absence of extraneous detail, and white wood trim on tower and spire.

These Strickland churches are typical of the first phase of the revival. Throughout the eastern states premature Gothic of this kind appeared wherever a builder possessed some knowledge of English architecture, a parishioner had traveled abroad and been pleased with what he saw, or Hopkins' book had found a friendly audience. As early as 1829 William Passman, an architect of Aulston, Yorkshire, built a Gothic church in stone at Arlington, Vermont.[14] In 1844 Augustus Cowman, having returned from a journey to England, con-

---

[13] Upjohn, *Richard Upjohn*, p. 209; rectory for the Reverend Henry M. Mason (1852–53).
[14] The Historical Records Survey, *Inventory of the Church Archives of Vermont, No. 1, the Diocese of Vermont Protestant Episcopal* (Montpelier: The Historical Records Survey, 1940), pp. 72–73. See Herbert Wheaton Congdon, *Old Vermont Houses, the Architecture of a Resourceful People* (Brattleboro: Stephen Daye Press, 1940), pp. 179–80, for a discussion and illustration of this church.

tributed heavily to a new St. James' at Hyde Park, New York, built in "the English country church" manner.[15] In 1831 St. Peter's was built at Waterford, Pennsylvania (Fig. VI–3); it resembled John Henry Hopkins' own designs, which he later published.[16] All these examples—the design by Strickland, the proposals made by Hopkins, and other churches of the same period and style— have symmetrical plans, towers in the center of the west front, and "carpenter Gothick" detail, which date them. In most cases the deep, recessed chancels were later added.

As the periodical literature of the period has shown, by the mid-1840's American architects and their clients were intrigued by and prepared to accept Gothic, but they did not know much about it. Books were an assistance to the

[15] Information provided by the Reverend Gordon L. Kidd, Rector, St. James', Hyde Park, New York.

[16] There can be little doubt that John Henry Hopkins had something to do with the design of the church at Waterford. In *The Life of the Late Right Reverend John Henry Hopkins, First Bishop of Vermont and Seventh Presiding Bishop*, by J. H. Hopkins, Jr. (New York: Huntington, 1873), p. 129, there is a quotation from a testimonial letter addressed to Hopkins when he left Pennsylvania for Massachusetts in 1831. It refers directly to Hopkins' work among the churches in what is now the Diocese of Erie. "Butler, Mercer, Meadville, Erie, Greensburgh, and Blairsville, will all remember the spirit and zeal which were infused by your visits to those places, and most of them have responded to your efforts by the erection of churches not surpassed in the elegance and taste of their workmanship." Built in 1831, the Waterford church would not have been mentioned in this letter; it was either under construction or not yet begun.

Other churches in this style are Christ Church, Brooklyn (1841–42), and the Church of the Ascension (1840–41), both by Upjohn; St. Paul's Church, Rahway, New Jersey (built 1842, enlarged 1860), of brick and brownstone; St. Peter's Church, Salem, Massachusetts (1837), by Gridley J. F. Bryant, of stone; St. Paul's Church, Camden, New Jersey (1834–35), of stone, attributed to John Notman; St. John's, Cleveland (see p. 59 and n. 40 above); St. John's Chapel, Miles River Crossing, Maryland (1841), now in ruins, of stone (this example has a receding chancel, however); Saint James', Wilmington, New Hanover County, North Carolina (1839), by Thomas U. Walter; Chapel of the Cross, Chapel Hill, Orange County, North Carolina, by Francis L. Hawks, from Hopkins' book (see F. B. Johnson and T. T. Waterman, *The Early Architecture of North Carolina* [Chapel Hill: University of North Carolina Press, 1947]); and Episcopal Church, Greensboro, Georgia (*ca.* 1852) (see F. D. Nichols and F. B. Johnson, *The Early Architecture of Georgia* [Chapel Hill: University of North Carolina Press, 1957]). The following buildings cited by the Reverend George W. Shinn in *King's Handbook of Notable Episcopal Churches in the United States* (Boston: Moses King, 1889) also fall into this category (page references are to Shinn): St. Luke's Church, Rochester, New York, (1825) (p. 54); Church of the Epiphany, Washington, D. C. (1844, enlarged and remodeled 1857 and 1874) (p. 64ff.); St. Mark's, Frankford, Philadelphia (1846) (p. 65ff.); and Trinity Church, New Orleans (1851–53) (p. 74ff.).

Figure VI-1. Christ Church, Easton, Md., as it appeared before 1878. William Strickland. 1840–48.

Figure VI-2. Christ Church, Easton, today.

Figure VI-3. St. Peter's, Waterford, Pa. 1831.

designer and the literate patron, but usually those who desired a Gothic church depended upon examples such as St. Peter's, Chelsea (see Fig. II–12), the illustrations and advice in Hopkins' *Essay*, or the plans for Trinity Church (Fig. VI–4). The second phase of the Gothic revival in America really belongs to Trinity, which, in spite of its rich detail and great size, was a large, urban, and expensive version of the early symmetrical church type which has been described. As soon as Trinity was begun, many cities acquired at least one big church in its manner.

These new churches were not always the property of the Protestant Episcopal community, for not until the late 1840's did English Gothic have so narrow an association. Another denomination had introduced Gothic into Maryland before Bishop Whittingham began his campaign. A group of German and Austrian Redemptorist Fathers arrived in Baltimore to work among the Roman Catholic population settled there. Shortly after Whittingham became bishop, Robert Cary Long, Jr., was commissioned by the Redemptorist Fathers to build St. Alphonsus' Church in Baltimore. (This church was originally called the Church of the Immaculate Conception.)

Conservative by nature, Baltimore was slow to adopt Gothic. Its taste was dominated by the examples of the great Roman Catholic Cathedral (1810–21) by Latrobe and the Unitarian Church (1818) by Maximilian Godefroy, both masterpieces of the neoclassical style. St. Alphonsus' was only the second major Gothic building built in Baltimore; the first, the Chapel for St. Mary's Seminary (1807), by Godefroy, was so much earlier in date and so exotic an amalgam of Gothic and other styles as to have almost no relationship to the project upon which the younger Long set to work in 1842.

The building of St. Alphonsus' was an exciting commission. The Redemptorist Fathers were missionary priests accustomed to large churches designed as chambers for preaching. Upon their arrival Archbishop Eccleston had given the Fathers St. John's Church as the center for their activities. Within a year after the first members of their party were settled, the Fathers decided to build a new church. The Reverend Joseph Salzbacher, Canon of the Cathedral of Vienna, officiated when its cornerstone was laid in May, 1842.

Long had been well trained, first by his father and later by Martin Euclid Thompson of New York City. He had traveled in Europe and had spent several years in Baltimore completing work his father had left unfinished when he died in 1833. St. Alphonsus' was a large, demanding, and important task, in many

Figure VI-4. Trinity Church, New York City, as it appeared in 1847. "Birds-eye view."

SOME BUILDINGS AND ARCHITECTS

ways a test for its architect. It was Long's first major commission. He was thirty-two when he began to work closely with the Reverend Alexander Czvitkovicz, C.Ss.R., who possessed a natural feeling for architecture.

The national background of the Fathers and the members of their congregation suggested that the new church should be in the South German Gothic style of the late fourteenth or early fifteenth centuries, and Father Czvitkovicz felt that St. Alphonsus' was. In 1844, in a letter to the Archbishop of Vienna, he described it as "a beautiful monument of German art, because it is designed and is being executed after German models."[17] However, Long described it as English Perpendicular.[18] St. Alphonsus' was actually a little of both.

The money for the building came from abroad; in addition to funds contributed by the Munich Ludwigs Missionen Verein, the Leopoldinen-Stiftung of Austria sent at least twelve thousand dollars to help with the costs of construction.[19] Father Czvitkovicz went abroad to solicit further assistance at least once while the church was building, had an audience with King Louis of Bavaria, and received promises of aid. As soon as building began he moved into a house near the site so that he might supervise operations. His connection with the church ultimately became so close that in some quarters the actual design was attributed to him. Certainly he and his colleagues expressed definite preferences and requirements concerning the arrangement of the interior space and the appearance of the exterior.

[17] The Reverend Alexander Czvitkovicz to the Archbishop of Vienna, Eve of Pentecost, 1844 (information supplied by the Reverend R. N. Reiss, C.Ss.R.). For further information on the connections between Austria, Germany, and American Roman Catholics in the mid-nineteenth century, see Benjamin J. Blied, *Austrian Aid to American Catholics* (Milwaukee, Wis.: By the author, 1944). Canon Joseph Salzbacher visited the United States in 1842 to make a study of Catholic activities for the Austrian public. His observations were published in 1945 as *Meine Reise nach Nord-Amerika im Jahre 1842 mit statistischen Bemerkungen* (Vienna: Wimmer, Schmidt & Leo, 1845). Blied includes statistics on the sums sent to America by the Leopoldine Society. The largest contributions were made between 1832 and 1861, three decades in which approximately four hundred thousand dollars was sent to assist American parishes. Baltimore received over twenty-one thousand dollars from this source.

[18] "Gothic Architecture—A New Church," *United States Catholic Magazine*, 2 (May, 1843):297–304.

[19] The Reverend R. N. Reiss, C.Ss.R., Archivist of the Redemptorist Order, provided this information, which is from the *Berichte der Leopoldinen-Stiftung im Kaiserthume Oesterreich*, 18 (1845):25–27.

Confronted with clients who wished to have a German Gothic church, Long need not have been at a loss, for in 1830, in his *Denkmäler deutscher Baukunst*, Georg Moller had included careful illustrations of the churches at Marburg, Freiburg im Breisgau, Limburg, Oppenheim, Gelnhausen, and Ulm. But Long's sources were not exclusively German. In 1843, when he wrote an article on his plans for the new church in Baltimore,[20] he discussed his interest in the English literature on Gothic and specifically mentioned A. W. Pugin as one who had "met with great and deserved success." It is quite clear that he knew Pugin's drawing style and patterned his after it, for he borrowed both the manner of illustration and the elegant details, such as the angels which support the scroll bearing the name of the church, from Pugin's *Dublin Review* articles (see p. 20, n. 29, above, and Figs. VI–5 and VI–6). Long also referred to the progress in "preservation and restoration of the long neglected and abused remains" of Gothic art in England. His account of the history and traditions associated with the internal arrangement of Christian churches resembled that of Thomas Hope,[21] and his recital of the characteristics of each of the major English Gothic styles precisely followed John Rickman.[22] The interior of St. Alphonsus' is, in fact, very like Rickman's Plate XIII, "a composition showing a Decorated interior with three aisles, all of the same height, and groined"[23] (Figs. VI–7 and VI–8). Finally, there was another English resource upon which Long might have drawn, for, in some ways, St. Alphonsus' resembles an English Commissioner's church of the 1820's.[24] But Father Czvitkovicz was also correct when he said the church was German. St. Alphonsus' is a hall church with a shallow, rounded apse containing the high altar and two flat apsidal areas on either side of it at the ends of the aisles, each equipped with an altar (Fig. VI–9), an internal plan usual in Germany.

The interior is a rectangular space through which the columns rise 50 feet in the nave and 40 feet at the side walls. As in other churches by Long there is a narrow, low vestibule between the three outer doors and the entrances to the

[20] "Gothic Architecture—A New Church," pp. 298–99.
[21] *Ibid.*, pp. 300–2. On Hope, see Carroll L. V. Meeks, "Romanesque before Richardson in the United States," *Art Bulletin*, 35 (March, 1953):19ff.
[22] "Gothic Architecture—A New Church," pp. 299–300.
[23] *An Attempt to Discriminate the Styles of Architecture in England from the Conquest to the Reformation* (London: Longmans', 1825).
[24] See M. H. Port, *Six Hundred New Churches*, Plates III–A, III–B, V–D, and VIII–A.

nave. Originally only the center door opened into the nave; a baptistry occupied the right-hand portion of the chamber, and the stairs to the gallery filled the left, an awkward arrangement which has since been corrected. The façade was close to the street and raised the height of a wide flight of steps. It seems, if the drawing of 1843 is correct (see Fig. VI–5), that Long did not originally plan to surround his church with a cast-iron fence.

Within a few years after St. Alphonsus' was completed, a school, residence, and offices were added in a style similar to that of the church. With it they constitute a unified, urban composition, their walls flush with the building line. All the buildings are enriched only by the low relief details above the lancet windows and doors.

The interior of St. Alphonsus' is a virtuoso performance which suggests in its dense, glittering exuberance the fabulous interiors Charles Barry and Pugin developed for the Houses of Parliament a few years later. The roof is supported by clustered columns of complex section, painted rose brown and marbleized. They are plaster over a cast-iron core. Confessionals stand against the walls between the engaged columns. The vaulting is arranged in an orderly pattern of ribs, with bosses at their intersections and a prominent ridge rib down the center of the nave and each aisle. The entire roof is now painted in patterns which resemble those at Ulm and Annenburg. Though it was plaster, Long was so pleased with his vaulting that he said, "We are not aware of any church yet executed in this country that has a ceiling so elaborately ribbed as this will be."[25] The windows, which have cast-iron tracery, are tall and slender.[26] The pulpit presently in the church is the original one, for Long described it; it is attached high on the column to the left of the altar and is reached by a spiral staircase.

Though less assertive and ornate than the interior, St. Alphonsus' exterior is equally remarkable. Long employed the components of a tower such as that at Bern but made no attempt to reproduce the ornament of his model, for he

---

[25] Long, "Gothic Architecture—A New Church," p. 303.

[26] All the tracery, the window frames, and the exterior moldings are of cast iron of surprising delicacy and craftsmanship. The lists of materials and costs for the church included an item of $1,254.09 for iron, which probably represents the cost of the supporting elements of the columns and vaults. The cast-iron tracery was one of the major items of expenditure—$5,229.43—and $10,794.54 was spent for brick and bricklaying. The granite for the foundation and external podium cost $5,400 (information from the Reverend R. N. Reiss, C.Ss.R.).

Figure VI-5. St. Alphonsus', Baltimore. Robert Cary Long, Jr. Cornerstone laid 1842. Etching by Long (1843).

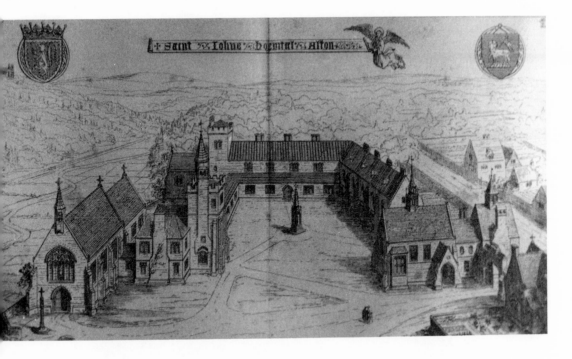

*Figure VI-6. St. John's Hospital, Alton, Staffordshire. A. W. Pugin. 1841–43.
From Pugin, Present State.*

Figure VI-7. "A Decorated Interior." From Thomas Rickman, Styles of Architecture *(1825).*

Figure VI-8. St. Alphonsus', Baltimore.

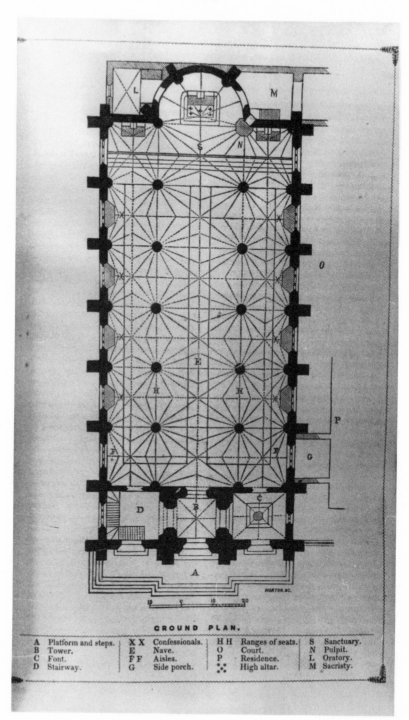

GROUND PLAN.

A	Platform and steps.	X X	Confessionals.	H H	Ranges of seats.	S	Sanctuary.
B	Tower.	E	Nave.	O	Court.	N	Pulpit.
C	Font.	F F	Aisles.	P	Residence.	L	Oratory.
D	Stairway.	G	Side porch.	.·.	High altar.	M	Sacristy.

Figure VI-9. St. Alphonsus', Baltimore.

could not do so in brick and with the available craftsmanship. He described the tower of St. Alphonsus' (Fig. VI–10) as "of the tabernacle kind; one section rising out of the other like the joints of a telescope,"[27] a form for which there were no precedents in English building but many in German. The tiny spire, which is cast iron and by no means as elaborate as the one Long had first proposed (see Fig. VI–5), rises from the top of the tiered tower like those of Germany, but for the sake of economy it is not pierced, as are the stone spires at Bern and Freiburg im Breisgau. The tower and spire are 200 feet tall, 50 feet taller than the church is long. The architect wished its height to contrast brilliantly with the Roman Catholic Cathedral nearby.

The ogee crocketed hood moldings over the lancets and on the spire could have been derived from any number of German examples, but in view of Long's written description and discussion of the church, it would seem that they were freely adapted from the volumes of Gothic detail published in England. A lack of coherence between the general pattern, which is, at least in part German, and the English character of much of the detail is nowhere clearer than in the treatment of the sixteen ribs which rise from each pier in the interior and in the details of the curious rosettes which fill the space immediately beneath the head of each ogee molding on the exterior. The battlemented parapet seems English, but a termination of this sort is present in some German churches. The flat front in which the tower is embedded is German. Finally, the rounded apse (Fig. VI–11) appears in German examples but is never treated in so declarative a fashion.

St. Alphonsus' and its satellite buildings are brick, now painted a warm putty color, the buttresses darker than the walls and the hoods and all details picked out in a soft gray-rose. Whether these colors are those originally designed by Long is uncertain, but he did intend, for both practical and artistic reasons, that the brick should be painted, for he felt that the projections and corners were bound to be chipped and that repairs to the rough cast details would be unsightly. In any event, he liked painted brick. There was "an *honesty*" about brick which, he said, "certainly recommends its adoption in a building sacred to the cause of truth, where all imitation and false appearance, in every respect, should be carefully avoided."[28] He urged brickmakers to "turn their attention

[27] "Gothic Architecture—A New Church," p. 303.
[28] *Ibid.*, p. 305.

Figure VI-10. St. Alphonsus', Baltimore.

Figure VI-11. St. Alphonsus', Baltimore.

to the making of bricks of some good neutral color, like the fire-brick, instead of their present intense and glaring red, so that the outside painting now necessary might be dispensed with" and to experiment with molded bricks "of every shape and variety required for architectural forms." Long believed that "the universal adoption of Gothic" was " 'a consummation devoutly to be wished' by every architect of just taste," and he hoped that innovations, such as the use of brick, would tend to reduce the impediment of cost, which restrained many people from use of the style.[29]

Long mentioned Trinity Church, New York, and used it as a standard against which to measure his own achievement. Trinity was of the utmost importance, he said, because it was large; he felt that "the great difficulty that has hitherto stood in the way of Gothic design is the smallness of the scale on which churches are constructed in the present day." Unlike the Greek temple style, in which "the same proportions are observed, whether the building be large or small; like the form of a man, which, whether colossal or lilliputian, has the same number of parts and the same general outline," Gothic, "which more resembles the form of vegetative life," required size for its full realization.[30] Although Long admired Trinity, he felt that Upjohn had failed. Though he had worked in the style "at greater expense than any specimen hitherto attempted in this country," it was regrettable that he had made his vaults of plaster, when he had had the money to make them of stone. In doing so he had upset the entire composition, in Long's view: "The architect there had it in his power to execute, what has never been seen among us—a groined roof of stone." By rejecting his opportunity, Upjohn had built a church, Long said, in which "the buttresses and lofty pinnacles on the sides of the building have now no meaning, for their design and intention is to support the stone vaulting of the interior by providing an adequate resistance to the lateral pressure of the arching, and, having left out this desideratum, their use is gone, and, with their utility, their appropriate beauty." Clearly, Long had studied and learned Pugin's principles. The simplicity of the exterior of St. Alphonsus' indicated that the walls supported only plaster vaulting.

At about the same time that Baltimore acquired its Redemptorist church, the Fathers were building St. Philomena's in Pittsburgh (Fig. VI–12) in a style so

[29] *Ibid.*, p. 300.
[30] *Ibid.*, p. 298. Long twice speaks of the Gothic as "vegetative."

SOME BUILDINGS AND ARCHITECTS

Figure VI-12. St. Philomena's, Pittsburgh.

close to that of St. Alphonsus' that Long may well have been its architect.[31] St. Philomena's had a clerestory. Since in 1843 Long had said that Trinity was, to the best of his knowledge, the only church in America with this feature, St. Philomena's can be dated after 1843. Its relationship to Trinity is obvious, both in the design of the spire and tower and the masses of the nave and aisles.

St. Alphonsus' brought Long local fame, commissions, and a leading position in the small architectural community in Baltimore. Though the flatness of the exterior and the primitive use of Gothic ornament in low relief, applied like embroidery to the container which held the interior drama of the nave and apse, were signs of early, provincial revivalism, the church showed that its architect was gifted as well as informed. In 1844 Long was one of four architects considered by the officers of a Scottish Presbyterian congregation which planned to build a new church at the corner of Franklin and Cathedral Streets in Baltimore, only two blocks from St. Alphonsus'.[32] Long, who won the commission, impressed the building committee by his explanation that Classical architecture, which the committee had at first wanted, would cost more than Gothic if it were constructed properly. For his Presbyterian clients Long astutely selected not Gothic, as at St. Alphonsus', but Tudor, which possessed a certain relevance to Presbyterianism, was roughly of the same date as the foundation of the denomination, and was eminently Protestant. A broad, spacious hall with no formal chancel could be well contained in a brick building with a flat timber roof. The choice of Tudor and Long's manipulation of its elements demonstrate how expert he had become by 1844.

From the beginning Long had trouble with the Franklin Street commission. The building committee grumbled because the detailed drawings were slow in coming and the church cost more than estimated. Money was short and was only grudgingly expended; in the end Long received but a part of the fee due

---

[31] The archives of the Redemptorist Order contain little information about St. Philomena's, though they confirm that it was built in the mid-1840's. The church was razed in 1922.

[32] See W. H. Hunter, "Robert Cary Long, Jr. and the Battle of Styles," *Journal of the Society of Architectural Historians*, 16 (March, 1957):28–30; A. A. Lambing, *A History of the Catholic Church in the Dioceses of Pittsburgh and Allegheny from its Establishment to the Present Time* (New York: Benziger, 1880), p. 151. H. E. Dickson, "The Baker Mansion, Altoona, Pennsylvania," *Journal of the Society of Architectural Historians*, 17 (March, 1958), establishes that Long was working elsewhere in Pennsylvania in 1844 and 1845. See also R. H. Howland and E. Spencer, *The Architecture of Baltimore* (Baltimore: Johns Hopkins, 1953), on other works by Long.

him, and his reputation in Baltimore was damaged by the complaints of these clients. He moved his office to New York before the job was finished, and after this episode building committees tended to choose architects who lived in Baltimore.

Though the church was an affliction for Long, aesthetically it was worth the struggle. The Franklin Street Presbyterian Church (Fig. VI–13) is a sturdy brick structure with an extremely successful street front, for Long was particularly adept at adjusting the façades of buildings to their sites, no matter how demanding or difficult the situation. When it was built the church stood in a neighborhood of town houses and churches, including the Roman Catholic Cathedral and the Unitarian Church. The presence of the latter may well have suggested a style other than Classical: with such competition it was better not to compete.

Like St. Alphonsus', this is a church without aisles, but there the resemblance between the two ceases, for the Presbyterian Church is as low and horizontal as St. Alphonsus' is tall and slender, and it possesses no tower or spire. The material is good red brick, with stone trim used sparingly and in functional situations on the parapet, in courses, in the offsets of the buttresses, and in the enrichment above and beside the doors. The exterior design is effective because it depends upon the repetition of a series of simple, well-proportioned openings and masses. The front is made up of five parts, of which four are two identical pairs. The interior consists of a shallow, low, and undecorated vestibule and the main hall, which has a gallery at its rear. There is no chancel. The roof is paneled wood supported on corbels.

Long's sources are obvious. Not in its detail, but in its character and the manner in which the parts are related, the façade is indebted to illustrations of Italian architecture contained in *An Historical Essay on Architecture*, by Thomas Hope. Pugin's *Specimens of Gothic Architecture* and *Examples of Gothic Architecture* supplied ample material from which to extract the details. As early as 1837 John Notman could have considered a number of American and English early Gothic revival churches when he composed a front for the Laurel Hill Cemetery Chapel,[33] and there is no reason to think that Long did not know the same examples in 1844, when he put together his facade of octagonal towers and crenelated parapets.

[33] See p. 46 and n. 28 above.

Figure VI-13. Franklin Street Presbyterian Church, Baltimore. Robert Cary Long, Jr. Ca. 1844.

Long was an obvious candidate for Protestant Episcopal favor, for these two important Baltimore churches were establishing his reputation just as Whittingham settled in and initiated his church building program. It is, therefore, not surprising that while he struggled with the Franklin Street commission Long was also engaged in building five churches in the Episcopal Diocese of Maryland. Bishop Whittingham approved of Long's tastes and abilities and praised him in his annual reports to the diocese. Before he left Baltimore to begin practice in New York, Long had encountered, in the course of his acquaintance with the Bishop, the concepts of the parish church revival.

St. Alphonsus' and the Franklin Street church reveal a good deal about Long. He was singularly responsive to the history of architecture and thoughtfully engaged in putting his knowledge of it to good use. Beneath his eclecticism there was considerable originality, for he rarely lifted a detail intact from the illustrations in the literature at his disposal. Experimentation with building materials interested him and, finally, he enjoyed writing about his buildings and those of others.

In 1847 and early 1848 Long was in the process of moving his office to New York City, where, by October, 1848, he was established and ready to receive clients.[34] At about the same time George Duyckinck, who was later a contributor to the *New York Ecclesiologist*, became proprietor and editor of *The Literary World* and resolved to increase the number of its articles on the fine arts, and particularly on architecture. His taste ran to Gothic. The tone of the review of Grace Church, Newark, which he published in October was in no way unusual in American periodical literature, for it opened with praises for Gothic, which it said had come to replace "the wretched, abortive Grecian Temples, of whitewashed pine boards, which have so long been an eye-sore to the judicious,"[35] along with an obeisance to Upjohn as the architect of Trinity, a church of "acknowledged purity and beauty . . . in spite of some defects."

[34] *The Literary World*, 3 (October 14, 1848):759, contains an advertisement by Long describing himself as "late of Baltimore" and giving his address as 61 Wall Street. On April 3, 1849, he addressed the New York Historical Society on "Ancient Architecture of America," and his comments were published as a book in 1849 (see Hitchcock, *American Architectural Books*, Item 734).

[35] "The Fine Arts. Church Architecture. Grace Church, Newark, New Jersey," *The Literary World*, 3 (October 14, 1848):733. See p. 184 above for discussion of a review of Grace Church in the *New York Ecclesiologist* for April, 1849.

The author of this article, who was either Duyckinck or Long, then attacked Upjohn ferociously for his use of color in the interior. Among other disasters, he said, it made the altar look like "a Yankee pedlar's notion wagon."[36] In the end the review, which had begun on a reasonable note, called Grace Church "a miserable paltry attempt at something which it is not, a specimen of lamentable taste, defacing what, if simple, had been perfect, and altogether *Gothic*, only as a piece of veritable *Gothicism*." The author concluded that vain attempts at originality were a hazard for American architects, who would be better off if they abided by "ancient and established models," a suggestion with which Duyckinck was himself to disagree a few months later in his address before the New York Ecclesiological Society.

The first of six articles by Long entitled "Architectonics" appeared in *The Literary World* in November, 1848, the last in March, 1849. (The series was left incomplete at his death from cholera in 1849.[37]) As early as 1841 Long had said that architects should "enlighten public opinion on the subject of their profession,"[38] had publicly defended his art against charges of "degeneracy," and in 1843 had presented a full explanation of his design of St. Alphonsus', which has been discussed. His venture into journalism in 1848 was, therefore, no surprise.

Long believed that Gothic was the only style which expressed "a home, a holy place, a response to the inner voice, an utterance of all that is good, and lovely, and reverent." He regretted adventures into "Norman, Byzantine, and other proximate styles."[39] Having made these preliminary observations, in the second "Architectonics" he turned to criticism of St. George's, Stuyvesant Square (1846–50), by Blesch and Eidlitz, the newest and largest offender against his theories.[40] St. George's was a church in which it was easy to find "architectural anachronisms."

[36] *Ibid.*

[37] These articles are attributed to Long because George A. Frederick, a Baltimore architect, did so in notes for a memoir of his professional life and reminiscences of Baltimore and its personalities (manuscript in the Library of the Maryland Historical Society).

[38] "Architecture. On the Alleged Degeneracy of Modern Architecture," *Journal of the Franklin Institute*, 32 (October, 841):246.

[39] "Architectonics. No. I. Gothic Church Architecture," *The Literary World*, 3 (November 18, 1848):833.

[40] "Architectonics. No. II. St. George's Church, Stuyvesant Square," *ibid.* (November 25, 1848):853. See also Schuyler, *American Architecture and other Writings*, 1:136–42.

The third essay of the series dealt with the architecture of street façades. Though it was not concerned with Gothic or ecclesiastical art, it illustrates Long's architectural astuteness and his intelligent concern for problems of design, aesthetic principles, new building materials, and new building types and necessities. Architecture, Long said, was too serious to be treated solely as a fashion. Gothic, Roman, and Greek buildings had expressed the nature of the societies they served; the nineteenth century should find a similarly responsive and characteristic form for its secular buildings. The gabled house of medieval pattern had, in modern times, given way to the uniform façade because changes in society and in the form of cities required it. "Wherever long horizontal lines have been obtained," he said, "there we find the most certain advance in the correct ideal, *viz. the expression of the bond of each to all. . . .* A horizontal line bounding the front elevation, and a regularity in the recurrence of stories, gives a continuity of line for basements, windows, and attics, which is desirable, and is compatible with great diversity in minor details, expressive of the wealth, taste, and individuality of the owner of the mansion, the variety of each forming the perfection of the whole, and expressing more perfectly the idea of the unity of all."[41] Long felt that in Italy urban architecture had attained perfection. He did not approve the London terraces of John Nash, for he felt that in them the character of the individual house was lost in the larger identity of the whole.

Long struck out at Upjohn again in his fourth "Architectonics," which was a review of Grace Church, Brooklyn. While praising the integrity which Upjohn had demonstrated in his attempt to make his wooden interior expressive of its materials, Long condemned an indecisiveness which was manifest in Upjohn's design. There was too much horizontality, too much "thinness and meagreness," in some parts while others were "fashioned with a ponderosity of proportion, suggestive of a Thor's hammer among the carvers." The detail was incoherent, "the Go-thin alternating with the Go-thick, in a most remarkable way."[42]

The discussion of "Polychromy," the fifth in Long's series,[43] is both accom-

---

[41] "Architectonics. No. III. —Street Architecture," *The Literary World,* 3 (December 23, 1848):949.
[42] "Architectonics. No. IV. Grace Church. Brooklyn Heights," *ibid.,* 4 (February 10, 1849):131.
[43] "Architectonics. No. V. Polychromy," *ibid.* (March 3, 1849):193–94.

plished and literate. Long's theories had been enlarged by reading in Fergusson's *Historical Inquiry* and Ramée's *Histoire Générale de l'Architecture*; he was again prepared to generalize. An unfortunate de-emphasis of color in building had occurred because architecture was too often confused with sculpture, he said. "Architectural mass is imagined to be the same as a sculptured one, only made up of many stones instead of one, on account of its immensity. To resemble a stupendous monolith, not builded at all, but carved out of one solid body, this is the common notion of architectural unity; a simple oneness, which is, in fact, no unity at all." In his earlier essay on St. Alphonsus' Long had shown that he was approaching a conclusion such as this, for there he had commented that Egyptian, Greek, and Roman buildings were based on "form," while Gothic was a style founded upon "detail." Though they were essentially derivative, by 1849 Long's ideas were beginning to coalesce; he had begun to think in terms of a new style, or at least of original rather than eclectic stylistic solutions for certain modern problems. He clung to Gothic for churches, but he became more adventurous when he considered buildings for which there were no historical precedents. It is for this reason that the sixth and final "Architectonics"[44] is by far the most interesting of the series, for it is on shop fronts, a topic which, like the article on street façades, freed Long from tradition and left him at liberty to describe a kind of building which would be expressive of nineteenth-century America. In this discussion he mentioned ornament only once and made no reference to any of the historical styles. Two forms of front occurred to him. The first, in which the ground floor shop stood forward of the main block of the building, would state directly that it was non-load-bearing: "perfect freedom of design for the shop front would thus be obtained, the 'solids' or supports belonging to it could be attenuated to the last degree of visibility, without any hurt to the eyes from the ponderous mass of the front above." The second was to be used in cases where setback was impossible: the front of the shop, open and light, should "be used in each story, allowing either horizontal or arched headings, and varying the details as taste might dictate." In cases of this kind, Long said, "ornamentation might be used in the horizontal spaces, between the windows of the different floors, so as, by division and enrichment of surface, to remove all appearance and sensation of

---

[44] "Architectonics. No. VI. —Shop Fronts," *ibid.* (March 31, 1849) :297–98.

weight." He much admired similar solutions he had seen in the Ferdinand Strasse and Grossen Burstall in Hamburg.

Though the articles on shop fronts, street façades, and polychromy are not concerned with ecclesiastical architecture, they are of importance here because they illustrate well the growth and sophistication attained from 1841 to 1843 and 1848 to 1849 by one architect who was involved with the American Gothic revival. In the case of Robert Cary Long, Jr., it is possible, because of his literary penchant, to trace his development from the decorative revivalism of St. Alphonsus' to intellectual experimentation with design which was not eclectic but was based upon the "principles" that the Gothic revival had clarified.

It is possible to perceive that between the early Gothic of Strickland and Hopkins, before 1840, and the arrival of ecclesiological revivalism with the building of St. James the Less in 1846 to 1848 there lies a revival to which belong the churches of Long, Trinity Church and the other New York churches discussed in Chapter II, St. Mary's, Burlington, the Chapel of the Holy Innocents, and the churches in Troy and Highland Falls. Two influences were at work in these years. The first, Bishop Doane's attempt to follow the leadership of the English revivalists, was, though prophetic of things to come, the less important of the two in terms of the quantity of building it produced. The second, reflected in the design of Trinity Church, in Long's knowledge of Pugin and in Gilman's references to him, and in Renwick's achievement at Grace and Calvary, was the influence of Pugin, who dominated the American Gothic revival between 1841 and 1847, the years from the publication of *True Principles* to the construction of St. James the Less. Only the churches built by Doane and his friends, Upjohn's experimentation with the parish church style at the Church of the Holy Communion, and his thoughtful consideration of the ideas and policies advocated by Neale and Webb in the *Symbolism of Churches* and the *Ecclesiologist* indicated that a major change was occurring and new authorities were about to arrive on the scene.

Upjohn had drawn on Pugin's *True Principles* for the Trinity Church design, just as Gilman and other architectural journalists were accepting the ideas explored in it. His *Present State* contained thirty-six of the best plates he ever made. A short but significant period in American architecture ensued, dominated by Pugin's manner; it paralleled the appearance of his theories as an influence on American architectural writing. Though Upjohn, after Trinity Church, left Pugin and began to follow ecclesiological leadership, James Renwick, Jr., seems never to have forsaken him.[45] Long admired not only Pugin's ideas and designs but his literary manner and bearing; he seems to have consciously copied Pugin's pugnaciousness in criticism. Even after the arrival of the English parish church model, though Pugin's designs from the *Present State* were no longer as generally copied, a study of the *New York Ecclesiologist* will reveal that his theories retained their popularity. It is the influence of his illustrations on American church building between 1843 and 1847 which will be discussed here.

Long built three modest churches for the Episcopal Diocese of Maryland in 1845. Two were in small towns near Baltimore; the third was in the city itself. The Church of the Ascension, Westminster (Fig. VI–14), and St. Timothy's, Catonsville, were originally identical and reflected in their essentials Pugin's illustrations of St. Anne's, Keighley, and St. Mary's, Southport (Fig. VI–15). Bishop Whittingham approved of these churches by Long and described St. Timothy's as "the best model country church in Maryland" when he laid its cornerstone in 1845. Today the church has aisles and arcades, no clerestory, large transepts, a tower and spire, and Tiffany windows, all added in the late nineteenth and early twentieth centuries. The Westminster church remains exactly as it was first built. Trinity Church, Fells Point, in Baltimore, has not survived, though some idea of the design can be obtained from Whittingham's description of it: "Small in dimension, and moderate in cost, this building with its pointed ceiling, long narrow windows, receding chancel, and triple lancet chancel window of stained glass has a truly church-like air."[46] It seems, then, that Trinity resembled the others Long executed in the same year.

Pugin's position as the leading Roman Catholic architect in England in the early 1840's and his authorship of articles in Catholic periodicals such as the *Dublin Review* should have been enough to recommend him and his designs to American Roman Catholics. For a variety of reasons his work never was

---

[45] See p. 69 and p. 68, n. 52, above.
[46] See W. R. Whittingham's annual report in the *Journal of the . . . Annual Convention of the Diocese of Maryland of the Protestant Episcopal Church* (Baltimore: for the Convention, 1845), p. 38.

accepted by them. The majority of priests at work in the United States were, like their parishioners, of Continental origin; they were not familiar with the English parish church. The congregations for which churches were being built were large, often urban, missions. The small, rural Roman Catholic country church, which was something of a rarity in the United States, was most often the responsibility of the local priest and his flock. Finally, England had been long out of the sphere of Roman Catholic affairs; only between 1843 and 1846, as the Oxford Movement gained momentum, did it again figure prominently, and then Newman, who did not share Pugin's views, was its representative. By that time in the United States English Gothic had been appropriated by Protestant Episcopal church builders, who were richer in building funds and more historical in orientation than their Roman Catholic counterparts. But during the turmoil and immense activity of these years, a Roman Catholic Gothic revival style did evolve, and St. Alphonsus' fairly represents it.[47]

One notable Roman Catholic parish church requires comment here, for St. Peter's Church, built between 1842 and 1844 at Brownsville, Fayette County, Pennsylvania[48] (Fig. VI–16), approached the quality of St. James the Less. Talbot Hamlin correctly characterizes St. Peter's as "the most successful of the earlier Gothic revival churches in America."[49] Because the name of no architect is associated with its design, historians have speculated that its plans were brought from England or that the church was a rough, approximate copy of Pugin's illustrations in the *Present State* (see Fig. I–1). There is, however, another possibility: an American architect may have provided the plans from which local craftsmen, accustomed to and accomplished in building in stone, developed the finished building. The beauty of the church and the authenticity of certain of its details, particularly the newel staircase of stone, would seem to imply that there were architectural plans of some sort, for it seems hardly possible that its various refinements could have been executed by masons who simply worked from memories of churches they knew in England or Ireland,

[47] See John Gilmary Shea, *History of the Catholic Church in the United States*, 2 vols. (New York: Shea, 1892), for illustrations of St. Joseph's, New Orleans, built 1846; St. Peter's Cathedral, Cincinnati, built 1845; and the cathedral at Louisville, built 1849. In these years major Roman Catholic churches were also built in the neoclassical style.
[48] Charles M. Stotz, *The Early Architecture of Western Pennsylvania* (New York: Helburn, for the Buhl Foundation, 1936), gives full illustrations of the church in photographs and measured drawings (pp. 226–30); see also p. 216.
[49] *Greek Revival Architecture in America* (New York: Dover, 1964), pp. 276–77.

Figure VI-14. Church of the Ascension, Westminster, Md. Robert Cary Long, Jr. Ca. 1845.

SOME BUILDINGS AND ARCHITECTS

ST. ANNE'S, KEIGHLEY.

ST. MARY'S, SOUTHPORT.

Figure VI-15. St. Anne's, Keighley, Yorkshire, and St. Mary's, Southport, Lancashire. From Pugin, Present State.

and plans sent from England or Ireland would have been altogether more sophisticated than was the design of St. Peter's. In spite of its "reality," features of the church, such as the position of the tower in the center of the west front and the rectangularity of the heads of the windows, would seem to suggest an American nineteenth-century designer.

St. Thomas' Protestant Episcopal Church in Glassboro, New Jersey, by John Notman (Fig. VI–17) is enough like St. Peter's, Brownsville, to suggest that Notman either designed both churches or that he knew the Brownsville church and patterned his at Glassboro after it. By one usually reliable authority St. Thomas' is dated 1840;[50] Bishop Doane stated flatly that he laid the cornerstone in 1846, though the church records indicate that the ceremony occurred six years after the actual construction was completed. If St. Thomas' was indeed built in 1840, then it seems possible that Notman simply enlarged its design two years later for Brownsville. If St. Thomas' is correctly dated 1846, then the resemblance to St. Peter's could be founded upon Notman's knowledge of it.

Whatever the explanation, the two churches are much alike. St. Peter's is larger than St. Thomas' in every dimension, but the similarity of the two west fronts is too strong to be pure accident, as the handling of the point at which the nave roof of each meets the wall indicates. There are other similarities such as the buttresses on the north and south flanks and the design of the offsets on all the buttresses. The beautiful stone interior of St. Peter's and the wide and graceful chancel arch and recessed chancel are not equaled at St. Thomas'. Both St. Peter's and St. Thomas', early monuments of the American Gothic revival, could well owe their general form and character to the illustrations of Pugin's churches which appeared in the *Dublin Review* in May, 1841. St. Oswald's, Liverpool (see Fig. I–1) may have inspired them.

The parish church revival under the leadership of the English Ecclesiological Society began in earnest only in 1846 and 1847, with the arrangements for St. James the Less and the communications between Robert Ralston and

---

[50] The Historical Records Survey, *Inventory of the Church Archives of New Jersey*, p. 162: "Present site a gift of Mrs. Bathsheba T. Whitney acquired 1840, present church erected same year although the cornerstone and dedication ceremonies did not take place until 1846." See also p. 46, n. 26, above.

SOME BUILDINGS AND ARCHITECTS

Thorp and Webb in England which St. James elicited. The foundations for a full-fledged ecclesiological revival had, of course, been laid by the examples of St. Mary's, Burlington, which was under construction, the Chapel of the Holy Innocents, also in Burlington, the churches at Troy and Highland Falls, and the Church of the Holy Communion, in New York City, and by a wide and approving knowledge of Pugin's books and the works of Ruskin and other English authorities. The presence of a number of vigorous and well-informed Protestant Episcopal bishops in dioceses on the East Coast was also to be a major factor in the rapid growth of the revival. A corps of architects with some experience in the field of church design had begun to assemble. The churches which were built in the decade between 1846 and 1856 were either of wood, which was the choice of many a modest parish, of brick, or, more rarely, of stone. Frank Wills, John Notman, J. W. Priest, and Richard Upjohn were responsible for by far the largest number of them, either directly as architects or because a pattern church they supplied was followed by a local builder. It was the organization of the New York Ecclesiological Society in 1848 which supplied the momentum necessary to spread the influence of the style.

In Maryland Bishop Whittingham was particularly concerned about the eastern counties of the diocese, where the rural population was inadequately served by the Church. St. John's Chapel, Cornersville (Fig. VI–18), consecrated in 1853, is typical of the modest structures which were built to supply this need. Though of the greatest simplicity and without any ornamentation, it differs in fundamental ways from the eighteenth-century churches which remain in the area, for it is narrower in proportion to its length than they and has a distinct chancel. In eighteenth-century churches the pulpit, font, altar, and other ritual centers were distributed within the main rectangular chamber. At Cornersville the Gothic themes of pointed arches and timber roof survive in the triangular form of the opening into the chancel and above the windows. The roof is higher and more steeply pitched than in the earlier churches. The exterior is clapboard and has no buttresses or other pretensions to Gothic forms. St. John's Chapel was certainly the work of a local carpenter.

Hillsboro Church (Fig. VI–19), built in 1851, followed an altogether more sophisticated design. Its proportions agree with the ecclesiological precept that "in the structure of a Gothic church there is found *first* the chancel—and

PULPIT

BAPTISMAL FONT

WEST FRONT
Scale:

Figure VI-16. St. Peter's, Brownsville, Pa. Ca. 1840–46.

Figure VI-17. St. Thomas', Glassboro, N.J. John Notman. Ca. 1840–46.

Figure VI-18. St. John's Chapel, Cornersville, Md. Consecrated 1853.

SOME BUILDINGS AND ARCHITECTS

Figure VI-19. Protestant Episcopal Church, Hillsboro, Md. 1851.

by a chancel we mean no recess from the nave a few feet deep but a roomy house, a spacious tabernacle, in which the service of God may be solemnly, and if not always magnificently, yet *ever* with all due circumstance performed.''[51] Hillsboro Church is St. James the Less transferred to wood. All features necessary in stone but not in wood are omitted. It is a diagram of the parish church pattern respectful of ''reality'' and of the material of which it is built. This church compares interestingly with those at Maugerville, Burton, and Newcastle, New Brunswick (see Figs. IV–17 and IV–18), of the same date, in which the buttresses, offsets, and other stone requirements are reproduced in wood.[52]

Various characteristics of the church at Hillsboro suggest that Upjohn was its designer; he seems to have been willing to supply parishes which could not afford the complete services of an architect with designs at little or no cost. Credit for this and other sensitive, intelligent, and characteristically American transformations of a stone pattern to wood belongs to Upjohn. By 1847 so many requests for plans were arriving in his office that he resolved to publish a book illustrating churches he had designed and could recommend for parishes in need of correct but inexpensive models. In an advertisement for this publication he mentioned ''the increasing demand for Country Churches of moderate cost, and similar in style to St. Peter's, Stockbridge, Massachusetts, and others, which have been erected by the subscriber in several of the New England and Middle States,''[53] and he proposed to include plans illustrative of ''a mode of erection that should come within the means of the feeblest congregation, yet be in all its essential features, *a Church*—plain indeed, but becoming in its plainness. This demand, it is believed, the Churches referred to have generally met. When the means are limited, but little can be devoted to mere ornament; nor can ornament in any case commend itself to good taste, when it thrusts itself

[51] ''Editor's Farewell,'' *NYE.,* 5 (December, 1853):177.

[52] Frank Wills had discussed the correctness of retaining in wooden buildings features necessary in stone (see *Ancient English Ecclesiastical Architecture,* p. 90).

[53] The Whittingham Papers, now in the collections of Duke University, contain an advertisement for this book: ''*Proposals for Publishing by Subscription Designs for Country Churches. and Rural Houses, consisting of Plans, Sections, Elevations, Details and Perspective Views of Each Church & House: with Designs for Church Furniture—Decorations and Hints upon Stained Glass, etc.* By Richard Upjohn, Architect. March 1, 1847, New York.'' The quotations are taken from this prospectus.

on the observer with unmeaning intrusion, and has no connection with the purposes and utilities of the place." Upjohn then stated his philosophy of church design: "Without fitness of arrangement and adaption to the end proposed, no structure—however elaborate and costly—can be pronounced truly beautiful —and with these qualities the simplest and plainest edifice may claim the praise. Nowhere, perhaps, is this want of fitness more apparent, or more offensive, than in our Church architecture. How often do we look in vain for that air of tranquil repose, that sober and solemn aspect, which command even an involuntary respect, and tend to secure the sacred structure from irreverence and profanation."

An excellent example of Upjohn's wood church style remains intact in good condition in Maryland. In 1853 the headmistress of Hannah More Academy in Reisterstown built a chapel on the grounds of the school (Figs. VI–20, VI–21, and VI–22). Her taste pleased Bishop Whittingham because she had followed one of Upjohn's patterns. The influence of St. James the Less upon Upjohn first appeared at Calvary Church, Stonington, Connecticut, in 1848; it was built of stone. At St. Thomas', Amenia Union, New York (1849–51), he continued the form but this time in brick, and began to reshape its elements somewhat to suit his personal preference for unified masses, bulky shapes, and acute angles (Figs. VI–23 and VI–24). St. Michael's, Reisterstown, is representative of the same type in wood. Comparison of the three shows how sensitive Upjohn was to the logic of materials. The emphatic western façade with buttresses has disappeared in the wood version. In brick it is retained, indeed reaffirmed, in one tall, dramatic, and rising forward plane which tapers gradually to the bell cote.

Not until the 1850's did Gothic architecture in wood attain the originality and the brilliant understatement of which it was capable, and then it was largely because of Upjohn's experimentation with its possibilities. At Spotswood (1849) and Millburn (1853) in New Jersey, there are pretty examples of larger churches in wood (Figs. VI–25 and VI–26). The interior of St. Stephen's, Millburn (Fig. VI–27), which is an extraordinarily light, sophisticated, and delicate achievement, carried the potentialities of wood as an ecclesiastical building material beyond Gothic inspiration and into a fresh manner which, though it is reminiscent of medieval building, is linear in ways in which stone could never be. St. Stephen's and St. John Chrysostom's, Delafield, Wis-

THE GOTHIC REVIVAL AND AMERICAN CHURCH ARCHITECTURE

Figure VI-20. St. Michael's Chapel, Hannah More Academy, Reisterstown, Md.
Richard Upjohn. 1853.

Figure VI-21. St. Michael's Chapel, Reisterstown.

Figure VI-22. St. Michael's Chapel, Reisterstown.

SOME BUILDINGS AND ARCHITECTS

Figure VI-23. St. Thomas', Amenia, N.Y. Richard Upjohn. 1849–51.

Figure VI-24. St. Thomas', Amenia.

SOME BUILDINGS AND ARCHITECTS

Figure VI-25. St. Peter's, Spotswood, N.J. 1849, with later additions.

THE GOTHIC REVIVAL AND AMERICAN CHURCH ARCHITECTURE

Figure VI-26. St. Stephen's, Millburn, N.J. 1853.

Figure VI-27. St. Stephen's, Millburn.

consin (Figs. VI–28 and VI–29), built from 1851 to 1853 but consecrated in 1856, rank among the best surviving examples of the American parish church in wood. The history of St. John Chrysostom's, which has been somewhat mysterious, can now be clarified.[54] Robert Ralston Cox of Philadelphia, a founder and officer of the New York Ecclesiological Society, was instrumental in the establishment of the church and arrangements for the building. Local tradition has associated the design of the church with Cox, who was said to have followed either Greenstead Church, England, or "St. James" in Philadelphia. In view of the connections between Cox and St. James the Less and the fact that he was close to Robert Ralston, the sources of St. John Chrysostom's are so obvious as scarcely to require elaboration. Cox either commissioned Upjohn to do the design, which seems unlikely since the Upjohn papers contain only one letter concerning it,[55] or adapted a plan from Upjohn's *Rural Architecture*, keeping close to the Philadelphia building which had altered Upjohn's style. St. John Chrysostom's belongs to the St. James the Less parish church revival. Its size, the size of its nave in proportion to its chancel and sanctuary, the triplet window in the east, the placement of liturgical centers in the chancel, and the rood screen all follow the dictates of ecclesiology. The details of hinge designs, lectern, and finials on the pews are drawn from the *Instrumenta Ecclesiastica* prepared by William Butterfield for the Ecclesiological Society.[56] But the bargeboards, the board-and-batten exterior, the slenderness of its parts, and the acute angle of the roofs belong to wood and to American sensibility. The pattern of the English medieval parish church had traveled far and been greatly modified in its passage, but its essentials had not been lost. St. John Chrysostom's belongs to the Gothic revival because it follows Gothic "principles."[57]

Other architects also designed for wood construction; Frank Wills, for ex-

---

[54] See Richard W. E. Perrin, "Richard Upjohn: Anglican Chapels in the Wilderness," *Wisconsin Magazine of History*, 45 (Autumn, 1961):42.

[55] See Upjohn, *Richard Upjohn*, p. 209.

[56] See p. 105, n. 25, above.

[57] The *New York Ecclesiologist* published "the following list of wooden churches by Mr. Upjohn, and of the same general character as All Angels, Brunswick, Me.—Chelsea, Plymouth, Stockbridge, Mass.—Middletown and Newport, R.I.—Maspeth, Ravenswood, and Hamilton, N.Y.—Pulaski, W.N.Y.—one near Pittsburgh, Pa.—West Hoboken, N.J.—Racine, Wisconsin—one in Virginia. Also several others. In details, however, they differ. Proportions and size vary: some have not the turret: that in Brunswick, Me. is cruciform" (5 [July, 1853]:128). To these should be added Grace Episcopal Church, Bath, Maine

269

SOME BUILDINGS AND ARCHITECTS

ample, sent plans for an Early English church in wood to San Augustine,
Texas, in 1849.[58] But it was Upjohn who dominated the field of small church
design. It was work from which he derived little or no profit but which he was
willing to do. He supplied plans and particulars of construction for needy
parishes because he believed the religious and artistic obligations of the architect to be as Pugin and the ecclesiologists had defined them. Upjohn possessed a recalcitrant and assertive gift, which Long had spotted and defined
unkindly as "Go-thin and Go-thick." His buildings reveal this personal style,
for, however much he strove to qualify this manner and fit himself into the
mold of ecclesiological form, he was unable to do so. Wood construction, which
was so far removed from the original Gothic, released him. Wood was the
material of which he was fond and with which he had already experimented in
the interiors of his larger churches. The many small wooden churches inspired
by or built from Upjohn designs are modest but important. They record the
moment when American builders and architects, while improvising upon a
foreign style and the ideas that came with it, displayed their capacity to comprehend aesthetic principles and repeat not correct detail but the essential
constructive and spatial truths of the style in which they were working.

The churches built between 1845 and 1855 in brick and stone were inevitably,
because of their materials, closer to English patterns and richer in ecclesiastical
decorative arts than those in wood. Most were built by city rather than rural
parishes, and, unlike the smaller, less costly, and often anonymous country
churches, they can be identified as the work of specific architects. Two important Maryland churches were under construction in the mid-1840's. One
was in the earlier pre-ecclesiological Gothic; the other was the church that, in
1846, the *Ecclesiologist* had reported was being built "near Baltimore" from
the plans used for St. James the Less.[59]

(1852), as well as the various Maryland, New Jersey, and southern and midwestern
churches built from the plans which appeared in *Rural Architecture*. Also see "New
Churches," *NYE*, 5 (October, 1853):163, which attributes a wooden church, St. Mark's, in
Newark, New York, to Upjohn's design in *Rural Architecture*.
[58] *Ancient English Ecclesiastical Architecture*, Plate XVII. Wills's "Grace Church, Albany,
N.Y.," which he reproduces on p. 133, refers to two wooden churches by Wills, one in the
"south," another in New York City.
[59] See p. 97 and n. 4 above.

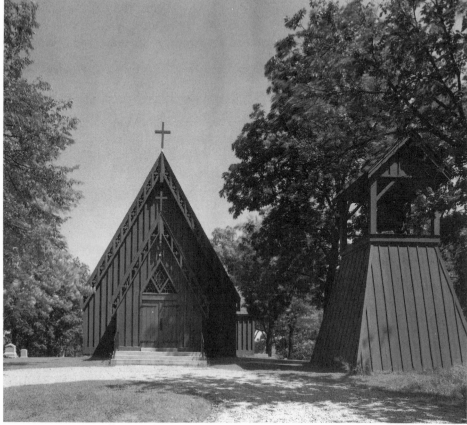

Figure VI-28. St. John Chrysostom's, Delafield, Wis. Richard Upjohn. 1851–53.

SOME BUILDINGS AND ARCHITECTS

Figure VI-29. St. John Chrysostom's, Delafield.

Between 1840 and 1850 Long was the only architect Bishop Whittingham mentioned by name in his annual reports to the diocese. He was grateful for the praise and support the Bishop gave him, and the two men were on formal but friendly terms. In April, 1847, when Long sent the Bishop a copy of Brandon's *Parish Churches*, he said in the letter which accompanied the gift that he was sure Whittingham would "be struck at first glance with the admirable simplicity, economy and beauty of the Churches here offered as models for imitation."[60]

Long's last church for the Protestant Episcopal community in Maryland was also his largest. The design for Mount Calvary Church, Baltimore (Fig. VI–30), was prepared in 1844, and the church was under construction in 1845. Again, as in his two earlier Baltimore churches, Long improvised, following no specific medieval or nineteenth-century model but suggesting the presence of many sources. Though Mount Calvary is as severe as St. Alphonsus' is exuberant and the Franklin Street Presbyterian Church is staid but rich, it is fundamentally the same building as those two. The tower is pressed back into the façade, a vestibule crosses the front, the interior is an open hall, and here again Long shows his ability to adjust the façade to the site, which was in this case a wedge-shaped piece of land, higher than the roads which pass on either side.[61] The details, which are not English, recall the illustrations in Thomas Hope's *Essay on Architecture*, a book which Long had used earlier. The unpainted brick of Mount Calvary and its square tower, decorated only by corbelled arches, are similar to those of Italian and German churches. The windows are pointed. The hall is set crosswise, parallel to the façade, and emerges on the sides like massive transepts.[62] Bishop Whittingham never commented on the architecture of Mount Calvary, but he did say of it that "there are larger, more costly, and more splendid churches in Baltimore, but there is none in my judgement so well adapted to make the worshipper feel he must 'keep his foot' for he is in the house of God."

In the summer of 1846 Whittingham visited Robert Ralston; the cornerstone

[60] Long to Whittingham from Baltimore, April 23, 1847, Duke University Collections.
[61] This idiosyncratic plan may be a result of the relatively shallow site.
[62] A great many changes have been made in Mount Calvary Church. The chancel was deepened in 1853; the spire, which blew down, was never replaced; to correct structural difficulties in the roof, a huge permanent timber scaffolding was installed in the nave. All that now remains of the original design is the front, minus its spire, and the wings of the nave which appear on the sides.

Figure VI-30. Mount Calvary Church, Baltimore. Robert Cary Long, Jr. 1844–45.

THE GOTHIC REVIVAL AND AMERICAN CHURCH ARCHITECTURE

of St. John's, Huntingdon, near Baltimore, was laid in April of the following year. It stood at the first tollgate on the York Road, beyond the Baltimore city limits, which tallies with the location which the *Ecclesiologist* had given, "near Baltimore." St. John's was the first in a series of American churches inspired by the plans of St. Michael's, Long Stanton, and St. James the Less. The English plans from which Ralston worked had had no vestry. In 1849 Frank Wills was asked to suggest how such an addition might best be made to St. John's.

The appearance of St. John's as it was built in 1847 will never be known, for in May, 1858, it was burned by an arsonist. The remains of the walls of the original church were incorporated into the rebuilding, which began at once after the fire. The plan was enlarged to include a tower.[63] The many alterations and additions which have gone on since the rebuilding have not obliterated all traces of the English plan; the characteristic arrangement of chimney and south porch survive (Fig. VI–31).

The influence of St. James the Less appeared elsewhere. Trinity Church, at Matawan, New Jersey (1851), repeats, in brick and brownstone, its bell cote, buttressed west front, and intimate scale (Fig. VI–32). Upjohn went on to develop the themes and feeling of St. James the Less: Christ Church, Elizabeth, New Jersey, built in 1854 (Figs. VI–33 and VI–34), is a combination of the cross form of Burlington with the nave and west front of St. James the Less; the Chapel of St. Mary the Virgin, at Nashotah Episcopal Theological Seminary in Wisconsin (Fig. VI–35), of 1859 to 1860 is a larger version of the scheme set forth first at Amenia Union (see Figs. VI–23 and VI–24). Together these churches demonstrate the size of the geographical area over which St. James the Less held sway and how long it dominated.[64] Upjohn employed

[63] The records of this church cannot now be found, and it is therefore impossible to know who reconstructed and designed it after the fire. The transepts and present chancel were added in 1878. Until then, save for the location of the tower and the absence of west buttresses, the church resembled the model which had appeared in the *New York Ecclesiologist*.

[64] See Shinn, *Notable Episcopal Churches*, for the Memorial Church of St. Luke the Beloved Physician, Bustleton, Pennsylvania, by Upjohn (1860–61) (p. 97), and the Cathedral of St. Peter and St. Paul, Chicago, built before 1861, architect unknown, but design similar to Nashotah (p. 241). See also Perrin, *Historic Wisconsin Buildings, a Survey of Pioneer Architecture, 1835–1870*, Milwaukee Public Museum Publications on History no. 4 (Milwaukee, Wis.: Public Museum, 1962), p. 39, on Holy Innocents', Nashotah, Wisconsin (1861) (p. 42), and St. Patrick's Roman Catholic Church near Adell, Wisconsin (1877) (pp. 74–75).

SOME BUILDINGS AND ARCHITECTS

Figure VI-31. St. John's, Huntingdon, Baltimore.

Figure VI-32. Trinity Church, Matawan, N.J. 1851.

SOME BUILDINGS AND ARCHITECTS

Figure VI-33. Christ Church, Elizabeth, N.J. Richard Upjohn. 1854.

THE GOTHIC REVIVAL AND AMERICAN CHURCH ARCHITECTURE

Figure VI-34. Christ Church, Elizabeth.

SOME BUILDINGS AND ARCHITECTS

Figure VI-35. Chapel of St. Mary the Virgin, Nashotah Episcopal Seminary, Nashotah, Wis. Richard Upjohn. 1859–60.

motifs from St. James the Less so frequently that they became one of the two church styles in which he worked. The second, which was derived from the type and form of the Church of the Holy Communion, owed much of its mature character and sensitivity to his observations of the materials and dignified informality of St. James the Less. St. Paul's, Brookline, Massachusetts (1852), a stone version of the design of St. Stephen's, Millburn, is a typical and refined example of this second manner.[65]

Having achieved remarkable success with St. Mark's, Philadelphia, John Notman acquired a considerable reputation as an architect of churches. His services were in demand from New York State to Georgia.[66] The building of the Baltimore and Ohio Railroad and the construction of the Chesapeake and Ohio Canal made Cumberland, Maryland, a prosperous place in the 1840's. Until 1841 Emmanuel Protestant Episcopal Church there had had to struggle to stay alive, but new wealth and a new rector, the Reverend D. Hillhouse Buel, convinced the vestry to undertake the building of a new church. The Reverend Mr. Buel was one of the first who appealed to the New York Ecclesiological Society for architectural assistance.[67] Frank Wills sent him a design, but by May, 1849, the decision had been made to build a large church and to hire Notman, who was present when the cornerstone was laid. He proposed to build "a cross church . . . with a noble tower and spire in the angle of the chancel and north transept, and a south porch." It was to have a "fine chancel 31 × 20 inside." The whole length of the nave and chancel was to be more than 130 feet; the nave was to be 39 feet wide and the transepts 60 feet wide.[68] When estimates for the church ran as high as ten thousand dollars, the project halted temporarily while Notman was approached to see whether he would be willing to work with the original Wills design. When Notman rejected this proposal, the rector and a majority of the vestry decided to proceed as

[65] Shinn, *Notable Episcopal Churches*, cites St. Thomas' Church, Hanover, New Hampshire (1876), by Frederick C. Withers, in the Upjohn manner (p. 169ff.), and St. Mark's Church, Mauch Chunk, Pennsylvania (1867), by Upjohn. In addition, Holy Trinity, Oxford, Maryland (1853), is by Upjohn.

[66] In September, 1849, Notman was negotiating with a parish in Savannah, Georgia (manuscript material in the possession of the vestry of St. Luke's, Carey Street, Baltimore).

[67] "Report of the Second Quarterly Meeting of the New York Ecclesiological Society held in the school room of St. Paul's Chapel, on Monday, July 3, 1848," NYE., 1 (October, 1848):16.

[68] Buel to Whittingham, May 22, 1849, Duke University Collections.

originally planned, though they recognized that the cost of the larger building would be a distinct strain on the resources of the parish. In March, 1850, Notman was in Cumberland interviewing local workmen. Everyone was enthusiastic and pleased with the attitude of the architect. The Reverend Mr. Buel wrote Bishop Whittingham to suggest that Notman's ability as an architect of churches be brought to the attention of the vestry of Grace Church in Baltimore, which was about to build.[69] By July, 1850, Notman was spending considerable time in Cumberland, and in January, 1851, the structure was roofed in and the interior was being completed.

Bishop Whittingham had predicted that Emmanuel Church would "take the palm" for plan and finish, and he was right. Notman had supervised its construction conscientiously; when he could not be present during construction, he left an agent in residence.[70] The rector and his vestry had invested their enthusiasm and hopes in the new church, which cost not ten but eighteen thousand dollars[71] and involved them in a debt which was to be a burden for decades.

The center of the town of Cumberland lies in a valley; at the top of a hill, overlooking the main business street, stood the ruins of an eighteenth-century fort with underground magazines. This was the site upon which the vestry resolved to set its new church, with the cellars of the fort forming the basement above which the church would stand on a platform of timbers (Fig. VI–36). Realizing that the east front would overlook the town and that the usual association of tower and entrance, or west end, would not be effective in this situation, Notman sought a design in which tower and chancel were together. The *Ecclesiologist* had supplied a useful illustration of St. Paul's, Brighton (1846–48), by R. C. Carpenter[72] (Fig. VI–37). Out of respect for the limited funds and capacities of the local workmen,[73] Notman omitted the carved stone and the tracery of St. Paul's, while retaining the essentials of the Carpenter design.

---

[69] Buel to Whittingham, May 23, 1850, Duke University Collections.

[70] Letters from the Reverend Mr. Buel to Bishop Whittingham make this clear. The vestry records ("Report of Mr. Semmes, Treasurer, May 7, 1851") of Emmanuel Church, Cumberland, show that Notman's fee was $1,350, a figure that must have included travel and other expenditures, for it was higher than his customary 5 per cent.

[71] *Ibid.*

[72] "New Churches," *E.*, 5 (April, 1846):154.

[73] The vestry records of Emmanuel Church show that the builder, Walton, and the mason, Lippold, were both local men and that Notman relied upon their abilities.

Figure VI-36. Emmanuel Church, Cumberland, Md. John Notman. 1850–51.

Figure VI-37. St. Paul's, Brighton. R. C. Carpenter. 1846–48.

He added transepts to improve the appearance of the church on its hill and to allow for the separate seating of slaves. Emmanuel Church is not quite as large as St. Mark's, Philadelphia, nor is it as elegant, but it compares favorably with it. The vestry commented with pride that "the singular beauty of the site, the fine proportions of the building, the variety and happy grouping of its different parts, chancel, tower, nave, transepts and south porch and its lofty and very graceful tower and spire render the new Emmanuel Church an uncommonly picturesque structure." They added that "though a building of moderate cost and humble pretensions" it would be an asset to the reputation of Mr. Notman.

Since Notman already had St. Mark's to his credit, it is odd that the *New York Ecclesiologist* never discussed Emmanuel Church. It is tempting to think that Frank Wills chose to overlook both it and Notman, who was not placed on its list of recommended architects until 1853. In the year and a half that Emmanuel was building, Notman also had in progress houses in Philadelphia and another large church, St. Peter's, in Pittsburgh.[74] In these months he was moving in several directions, producing both Italianate and Gothic designs. The drawings in the Historical Society of Pennsylvania collection indicate that he possessed a gift for styles other than Gothic.

The Reverend Mr. Buel's suggestion that Bishop Whittingham might intervene with the vestry of Grace Church in Baltimore on behalf of Notman was surely responsible for the church which was built in 1851 and opened for services late in 1852. Grace Church, now Grace and St. Peter's (Fig. VI–38), is a copy of St. Mark's, Philadelphia, in spite of the newspaper accounts of its consecration which stated that it was the work of the local architectural firm of Niernsee and Nielson. Though Notman could well have sold tracings of the plans to the vestry or to Niernsee and Nielson, it hardly seems possible that he would have permitted all credit for the design to go to them had this been the case. The plans could have been loaned, without the architect's knowledge, by the vestry in Philadelphia, a circumstance trying for Notman and unethical on the part of Niernsee and Nielson. The presence of this replica of St. Mark's

---

[74] J. Van Trump, "St. Peter's, Pittsburgh, by John Notman," *Journal of the Society of Architectural Historians*, 15 (May, 1956):19–23. Notman was already at work at Cumberland when he received the commission for St. Peter's. On this church see "New Churches," *E.*, 9 (October, 1851):432–33.

Figure VI-38. Grace and St. Peter's, Baltimore. Niernsee and Nielson. 1851–52.

reveals a good deal about architectural practice in mid-nineteenth-century America and indicates how stylish the eccesiological revival had become by 1851.

By the simple expedients of placing the tower on the left side of the entrance and turning the whole church around, Niernsee and Nielson tailored St. Mark's to its new situation.[75] The tracery in the aisle windows is identical with that in St. Mark's, but the exact position of a given pattern was not followed. The stone piers and the clerestory of the interior are the same, though Grace and St. Peter's does not have the dramatic stone interior which contributes so much to St. Mark's. There was about the new Baltimore church an authenticity and "Englishness" which pleased almost everyone and made Long's brick and cast iron seem old-fashioned. It is strange that Ferrey's design for St. Stephen's, Westminster, should have traveled so far and should have been twice reorganized to fit special circumstances in America.

Frank Wills had founded his New York practice in 1848. Since Robert Ralston Cox and Robert Ralston were involved with him in the organization of the Society, Wills must certainly have seen St. James the Less shortly after he arrived in the United States. Encouraged by the support of the *New York Ecclesiologist*, Wills's reputation prospered, and in 1851 he was able to report to Bishop Whittingham that because Henry Dudley of Exeter, "an English gentleman who for twenty years past has been engaged in the erection of many of our best churches in England," had joined him in partnership, he would be "the better enabled to give that attention to my work distant from New York, which otherwise I could not have done."[76]

---

[75] Grace and St. Peter's is nearly the same over-all length as St. Mark's, about 137 to 140 feet, and the width of the nave, with the aisles, is 63 feet. St. Mark's nave is 61 feet wide. On the Baltimore site correct orientation was impossible because the long dimension of the property ran north to south. Because of an existing alley at the north, the original chancel at Grace and St. Peter's was meager. In 1903 it was repaired, extended, and thoroughly rebuilt by Henry M. Congdon and Son, architects of New York City. A chapel has been added off the west side of the chancel end. Probably because the south door opened so abruptly onto the street, it was supplied with a small porch, a feature not present at St. Mark's.

[76] Wills to Whittingham from 298 Broadway, New York, June 3, 1851, now in the Duke University Collections. The view of Trinity Church, San Francisco (1849), recorded Wills's office address as 166 Broadway; also see p. 185 above.

SOME BUILDINGS AND ARCHITECTS

Wills possessed a personal style which influenced American church building in two ways: first, through the designs which he prepared in response to specific commissions, and second, through his position as architect for the New York Ecclesiological Society, where he was called upon, as was Upjohn in his practice, to supply plans for parishes too poor to afford original drawings. In the United States and Canada there are a number of Wills churches which originated in this second way.

In 1849, when Wills published a view of his proposal for Trinity Church, San Francisco (Fig. VI–39), characteristics of his mature manner were already apparent. Like the towers of his earlier wood churches in New Brunswick[77] and the later designs for The House of Prayer, Newark (1850–51),[78] and St. George's, Milford, Connecticut (1850–51) (see Fig. V–2), the tower at San Francisco was low and square, embellished by a polygonal spire. Also, as at Milford and Newark, there was a door in the side of the tower. At Milford and San Francisco the tower stood at the west, but at Newark, "owing to the peculiarity of the site," Wills was forced to arrange it next to the chancel, an expedient for which he apologized in his discussion of the design.[79]

Trinity Church is typical of the solution Wills supplied when he was called upon to produce a large stone church. His design, which contained all the ecclesiological essentials, was, though "somewhat plain," generally "Middle Pointed," and it had paneled ornament in the spire, an enrichment he used whenever he could. Both the *Ecclesiologist* and the *New York Ecclesiologist* were distinctly reserved in their praises of this design. The *New York Ecclesiologist*, feeling that "Christian Architecture" had "no cast-iron mould" and that "circumstances" should within limits guide its development, implied that Wills's scheme was too authentically English for the climate in California.[80] The *Ecclesiologist* found it could "not speak in very high terms of the design," which it called "common-place" and "destitute of individuality," and employed a number of qualifying adjectives such as "meagre." The review and discussion

---

[77] See Hubbard, "Canadian Gothic," p. 105, for an illustration of the Burton church.
[78] See Wills, *Ancient English Ecclesiastical Architecture*, Plate XVIII and p. 115. This church, which is extant, was rehabilitated and restored in 1966.
[79] *Ibid.*
[80] "New Churches," *NYE*, 1 (June, 1849):149.

Figure VI-39. Proposed Trinity Church, San Francisco. Frank Wills.
Lithograph by Wills (1850).

of the proposal ended by saying, "Whatever faults we may have found, this design for a Pointed church in California is sufficiently good to command our sympathy in its success."[81]

The model church which was illustrated in the *New York Ecclesiologist* in 1849, the year of the Trinity Church proposal, was certainly by Wills.[82] Upon the recommendation of the New York Society a number of parishes accepted it and its architect. The Reverend William Francis Brand, a friend and biographer of Bishop Whittingham, was encouraged by the Bishop to establish a parish, build a church, and collect a congregation at Emmorton, Maryland. St. Mary's is the model church of the *New York Ecclesiologist* with additions and changes which show that Brand was personally familiar with St. James the Less (which was, of course, not far away). Though decorative enrichments have been added in the chancel, this stone church, with its western buttresses, tiny nave, and south porch, remains essentially as the Reverend Mr. Brand left it (Figs. VI–40 and VI–41). Modest and charming, St. Mary's is truly notable because Brand purchased, a few at a time, from 1851 to 1870, as he could afford them, fifteen matched windows by William Butterfield from Gibbs of London. The series begins in the south wall of the chancel with the Annunciation and continues over the altar, where the Nativity, the Adoration of the Shepherds, and the Adoration of the Kings fill the three lancets (Fig. VI–42). The north windows of the nave illustrate the life of Christ, the west window the Crucifixion, and the four on the south of the nave the Descent from the Cross, the Resurrection, and the Ascension. A double window in the south wall of the chancel is a later addition and is not by Gibbs.[83] St. Mary's is the finest rural church in the diocese of Maryland; its glass is unique—the only program of its kind by Butterfield in North America.

[81] "New Churches," *E.*, 7 (November, 1849):234. See also the extensive review of Wills's illustrations in *Ancient English Ecclesiastical Architecture* in "New Church," *E.*, 8 (October, 1850):201, in which St. George's, Milford, is described as a "very miserable whole"; Grace Church, Albany, is called "a very unfortunate mistake"; and The House of Prayer, Newark, is characterized as "a very unsatisfactory building." In defense of Wills it should be noted that these disparaging remarks were made after the *New York Ecclesiologist* had offended the *Ecclesiologist* (see Chapter V above).
[82] See Chapter V above.
[83] The chalice and paten in this church were made by John Keith of London (1850–51). The mosaic decoration in the chancel, new pews, and other furniture were added late in the nineteenth century.

Figure VI-40. St. Mary's, Emmorton, Md. Begun 1851.

SOME BUILDINGS AND ARCHITECTS

Figure VI-41. St. Mary's, Emmorton.

Figure VI-42. St. Mary's, Emmorton. Chancel windows by William Butterfield.

There are small Wills churches elsewhere; Christ Church, Oberlin, Ohio,[84] is by him, as are the Chapel of the Cross, Annandale, Mississippi,[85] and Christ Episcopal Church, Napoleonville, Assumption Parish, Louisiana[86] (Figs. VI–43 and VI–44). All are small, neat, correct renderings of the parish church model and date from the 1850's.[87] For the career of Wills, they are the equiv-

[84] Christ Church was built in 1855. The letters of the Reverend Francis Granger, who was then rector of the parish, are preserved in the archives of the Diocese of Ohio. They show that it was he who recommended Wills because he had been impressed by a Wills church he had visited.

[85] This church is attributed to Wills by the *New York Ecclesiologist*. After years of neglect, the Chapel of the Cross is now in a reasonable state of repair. It is brick, has a fully expressed chancel, a triplet window over the altar, a bell cote over the west end, and a south porch. The original chancel furniture is preserved.

[86] Dated 1853.

[87] Other churches by Wills are as follows. St. Mary's Church, Castleton, Long Island (1853), burned in 1947. The nave was later restored to its original form. Christ Church, Corning, New York, burned in the 1880's and was abandoned. Grace Church, Albany (illustrated in Wills, *Ancient English Ecclesiastical Architecture*, Plate XVII and p. 113), built in 1850, of wood, was demolished in 1951. The cornerstone of the Church of the Holy Innocents, Albany (illustrated in Wills, *Ancient English Ecclesiastical Architecture*, Plate XIX and p. 117), was laid in 1849 by Bishop Whittingham, and the church was opened in 1850. The interior is illustrated in Joel Munsell, *The Annals of Albany* (Albany: Munsell and Rowland, 1859), pp. 432–39; Munsell says that the font was made in Exeter, England; the glass was by Bolton, of New Rochelle, New York; and the roof of the chancel was "beautifully painted and ornamented with a blue ground, bearing stars in gold and white lilies." Around the walls of the nave the *Te Deum* was painted, and over the chancel arch Verse 4 of the Twenty-third Psalm appeared. This church is now the property of the Russian Orthodox Church. Wills also added a font and an altar to the Church of the Advent, Boston. The *New York Ecclesiologist* attributed Emmanuel Church, Adams, Jefferson County, western New York, to Wills (3 [September, 1851]:167).

In an article on "Practical Matters Connected with Church Architecture" in the *New York Ecclesiologist*, Priest alluded favorably to an eastern triplet window Wills installed in St. Stephen's Church, Pittsfield, Massachusetts. Upjohn (*Richard Upjohn*) mentions the church in Claremont, New Hampshire, saying that in 1853 the commission for it was given to Wills and Dudley after it had been promised to Upjohn. Plans for a church for Waukesha, Wisconsin, were submitted by Wills at the request of Robert Ralston Cox. The church in Waukesha is ecclesiologically inspired, but it is not by Wills. R. A. Gilpin, of Philadelphia, was the architect, Wills's plans being too expensive to build. John Coolidge, in an unpublished thesis ("Gothic Revival Churches in New England and New York," Harvard College, 1935), includes a list of buildings by Wills. He adds to the churches mentioned here only St. John Baptist, New York City (1849). Alan Burnham (*New York Landmarks* [Middletown: Municipal Art Society of New York, 1963], p. 386) attributes St. George's Episcopal Church, 135 Thirty-eighth Avenue, Flushing, to Wills and Dudley. The *New York Ecclesiologist* ("New Churches," 5 [October, 1853]:163) attributed the Church of St. James, Syracuse, then nearly completed at a cost of eighteen thousand dollars, to Wills and Dudley.

Figure VI-43. Christ Episcopal Church, Napoleonville, Assumption Parish, La.
Frank Wills. Ca. 1850.

SOME BUILDINGS AND ARCHITECTS

Figure VI-44. Christ Church, Napoleonville.

alents of Upjohn's small churches and chapels, and like them they exhibit, in an understated way, the traits and preferences of their designer. Wills could not resist the excitement of slender, tall shapes, and if he was given the least latitude, he digressed into applied ornament. His feeling for masses was sound, but as the *Ecclesiologist* correctly observed, it was more commonplace than original and was derived from his familiarity with English medieval building. Though his project for St. Peter's Church, Philadelphia (Fig. VI–45), was never used, it is characteristic of Wills's concern for decoration, massing, and feeling for the English church with which he had worked before he came to North America. In practice as well as in architectural theory, Wills was close to Pugin.

The later years of Wills's professional life are somewhat obscure. He seems to have dissolved his partnership with Dudley, and by 1856 he was settled once again in Canada, where he died while at work upon Christ Church Cathedral in Montreal.[88] But within the American Gothic revival traces of his style survived: whether or not it is by Wills and Dudley, the Church of the Annunciation, which stood on Fourteenth Street, New York City, was enriched with Wills's square tower and polygonal spire and massed lancets in its western façade;[89] St. John's Church, Troy, New York (1853),[90] is close enough to Wills's typical pattern to indicate that, if it was not actually by him, he had a following there. Though he practiced in America for less than a decade, Wills accomplished a great deal. At the very least, his churches were, like St. Anne's, Fredericton, charming and distinctive both in their larger forms and in their details. Montgomery Schuyler perceived this when he described a little Wills church in Greenwich, Connecticut, as "extremely pretty" and characterized Wills as "one of the most accomplished of the Anglican revivalists."[91] Through his writing and his designs Wills brought to North America a talent which embellished the revival and encouraged widespread acceptance of its exciting general principles.

[88] Illustrated in Hubbard, "Canadian Gothic," p. 105. In *The Annals of Albany*, p. 437, Munsell provides a terminal date for the career of Wills. He died in Montreal in 1856, while he was at work upon the cathedral there.

[89] Illustrated in *Putnam's Monthly*, 2 (September, 1853):244.

[90] Illustrated and described in Shinn, *Notable Episcopal Churches*, pp. 86–88, and dated 1855.

[91] *American Architecture and Other Writings*, 1:147. He does not identify the church he describes.

Figure VI-45. Proposed St. Peter's, Philadelphia. Frank Wills.

J. W. Priest, another of the architects recommended by the New York Ecclesiological Society, is a more elusive figure, but his attitudes on matters connected with the practice of architecture and his capacities as a designer may be determined by tracing the history of St. Luke's, Carey Street, Baltimore, where the old and new Gothic came into conflict. In 1847 the vestry of the parish embarked upon a program of building. At first Robert Cary Long, Jr., won the approval of the building committee with his "drawings and specifications for a handsome Gothic Church." But by April, 1848, the building committee had decided that a design "would be submitted by another gentleman."[92] Though Long tendered specific estimates, which included the cost of stone, in September, 1848, a decision was deferred. Discussion of the merits of various architects continued into 1849. By that time Long's death had eliminated him from the competition. In March, 1849, John Notman appeared in pursuit of the commission. He wrote that he would "prepare a plan or plans suitable to the expenditure and purpose; but I will expect the plan after adoption, to be carried out and I to be employed to do so, by contract or otherwise and to be paid for it, as I cannot afford to give my time on a risk or chance of adoption. If I contract for the church no charge will be made for the drawings." He offered to visit the vestry and discuss the project as he passed through Baltimore on his way home from the presidential inauguration in Washington. As yet unwilling to pay for anything, the vestry did not accept his proposition. Not until September, 1849, did it resolve to deal with Notman, and in the year that followed there ensued an exchange between Notman and the vestry which illustrates why architects required the protection of a professional association.

Notman had carefully explained that the price of working drawings would be $\frac{1}{2}$ of 1 per cent of the estimated cost of the church but that he would charge 5 per cent if he supervised the construction.[93] He asked, not unreasonably,

[92] All quotations and information concerning the building of St. Luke's are from the manuscript vestry records in the possession of the church.
[93] Notman wrote: "I will with pleasure carry out the plan if adopted, for which the established charge by good and bad architects is 5 percent on the cost, with all expenses of travel, etc. paid. I cannot be directly the contractor when every thing and every person is strange to me in Baltimore, unless to ask you a speculative price to cover all my risk. I am quite uninformed as to difference of prices of building and materials between this and Baltimore but I could readily know if your adoption of the plan renders it necessary or desirable."

that the vestry make a final decision so that he could have his plans back in order to send them to Savannah, Georgia, where his tracings had been well received. Apparently, he flatly refused to contract for the church, build it, and charge a fixed amount, a risk the vestry seemed to feel it might ask him to assume.

Having found Notman recalcitrant on the question of fees, the vestry approached him from another angle. Though it wanted his design, the vestry asked at what price Notman would furnish the plan and all specifications so that they could be executed by a local contractor. Notman was understandably annoyed. He needed the plans, the vestry had not returned them, and he was not at all sure that he wanted his church built by a local contractor. To resolve the matter, he preferred to compromise "rather than have my design carried out by mere builders who seldom preserve the spirit of the style." For 1 and ½ per cent, or $225 on a $15,000 estimate, he would part with the drawings, and he offered to reduce even that amount by a third because St. Luke's was a mission church.

Foregoing the luxury of supervision, the vestry agreed on the sum of $150, demanding full specifications as part of the bargain, a proposal which Notman refused. The fact then emerged that the vestry expected the architect to provide drawings and specifications not only for the building but for the furniture it would contain.[94] Notman was exhausted with the business. He wrote to his erstwhile clients that he was "not surprised at your now seeing that employing

---

[94] Notman said that he had not intended to let the vestry have full specifications for the price he had quoted and that all they were purchasing was the set of drawings they already had. The vestry was furious, pointing out that the drawings were useless without the specifications. In February, 1850, Notman gave in, sent the specifications, and complained wistfully that he had lost the commission for the Savannah church because of the delay. He added that, because his building was to be built by somebody else, he had had to give more specifications than would otherwise have been required. The vestry answered: "We adopted your design with the understanding that we should be favoured with all needful drawings and illustrations for placing the entire work under immediate contract for we determined that nothing should be left open for doubt or litigation." In making these comments, it added: "We have had a most unpleasant case in our state where the vestry of a church built in our city have been subjected to a suit for damages by the Contractors on the ground of failure or delay on the part of the architect to furnish in time the additional drawings, illustrations and explanations not given by him in the first instance, but promised to be sent when wanted." This undoubtedly was a reference to Robert Cary Long, Jr., and the Franklin Street Presbyterian Church.

an architect in part is not the best mode of proceeding." The vestry in its turn declared it had not been treated "with proper frankness and ingenuousness" and threatened suit. Notman did not get his money, and it is uncertain whether the drawings were ever returned.

Since the vestry found itself once again without an architect, in the summer of 1851 it decided to approach Frank Wills, only to discover that his "terms as to commissions and expenses appeared not feasible." At last Niernsee and Nielson of Baltimore was given the job. The firm agreed on a 2 and ½ per cent commission which would be raised, on paper, to 5 per cent "if the architects gave a contribution of money or materials equivalent to the additional rate." The cornerstone was laid in 1851 and services were held in 1853, though only the nave had been built and the tower had been carried only to the first stage. The church was singularly cold and drafty, and other peculiarities about it were beginning to cause some alarm.

So matters rested until 1857, when the rector of St. Luke's approached Priest, who stated that he would expect a fee of 5 per cent and travel expenses, and that if he came to Baltimore to consult on the problem but was not hired, he would ask his expenses and five dollars a day for his time. He stated flatly that 5 per cent was cheap rather than dear, for such "was the rate for new buildings and old ones were harder to manage." In February, 1857, Priest arrived and reviewed the situation in devastating terms: the plans Niernsee and Nielson had proposed, he said, would have resulted in a church "abnormal in design and grotesque in execution." The nave was too high for its width, and he recommended that at least two bays be added in an attempt to obtain better proportions. When Priest reviewed the condition of the nave to see if the heating could be improved, he found that the building was structurally inadequate and built of poor materials.[95] St. Luke's was in the end the creation

---

[95] As designed by Niernsee and Nielson, a chancel measuring 47 feet by 21 feet would have been added to the nave. The transepts, each 24 feet by 17 feet, would have been attached to the chancel. The north transept would have housed the choir, and the one on the south the Sunday school. Of this arrangement Priest said, "The addition of transepts to a chancel for parish churches is somewhat of an anomaly in architecture. Their proper place being with the nave."

Much was wrong with the structure. The roof and walls had not been properly sheathed, and at several points Priest found "a wide open area through which the cold could come in." The plaster walls had not been carried down behind the wainscoting, and the cold came

of Priest, for he corrected its proportions and converted it from a troublesome "anomaly" to an adequate ecclesiological church. After the death of Priest in 1858, the Reverend Charles W. Rankin, working with H. M. Congdon, who had been Priest's partner,[96] brought the project to its conclusion.

St. Luke's was, at the time of its completion, the largest Protestant Episcopal church in Baltimore and the most complex in plan (Figs. VI–46 and VI–47). It was also the richest in stained glass. The great window over the altar (Fig. VI–48) was made by Wailes of Newcastle, and it is said, perhaps incorrectly, to have been designed by William Butterfield.[97] All but two of the aisle windows and the north transept window came from Gibbs of London and were by Butterfield.[98] The westernmost window in the south aisle is by Gibbs, and it is dedicated "to J. W. Priest, the architect who constructed the chancel of this church."

But St. Luke's had been so long in building that by the time it was completed the stylistic enthusiasm of which it was an expression had begun to wane. Though it represented well the ecclesiological dicta, it was a composite work by several architects and had little of the vigor, freshness, or power possessed by St. Mark's, Philadelphia, to which it was comparable in style and elegance. Nor did it have the accuracy, authority, and charm of St. James the Less. St. Luke's is important, however, because of its association with Priest.

---

in along the walls. The doors were not properly fitted, and Priest advised that they, as well as the ventilators in the windows, be replaced. The timbers supporting the floor were of inferior quality and required immediate attention, for they had been inserted in the walls with no protection against the damp and were rotted.

[96] Congdon received a bachelor's degree from Columbia College in 1854 and immediately began to work with Priest in Newburgh, New York. He practiced architecture until his death in 1922. Mr. Herbert Wheaton Congdon, who kindly supplied information about his father, says that his grandfather, a merchant, was much interested in ecclesiology and gave H. M. Congdon a number of books on the subject. The architectural practice of the Congdons was large and "stretched from Maine to Idaho and as far south as Baltimore." There are a number of churches in Connecticut by the firm of H. M. Congdon. That at Ansonia is a good example of his work. The Reverend Mr. Rankin had long been in touch with the New York Ecclesiological Society. In 1851 he obtained an altar service through the Society for St. Peter's, Morristown, New Jersey, where he was rector.

[97] The window arrived in Baltimore during the Civil War and remained in storage until the end of hostilities. It was finally installed after a long argument over the payment of tariff on it.

[98] The two windows not by Gibbs are German. The windows in the south chapel are by Bolton of New York.

Figure VI-46. St. Luke's, Carey Street, Baltimore. Niernsee and Nielson and J. W. Priest. 1847–57.

SOME BUILDINGS AND ARCHITECTS

Figure VI-47. St. Luke's, Baltimore. Interior by J. W. Priest.

Figure VI-48. St. Luke's, Baltimore. East window.

St. Mark's Church, West Orange, New Jersey (Figs. VI–49 and VI–50), represents the beginning and the end of the ecclesiological style in the United States. The Reverend W. R. Whittingham was rector from 1827 to 1830, the years in which the church was begun and consecrated,[99] yet the tower, spire, and interior of the nave and chancel must have been rebuilt later, when the English influence was at its height. The assurance and competence of the design suggest that it was Notman, Priest, or Upjohn who completed the building Whittingham had begun; there is no trace of Wills in it. Though anonymous, St. Mark's is poised and dignified, typical of the Protestant Episcopal churches of its generation and its style, and the connections between it and the early years of the career of Whittingham enrich its significance. But St. Mark's can also be seen as the end of the parish church Gothic revival. The style was to continue, but the capacity to excite and educate had passed. The Romanesque and Italianate manners the ecclesiologists so much disliked and feared had arrived.

When St. Paul's Church in Baltimore was severely damaged by fire in 1854, Upjohn was commissioned to build a new church, using in his construction such elements of the earlier building as proved sound. He was at work on St. Paul's from 1852 to 1856.[100] The earlier church had been neoclassical; Upjohn's was Italian Romanesque.[101] St. Paul's (Figs. VI–51 and VI–52) is subtle and refined. Though the loggia may have been a device carried over from the earlier building, it emerges in a fresh context in Upjohn's façade, which recedes comfortably at street level. Unfortunately, the tower was never built,[102] for it was a beautiful and balanced design, kindred to, but not copied from, those of Roman churches. Upjohn suppressed the horizontal courses of his models, emphasized the thickened walls of the corners, and so stressed vertical movement. The interior, though almost ponderous, escapes it; the mass of the arcades with their coffered arches is qualified by the presence of two clerestory windows and two aisle windows for each bay.

[99] The Historical Records Survey, *Inventory of the Church Archives of New Jersey*, p. 319.
[100] Upjohn, *Richard Upjohn*, p. 198.
[101] Meeks, "Romanesque Before Richardson in the United States," gives a general review of the first manifestations of the vogue for Romanesque.
[102] See Howland and Spencer, *The Architecture of Baltimore*, p. 135, for an illustration of the tower.

Figure VI-49. St. Mark's, West Orange, N.J.

SOME BUILDINGS AND ARCHITECTS

Figure VI-50. St. Mark's, West Orange.

Figure VI-51. St. Paul's, Baltimore. Richard Upjohn. 1856.

SOME BUILDINGS AND ARCHITECTS

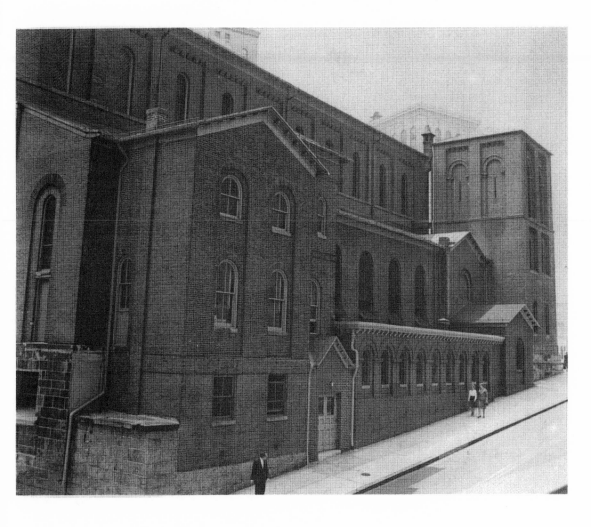

Figure VI-52. St. Paul's, Baltimore.

THE GOTHIC REVIVAL AND AMERICAN CHURCH ARCHITECTURE

After the informality and decorative diffuseness of the Gothic revival, St. Paul's seems dramatic, diagrammatic, and bold. The flat walls, blind recesses, sharp-edged shadows, and declarative masses of Romanesque composed façades assertive enough to survive in the increasingly dense American urban scene. By the mid-nineteenth century cities had begun to achieve a style of their own, but it was one in which the parish church in its churchyard was not at home. In 1850 James Fenimore Cooper observed with pleasure that in New York "whole squares may now be seen in which the eye rests with satisfaction on blinds, facings, and bricks, all brought to the same pleasing sober architectural tint," and he praised "the chaste simplicity" of the new streets.[103] It was these vistas which called for Romanesque to assume the place Gothic had earlier held as a reigning and revolutionary ecclesiastical style. But the revival did not disappear; it merely took second place, retreating to the smaller towns, where it continued to flourish. Behind it lay a decade in which the stringent standards of the ecclesiologists and the ideas of English theorists had stimulated American architecture to move out of provincialism into independence.

[103] *The Ways of the Hour* (New York and London: Cooperative Publication Society, n.d.), p. 10.

VII

Contributions of the Parish Church Revival

Because of Protestant Episcopal requirements and preferences, the Gothic revival found widespread and refined expression in North America, taking the form there of the acceptance of the English parish church style. The history of how, when, and where acceptance of this pattern took place provides tangible evidence of the depth and breadth of the contacts which existed in the mid-nineteenth century between American clergy and laymen and a group typical of the intellectual and artistic leadership of early Victorian England. Though the high feelings that characterized preoccupation with ceremonial and architectural matters in the nineteenth century seem somewhat incomprehensible today, they were, in their time, symptomatic of significant currents in and outside of the Church. In England and abroad the revival was a result of the High Church inclinations and convictions which were, in their turn, manifestations of the historical orientation of late romanticism.

The speed with which, after its initial appearance in England, the new church style arrived in the United States and the ease with which it established itself here did not mean that North American churchmen and architects were prepared to follow any and every English whim in matters of taste. They were aware of the historical arguments which supported the choice of the parish church as a model; they understood the abstract, rationalist architectural theories which accompanied reconsideration of medieval building. But, as the policies of the *New York Ecclesiologist* showed, when Americans weighed the historical argument which required an accurate revival against the architectural theory which contradicted it, it was the former which they found wanting.

Buildings were, therefore, but one of the achievements of the American revival: it intensified contact between American architects and laymen and English authorities and ideas; it brought latent American talents to maturity earlier than would have been possible without the stimulation afforded by the encounter with English doctrine and doctrinaires; it provided buildings and theoretical arguments which challenged and eventually ended the authority of the Classical revivals; it stimulated Americans to think for themselves; and it played a part in the creation of a new view of the profession of architecture.

Evidence of the presence and power of the parish church revival may be found in the comments upon it made by men as important as A. J. Downing. Until 1848 Downing had said nothing about church design. His discussions in his books and in *The Horticulturist* were confined to domestic architecture, and they included illustrations of houses and suggestions to those about to design or build one. However, in March, 1848, as the New York Ecclesiological Society was being organized, Downing published a picture of "an English country church" from the *Illustrated London News*.[1] He praised its style, materials, and proportions. Downing's intention was constructive, for he had resolved to do what he could to remedy an error in American taste. He had observed that "church architecture in our cities has been improved in the last ten years" and that New York and Brooklyn had acquired several in "a noble and pure style," but he was forced to report that "rural churches were sadly behind in taste and meritorious design." Those in the middle and eastern states were "heavy, rectangular wooden buildings, either ill proportioned and un-meaning, or crowned with steeples or towers, exhibiting the oddest possible combinations of architectural orders." As an authority on landscape, he also asserted that "there is nothing built by man's hands, which, if properly de-

---

[1] "Domestic notices. Design for a Rural Church," *The Horticulturist*, 2 (March, 1848):433.

signed, and properly kept, confers so much of dignity, poetry, and interest on a rural landscape, as a beautiful country church, —of sober, quiet color—embosomed in trees, and speaking volumes at a glance, of the religious feelings, the peaceful and refined habits of the inhabitants around it." Though Downing had decided that churches should be Gothic—"all its associations, all its history, belong so much more truly to the Christian faith"—he was certain that rural churches should never be diminutive versions of those suitable for cities. If rural churches were constructed of stone, which was permanent, they would, when covered with ivy, subside into quiet partnership "with the verdure and freshness of the whole country around." The English parish church provided "simplicity, greatness and truthfulness" at modest cost. Downing had specific examples in mind. "Three or four . . . in this simple Gothic mode," he said, had been built on the Hudson River and in Massachusetts between 1846 and 1848.[2] He had joined the parish church revival.

More than a year elapsed before Downing again discussed ecclesiastical architecture. When he did, he praised the Church of the Holy Communion, New York City, using the same arguments as in his earlier article.[3] *The Horticulturist* finally carried its first major comment on "country churches" in January, 1851. It left no doubt as to Downing's position. Though the architecture of the village church could establish the tone of the entire community, American churches were "the ugliest . . . in christendom," for their "bareness and baldness" expressed only the "hatred which originally existed in the minds of Puritan ancestors, against everything that belonged to the Romish Church, including in one general sweep all beauty and all taste."[4] Nor was Downing at all satisfied with the churches in the Greek temple form which had begun to displace the earlier, native manner. He advocated Gothic and described it as founded upon "upward lines . . . no weight of long cornices, or flat ceilings, can keep it down; upward, higher and higher, it soars, lifting everything, even heavy ponderous stones, poising them in the air in vaulted ceilings, or piling them upwards toward Heaven, in spires, and steeples, and towers." The unpretentious "right proportions, forms, outlines" of Gothic country churches would convey "true expression." Downing's commitment to English Gothic and the

---

[2] *Ibid.,* p. 434.
[3] "A Short Chapter on Country Churches," *ibid.,* 6 (January, 1851):9–12.
[4] *Ibid.,* p. 10.

parish church had come a decade later than his decision on domestic design, but it conformed to the pattern his thinking had assumed. The churches he preferred possessed aesthetic values close to those of his "cottage" style.

Downing was neither an original thinker nor a revolutionary. He said that he did not demand an "American style of architecture," that he was prepared to watch and wait until the nation produced "for itself a great national type in character, manners and art." He perfectly understood that exotic follies were part of a healthy "fermentation that shows clearly there is no apathy in the public mind."[5] He recognized that though it was foreign the English church satisfied certain American requirements.

Throughout his career Downing chose to follow only a selected group of English theorists. He had at first admired Loudon's imaginative and rational ideas. After travel in England in 1850 and 1851 he became fond of *The Builder*, from which he reprinted in *The Horticulturist* a series of long essays.[6] His choice was neither accidental nor casual; Downing endorsed the policy of the journal and agreed with the author of the essays.

While accepting the historical styles as suitable for some modern purposes, the writer, whom *The Builder* designated only as "S. H.," said that the architect need not "fetter his genius to the particular mode or style of any age or country past or present." Beauty did not reside solely in any "distant style." One should always remember that style was "the servant—an useful one—of architecture, but not its master." He could conceive of buildings which would be "real works of art" though they resembled no earlier style. Their design would be dictated only by use, climate, and situation.[7] Opinions such as these demolished the more authoritarian arguments which had been used in support of accurate Gothic revivalism.

Acquaintance with the parish church revival played a part in the development of Downing's ideas. By 1848 he had perceived that eclecticism in church architecture expressed an association between form and use. The essays in *The Builder* a few months later suggested that eclecticism was not the only way to

---

[5] "A Few Words on our Progress in Building," *ibid.* (June, 1851):251.
[6] "S. H.," "The Essence of the Fine Arts," *ibid.* (January, 1851):23–29; "On Expression in Architecture," *ibid.* (September, 1851):421–24; "The Beautiful in Art," *ibid.* (October, 1851):463–68; "Expression in Architecture," *ibid.* (December, 1851):562–67.
[7] "On Expression in Architecture," p. 424.

unite these two essentials. Downing had accepted this suggestion by the time that his career was cut short by death in 1852.

In American mid-nineteenth-century architectural commentary a desire to bring landscape and buildings together appears repeatedly. Though they resembled the English literature on landscape gardening, these American theories were original, indigenous, and respectful of the unplanned countryside in which the nation abounded. With or without the ecclesiologists, Americans who had traveled and knew England would have utilized the potentialities of the smaller English medieval church. Frederick Law Olmsted had perceived its place in rural England, through which he traveled in 1850 and 1851.[8] Downing emphasized the way English churches graced rather than dominated the landscape in which they were set. Enthusiasm for the revival thus came, for Downing and other Americans, from two sources. They were intrigued by and understood the historical justifications of Gothic as Christian in its forms and origins, and they liked the village churches because they were good, modest buildings which fitted organically into their settings.

In England, and later in the United States, ecclesiology encouraged acceptance of a new image of the practice of architecture. Barrington Kaye has pointed out that, though the Gothic revival appeared to offer "a return to art in architecture; an opportunity for imagination and fancy to be allowed to express themselves,"[9] it in fact gave the client unusual authority. The ecclesiologists certainly attempted to dictate matters of design; their criticisms of church buildings, such as those that appeared in the *Ecclesiologist* and the *New York Ecclesiologist*, restricted architects, limited their freedom to develop, and encircled them with dos and don'ts. Architects who departed from ecclesiological rules exposed themselves to public criticism and charges of ineptitude. Such gratuitous invasion of the autonomy of the artist was undoubtedly alarming. In their attempts to control the taste of client and architect, however, the ecclesiologists discussed ways in which the practice of architecture could and should

[8] *Walks and Talks of an American Farmer in England* (Columbus, O.: Jos. H. Riley and Company, 1859), pp. 310–11.
[9] *The Development of the Architectural Profession in Britain* (London: Allen and Unwin, 1960), pp. 83–87.

be reformed. Though they were sometimes tyrannical, their conclusions on such matters were, more often than not, favorable to the architect. When the *Ecclesiologist* attacked impediments to what it felt to be ethical architectural practice and responsible design, it entered an argument already in progress and increased the pressure for necessary reforms.

In 1836, in the first edition of *Contrasts*, Pugin included a plate critical of the practice of architecture, which he irreverently dedicated to "The Trade."[10] The training of architects was, he said, inadequate. An impoverished public taste received exactly what it deserved from a debased profession. Bad building was the order of the day. Competitions further corrupted an already sordid situation. Like others, Pugin was dismayed by the competition for the new Houses of Parliament. The Institute of British Architects, which had been founded in 1836, and the many pamphleteers who also attacked the Houses of Parliament competition were essentially in agreement with each of Pugin's points.

When the ecclesiologists sallied forth in March, 1842, to fight the competition system, reform architectural practice, and defend the integrity of the architect,[11] they were entering the fray rather late. In an age, said the *Ecclesiologist*, of "shares and tenders and contracts and companies and committees," a system as bad as competitions was to be expected. "But whatever may be the merits of this fashion generally, yet, when applied to churches, either new or old, it becomes so dangerous and mischievous, that it is a matter of high importance to show some reasons for rejecting it, and to recommend some less objectionable plan for adoption."[12] As the ecclesiologists contrasted past and present, they inevitably idealized the medieval method of choosing an architect, a process which they described as "an indenture, beginning most probably, '*In honorem DEI et Beati M—*' (the Patron Saint), set forth how Master Will. Horwood, freemason, undertook to build for the founder or founders a fair church, upon such and such conditions. He was not the preferred competitor, but the selected architect."[13]

---

[10] The plate was prepared for the 1836 edition and was included in the edition of the book which appeared in 1841.
[11] "On Competition Amongst Architects," *E.*, 1 (March, 1842):65–67, and 1 (April, 1842): 81–83.
[12] *Ibid.*, p. 65.
[13] *Ibid.*, p. 66.

CONTRIBUTIONS OF THE PARISH CHURCH REVIVAL

After an amusing, depreciatory account of the ill-informed nineteenth-century committees and the equally ill-informed architects who served them, the *Ecclesiologist* declared, "We may well regret the loss of free-masonry, and much more the absence of authority which could alone confer on the strictly worthy permission to exercise this noble art. At present there is nothing to hinder the most ignorant pretender from applying his unhallowed hands to so sacred a thing as church-building. Fresh from his mechanic's Institute, his Railroad Station, his Socialist Hall, he has the presumption and arrogance to attempt a church."[14] There was only one correct way to restore a medieval church, they said, and competitions could only compromise the result, cut prices, and tailor the work to the taste of a committee unsuited to make such a decision. In the case of new churches the results of commercialization could be even worse. "See the design, the melancholy first fruit perhaps of some beginner in church-building, at length laboriously though incongruously completed. It will be sent in at once to scores of competitions; and it would be hard if at some time, in some place or other, it were not selected."[15] The ecclesiologists called upon the profession to "dismiss every mercenary or selfish thought, be content to labour as in GOD's service without care for your personal fame, without thought of your personal sacrifices: strive in some degree to emulate your predecessors, whose names are perhaps now lost to memory, though their works—works of faith—remain in unapproachable excellence and in imperishable glory."

This discussion, which appeared in two lengthy parts, raised questions essential to a new concept of the profession which was developing, for the creation of an idealized image of the medieval architect was as much a part of the Gothic revival as the rebuilding of old churches and the design of new ones. Pugin had celebrated both the builder and the patron on the title page of *Contrasts*, where he illustrated Alex de Berneval and Erwin of Steinbach, each holding an architectural drawing and the instruments of his art.[16] The word

---

[14] *Ibid.*

[15] *Ibid.*, p. 82.

[16] This title page appeared in both editions of the book. In September, 1845, the *Ecclesiologist* printed an article from "A Correspondent." It resembles Pugin's wittier discussions and may well have been by him, for it included references to his favorite medieval architects and patrons of architecture, Wykeham, Wayneflete, Beckington, and Skirlaugh. The

"*cementarius*" appeared above them. In the central area between them William of Wykeham appeared studying architectural drawings as clerical attendants looked on. Other plates of *Contrasts*, which compared late medieval and modern buildings, developed the message implicit in the title page. Several years before the publication of *Contrasts*, however, Kenelm Digby had discussed medieval church building, designers, and donors in his protracted eulogy of the Middle Ages entitled *Mores Catholici*. He had quoted Vincent of Beauvais, who attributed the beauty of Gothic to "symmetry, proportion, and harmony of members, to disposition and to collocation, and elegance of composition, to invention and tempering of parts with regard to the effect of the whole, that the edifice may have solidity, usefulness, and beauty," and Digby added that "to an architect both nature, and learning and practice are essential."[17] The popularity of this Utopian image of the medieval builder had perhaps begun with Goethe's account of Erwin of Steinbach in *On German Architecture*.

Other scholarly studies which appeared in the 1830's and 1840's outside the immediate circle of the Catholic and Protestant Gothic revival also enriched the architect's view of the history of his art and deepened his belief in the nobility of its antecedents. In 1846 C. R. Cockerell read a paper entitled "The Architectural Works of William of Wykeham," which the *Ecclesiologist* approved: "Next to the investigation of the details and history of some great pile,

---

article began with the assertion that architecture was a trade, not an art, and described nineteenth-century practice:

This, called the design of the great and celebrated Mr.—, is despatched by railway to its destination, is much and ignorantly admired, and forthwith advertised to be contracted for; the drawings, to begin their lives well, lie probably at the principal hotel in the neighborhood. The tenders arrive, and that of the great Mr. Smith, the Unitarian builder, being fifteen pounds under any other, is selected. The foundation stone is laid; a band, perhaps that of the nearest regiment, is hired to preside and play some favorite air, sacred or not as the case may be. The architect arrives by the express train from town just in time, and takes his first view of the site for the new church; the service proceeds, and at its close a feeling address is made by the gentleman who condescends to use the trowel for the occasion, and after but few and irregular prayers, and still less of that reverence and form which should characterize so very important a ceremony, the committee and their friends adjourn to the discussion of a very *recherché déjeuner à la fourchette*.

[17] 11 vols., Am. ed. (New York: O'Shea, 1888–94), 3:404. Digby (1800–1880) received his bachelor's degree from Trinity College in 1819. His most important books were *Broadstone of Honour*, which appeared in three editions (1822, 1823, 1826–29), and *Mores Catholici*, the volumes of which were published at the rate of one each year through the 1830's. The third volume, which appeared in 1831, contained a long chapter on Gothic architecture.

such as the Middle Ages have handed down to us, and indeed often of equal value with it, is a concise description of the life and works of a great architect who had a hand in effecting one of these changes in style which have been turning points in the history of the arts."[18]

It would, of course, be inaccurate to attribute an all-powerful influence to the Gothic revival and the portrait of medieval life and the medieval architect which it fostered. Changes in class structure and economic reorganization were responsible for the problems which harassed the architectural profession and encouraged the discovery of the solutions which were ultimately found. Any picture of nineteenth-century architecture is, however, unbalanced, if it does not include the ethical and moral obligations which the Gothic revival placed upon architecture and its practitioners, for the revival was a major force pressing for change. To an age which admired engineering genius, growing comprehension of the complexities and structural brilliance of medieval buildings suggested that the men who constructed them must have had unique gifts. Through the critical years of the Gothic revival and even after it, the medieval builder remained a figure with whom architects identified themselves. The environment in which he worked, the patronage upon which he depended, the liberty from economic restrictions he seemed to have had, all contrasted with their own daily experience and provided an ideal which, though unattainable, was a constant challenge. Even as late as the 1890's, when the professionalization which had earlier been so ardently sought seemed to be discouraging rather than encouraging the free exercise of talent, complaints about the situation were phrased in terms to which the ecclesiologists and Pugin would have been sympathetic. "Any man whose calling it is to design buildings and carry them out," said R. N. Shaw and T. G. Jackson in 1892, "is an architect, a master-builder, an artist, and he owes it to Society to do it well and beautifully...."[19]

In the 1840's and 1850's there were within the Gothic revival as many or more amateur experts like Neale and Webb as there were architects. The power of these outsiders was, however, short-lived, and was restricted to the years of accurate revivalism and church restoration. The "autonomy" of the

---

[18] "Mr. Cockerell on William of Wykeham," *E.*, 6 (July, 1846):221–26.
[19] *Architecture as a Profession or an Art* (London: Murray, 1892), pp. 226–28.

architect, which Barrington Kaye has defined as "the possibility of disagreement between architect and client on matters of style and design," was limited as long as precise reproduction of Gothic was sought and required. Anyone who was sufficiently knowledgeable about the history of architecture could say whether or not a building was "correct." When architectural taste came to accept improvisation upon Gothic themes and principles, "autonomy" returned to the artist. Nowhere is this clearer than in the work of William Butterfield, whose career began in the reign of historical accuracy and matured in an atmosphere in which his personal, greatly admired, and much-sought-after style, which Sir John Summerson has called "fauvism,"[20] could flourish.

In the United States these English ideas and ideals about the responsibility of the architect and the social obligations it entailed found a welcome. In the 1840's and 1850's architecture was only beginning to establish itself as a profession in the modern sense. There were few more ingenuous declarations of the new attitude than that made by Frank Wills in *Ancient English Ecclesiastical Architecture*:

Now Architecture is a godlike art; it is a creative one, and we should do well to take the works of nature as our models. The greatest architects have done so, and assuredly we should not be ashamed to walk in the same paths with those whose labors have immortalized their names, and though they be dead yet live forever in some lofty dome or high embattled tower. In every beautiful building, in every edifice worthy to be styled an offspring of Architecture, there is not only a countenance so to speak, whose lineaments and features are graceful, but there is a soul that beams through the whole, and which renders it as expressive of the purpose for which it is intended, as do the smiles or furrows on the human face declare the thoughts or feelings of the mind.[21]

The Institute of British Architects was organized between 1834 and 1837 and received a royal charter of incorporation. Among its aims were the establishment of rules of accreditation for architects, investigation and control of the competition system, improvement of architectural education, establishment of standard minimum fees, and regulation of professional ethics.[22] American architects were aware of its existence, and in imitation of it a first American

[20] *Heavenly Mansions*, p. 174.
[21] P. 45.
[22] See Kaye, *Architectural Profession in Britain*, chaps. 5–8, for a history of the Royal Institute of British Architects.

association, the American Institution of Architects, was founded in December, 1836. It did not survive even though its members included Alexander J. Davis, Thomas U. Walter, William Strickland, and Isaiah Rogers.[23] In the two decades that followed, as American architects began to encounter problems identical with those that had made the Institute of British Architects necessary and enlarged their understanding of English speculation about the profession, its responsibilities, its nature, and its history, the idea of an association was revived. Bitter experience had taught them to dislike the "business-like spirit of the modern profession." Notman's difficulties with the vestry of St. Luke's, Baltimore, were certainly far from unusual.

Seventeen years of successful and productive practice and a position of authority as a senior architect whose reputation had been acquired largely in the dignified atmosphere of ecclesiastical design equipped Richard Upjohn to initiate discussions on the feasibility of an American institute. By 1857 he had the support in this project of a number of younger men who had either come from abroad to work in the United States or who were Americans returned, after training abroad, to begin their professional lives at home.

On February 23, 1857, an organizational meeting was held. In addition to the Upjohns, father and son,[24] those present were Henry Dudley and J. W. Priest, who represented the ecclesiological party (Frank Wills had died a few months before the meeting); Leopold Eidlitz, aged thirty-four, educated in Prague and Vienna, who had been in the United States since 1843; Richard Morris Hunt, aged twenty-five, who had returned in 1855 from the École des Beaux Arts; Wrey Mould, aged thirty-two, English by birth and training, who had arrived in New York in 1853 after working with Owen Jones; and Henry Cleaveland, who was following in the footsteps of Downing. Other members of the group were John Welch, who had his office in Newark; Joseph C. Wells, Charles Babcock, and F. A. Peterson were established in New York City. The thirteenth member, Edward Gardiner, is difficult to identify; by 1859 his name no longer appeared on the membership roll.

Peterson asked pertinent questions about the purposes of an institute and

---

[23] The "Proceedings of the American Institute of Architects" from 1857 to 1871 and other manuscript and printed materials in the library of the Institute in Washington are the principal source for this discussion. Upjohn, *Richard Upjohn*, also contains a chapter on the history of the Institute and the role of Upjohn in its foundation.

[24] Upjohn, *Richard Upjohn*, p. 159.

warned the founders to be careful, for there were "many who exercise our profession" and jealousy might result were their capacities in any way impugned. His suggestion that all architects in New York be informed of the plans which were afoot received a cool response from Wells, who felt it was not advisable to bring into the association "all who styled themselves architects."[25] Mould reassured everyone that the foundation of an institute would give the profession status in the American community; such had been the result with similar organizations in Europe. Acting on a motion by Hunt, the meeting decided to extend membership invitations to eleven men, of whom John Notman was one. Thomas U. Walter, A. J. Davis, and Calvert Vaux were others. Vaux, who was of the same generation as Mould, Eidlitz, and Hunt, had recently emigrated from England; he had been associated with Downing in the last months of the latter's life. When a full list of members, of which there were thirty-seven, was published in 1859, it included other "young lions": Arthur Gilman of Boston; James Renwick, Jr., of New York; T. A. Tefft of Providence, who was thirty-three and already near the end of his short but significant career; Henry Van Brunt, twenty-seven, fresh out of Harvard and at the beginning of his; Frederick C. Withers, another Englishman, trained by T. H. Wyatt and working with Calvert Vaux; Edward C. Cabot of Boston, at forty-one somewhat older than the others, who had come late to architecture; and Detlif Lienau, forty-one, a Paris-trained Dane. Priest properly belongs with this group for he was only thirty-four at the time of his death, which occurred five months after the appearance of this list of members.

The Institute, then, was founded by both senior members of the profession and new men who were alert to European ideas. Conspicuously absent from it were architects such as Mettam and Burke, whose Historical Society Building in New York the Institute reviewed ferociously in *The Crayon*. Among other unpleasantries, the review said that "even with an abundant allowance for human imperfections, we could not connect it with any acknowledged style of architectural art without doing violence to the style, if not to the building." The Institute added, in discussing the design of the front, that it supposed its three parts represented "*fact, fancy* and *fiction*, fact and fancy on each side, and fiction in the centre."[26]

---

[25] From "Proceedings of the American Institute of Architects."
[26] "The Historical Society Building," *The Crayon*, 5 (March, 1858) :79–80.

Two subjects preoccupied the Institute in its early years. The first was the nature of the profession, establishment of its standards, regulation of education and behavior, and the pros and cons of the competition system.[27] The members resolved to offer membership to persons "distinguished in different branches of the Arts related to architecture, such as Decoration, Landscape Gardening and the like."[28] A constitution was prepared. Richard Upjohn defined the nature of the problems arising in the practice of architecture.[29] He raised the question of the ownership of drawings, and the members decided that "drawings are but the instruments of service, and therefore belonged to the architect, unless otherwise specially provided."[30] C. Babcock said that "there was no reason why architecture should not be esteemed by the side of divinity, medicine and law" and that, regrettably, the public still recognized "as qualified members of the profession any full grown boys or aspiring carpenters, who hang out their signs and proclaim themselves architects."[31]

The Institute also proposed to encourage the further education of its members and to offer them the opportunity for intellectual companionship. A committee was established to arrange for the presentation of papers by members and illustrious outsiders who would be invited to participate. Since these discussions, which appeared as articles entitled "Architecture" in *The Crayon*, reflect the quality, character, insight, and interests of the participants, they will serve as fair representatives of the ideas of the leaders of the architectural profession in America at the end of the 1850's.

Calvert Vaux led off with a lively account of the design of city houses and apartments in Europe. He compared land values and street patterns in Edinburgh and on the Continent with those in New York and observed, in passing, that Americans would never tolerate the Scottish system of renting the top floors of high buildings to "the lower class of tenants."[32] R. G. Hatfield read a paper on the problems of construction for weight-bearing,[33] a subject prompted by the recent collapse of at least three buildings in New York and several others elsewhere in the United States. Reviews of recent buildings, including a lauda-

[27] See "American Institute of Architects," *ibid.*, 4 (November, 1857):339.
[28] *Ibid.*
[29] "Architecture," *ibid.* (May, 1857):151, and (June, 1857):182–83.
[30] "Architecture," *ibid.*, 6 (May, 1859):182.
[31] "Architecture," *ibid.*, 4 (December, 1857):371.
[32] *Ibid.* (July, 1857):218.
[33] *Ibid.* (December, 1857):371–72.

tory description of the Church of All Souls by Wrey Mould,[34] less enthusiastic comments on Dr. Spring's church by the firm of Thomas and Son,[35] an amusing account of a journey to study Eidlitz's St. George's Church by moonlight, and a description of Bowen and McNamee's Store, by J. C. Wells, filled out the presentations of the newly organized group. Simultaneously, stimulated by the accounts of the activities of the Institute, which it published on a regular basis, *The Crayon* enlarged its own coverage of architectural matters. It described the terms of the competition announced by the Peabody Institute in Baltimore and condemned the Peabody trustees for their decision to award prizes while at the same time stipulating that "they will not be obligated to employ the party to carry on the work whose design may be the most acceptable."[36] In the interests of painting and criticism, as well as architecture, it printed a thoroughly angry statement on Ruskin. He was, *The Crayon* said, "a man with a meaning, confident of his cause, and devoted to it with all his faculty"; he had "reduced architecture to its elements, and written the first modern book on building which contains a principle"; but he was also full of "paradox," "dogmatism," "cant," and "inconsistency" and was underendowed with "largeness of nature." It warned its young readers to distrust Ruskin's "statements and estimates" while accepting his principles "as approximations and hints, not laws."[37]

The papers read before the Institute of Architects in 1858 and 1859 illustrate how sophisticated American ideas about architecture had become in the eighteen years since Doane and his friends had visited Leeds and the churches of England in 1841. They also show which European theorists and theories had contributed most to American attitudes. The doctrine of the ecclesiologists had been left far behind by the younger generation of American architects; they had learned its lessons and passed on to the generalizations and "principles" the ecclesiologists had been too timid and too dedicated to history to consider.

Over and over again Eidlitz, Lienau, Van Brunt, and Hunt emphasized several major ideas in their lectures and in remarks upon the papers of others.

[34] *Ibid.*, 5 (January, 1858):20–22.
[35] *Ibid.*, p. 22.
[36] *Ibid.*, 4 (August, 1857):249.
[37] J. G. Brownlee Brown, "John Ruskin," *The Crayon*, 4 (November, 1857):329–36.

There was general agreement with Eidlitz when he deplored a historical approach to architecture in which "limited periods of its progress in time, as well as in space, have been selected for artistic disquisition,"[38] and all hoped that this approach would soon be replaced by a system of thought which would begin its consideration of the historical styles with a definition of "style in architectural art" as "the characteristic and peculiar mode of representing and expressing in the organism of a structure, the idea which has given rise to its erection, assisted at all times by a certain degree of progress in the science of construction."[39] The membership deplored the fact that "architects study styles instead of architecture" and that when they encountered "a style which requires much application to become properly initiated in it," they avoided it and turned instead to "another which gives them more license."[40] The members were agreed that mastery of "the history of architecture as a whole" and study of "the rules of aesthetics, which are as immutable as the laws of nature"[41] must form the foundation for future action and architectural education.

The defense of Gothic which prevailed in the 1840's was made obsolete by arguments such as these: clearly, it was to Pugin, the ecclesiologists, and Ruskin that Eidlitz referred when he said that "prejudice has acted injuriously upon the progress of architecture by forcing a rigid adherence to pre-conceived notions—in spite of the progress of ideas in the abstract—from devotion to time-honored usages and aversion to innovation. This, however, though a prejudice, has the redeeming quality of being an honest prejudice."[42] At the same time, it was to medieval building and the architecture of the Greeks, both of which had been burdened with "honest prejudice," that these young critics turned for inspiration and documentation of their ideas.[43] They were not opposed to the styles themselves, but rather to the use that had been made of them. They sought "the rules of aesthetics," for they had left behind not Pugin's principles but his Roman Catholic dogmatism. They were not opposed to the parish church revival as such, but they were opposed to ecclesiology.

[38] "Architecture," *The Crayon*, 5 (May, 1858):141.
[39] *Ibid.*, p. 139.
[40] *Ibid.*, p. 142.
[41] *Ibid.*
[42] *Ibid.*, p. 140.
[43] See *ibid.*, p. 141, and articles entitled "Architecture" for February, 1858, pp. 53–54; June, 1858, pp. 168–69; July, 1858, pp. 199–200; and November, 1858, p. 320.

They proposed to see Gothic as "that style of architecture which teaches construction adapted to purpose and organization, with ornamentation to express the construction." They were able to appreciate Greek and medieval building because "all three great art worlds, Grecian, Medieval Revival of Art, and Modern, have one great common centre from which they proceed, and around which they revolve. That centre is the love of truth. All art chaos has also its single centre, which is love of effect."

The possibilities of this kind of thinking did not attain full statement until December 7, 1858, when Henry Van Brunt presented a paper entitled "Cast Iron in Decorative Architecture,"[44] in which he described an architecture based on the principles and "rules of aesthetics" that the Gothic revival had helped to uncover. He did not propose, however, to resurrect the historical affiliations which had accompanied the revival. Van Brunt was twenty-six when he prepared his lecture. He had read Ruskin. *The Discourses on Architecture*, by Viollet le Duc, which he was to translate, had not yet been published.[45]

At the outset Van Brunt announced that he was willing to be instructed by history but not to copy past discoveries, for "the purest eras of architecture have been those in which building material has been used with the most honest regard for its nature, attributes and capacities" and "decline of every pure style" had come with "the improper uses of the constructive means." Thirteenth-century Gothic was beautiful because in it man and nature were in balance; neither the materials nor the builder predominated; it was "a perfect stone architecture. There is nothing in it which makes us forget the quarry." Decadence overwhelmed Gothic only when "the stone was taught to forget its native frown of power, its preadamite sternness, and was made to smile and flutter under the chisel." He found "misapplied skill" fascinating but fatal. Man and nature lived in constant collaboration, and architecture, of all the arts, must give visual form to the products of this union. Reproduction of the styles of the past had nothing to do with the present:

[44] *The Crayon*, 6 (January, 1859):15–20. This paper by Van Brunt elicited a long response from Eidlitz, to which Van Brunt in turn replied.
[45] The connections between Henry Van Brunt and Viollet le Duc were examined by Professor John Jacobus at the 1954 Frick Symposium in New York (see *Eugène Viollet le Duc, 1814–1879* [Paris: Caisse Nationale des Monuments Historiques, 1965], pp. 231–32). In 1859 Van Brunt could have read Viollet le Duc's *Dictionnaire raisonné de l'Architecture* (vol. 1 was published in 1854, vol. 2 in 1856, and vol. 3 in 1857).

CONTRIBUTIONS OF THE PARISH CHURCH REVIVAL

Architects become antiquaries when they feed exclusively upon the past, and are content to reproduce archaeological curiosities and copy shapes, however beautiful, of a fossil art, without reanimating them with the breath and spirit of the present. And when, through this respect and love for old things and old ways of doing them, the powers of architectural invention are suffered to lie dormant, amid intense intellectual activity as regards the arts of utility, the result is necessarily that architecture exists merely as a cold respectful reminiscence, a lifeless system of imitation and eclecticism.[46]

Van Brunt's disavowal of eclecticism and his insistence that the history of architecture could assist one to understand the present are typical of the second generation of nineteenth-century architectural theorists to which he belonged. When he said, "It becomes *us* then to look around us, and to ask ourselves with special solicitude if in our architectural works we are expressing the character of the age in which we live. Are we properly expressing our high and peculiar prerogatives of monumentalists? Is ours a *representative architecture?*" he was asking the question Fergusson and Lord Lindsay had raised in the late 1840's. The nineteenth century was, said Van Brunt, unlike what had come before it. New building materials and techniques were available to satisfy requirements and functions which had not previously existed. It was "an *iron age*—for no other material is so omnipresent in all the arts of utility." Though "men have a right to expect new expressions from esthetics, as fast as they get new revelations from the sciences," he was dismayed that "architecture, sitting haughtily on her acropolis," had failed to make "an honest system of architecture out of a material which is found so invaluable in the gravest exigencies of construction." If the nineteenth century was, as some critics had derisively called it "a cast iron age," then, said Van Brunt, let there be "a cast iron architecture to express it."

Van Brunt felt that though Ruskin's statements on the nobility and beauty of "perpetually varied ornamentation" were applicable to an age of handicraft and were sound observations on the art of the Middle Ages, they did nothing to assist the nineteenth century, which was an age of "aggregates" rather than "individualities." Machines had replaced the labor of men: "we have mechanics now, not handicraftsmen, who work not so much out of devotion to any

---

[46] "Cast Iron in Decorative Architecture," p. 15.

craft, as for the homely necessities of life. Labor now is the means and not the end of life."

Van Brunt disavowed all allegiance to Gothic revivalism. The idea of the "Liberty of the Workman," he said, would be as out of place in the nineteenth century as feudalism, were it revived:

However lovely it may be with all its poetic and romantic association in cathedral architecture, it is of another age, and we cannot and should not hope to revive it. When from amid the great bustle and activity of our times, we look back upon the Gothic age, and contemplate its serenity and statuesque repose, its deliberate and dreamy thoughtfulness, as it were, in all those matters of science and art embodied in architecture; when we behold how slightly time and labor were considered in questions of high art, how years passed by as days, and all effort was patient, simple, earnest and slow, we at once comprehend the secret of the success of Gothic art. Yet may not our own spirit, though apparently prosaic and leaning too much toward mere utilities, though rejoicing in clamor and hurry, may it not have its own peculiar high capacities for artistic expression?[47]

Henry Van Brunt, born in 1832, and William Morris, born in 1834, stood as far apart in 1859 as had Priest and the editors of the *Ecclesiologist* in 1849.

A declaration of independence from the ideas of his forebears and contemporaries was not enough for Van Brunt; he went on to describe the architecture of the new age. It would be one of "strict unities and formal repetitions . . . the pure architectural expression of fitness for its peculiar purposes," and "the principle of monotony, usually so repugnant to stone architecture, may under those more favorable circumstances be elevated to a beauty and an honor." His speculation on the use of iron is even more interesting. Aware that it should not be cast into units that resembled masonry, he proposed a system of building which would be expressive "either by drawing attention to the constructive expedients which this quality demands, such as rivets and anchors, or by permitting the *backing* material (the use of which has been found to be absolutely essential to comfort in this climate) to be honestly apparent in solid buttresses or through the open work in the iron. Here are presented means for an entirely new architectural expression, arising directly out of that only pure fount for all such expressions—constructive necessity." Van Brunt then described the decorative possibilities of iron:

[47] *Ibid.*, p. 17.

How appropriate to the peculiar conditions of our material, that the solid wall which does the serious work behind, should be plainly seen and acknowledged, and that decorative openwork should beguile its surface with everchanging shadows, and half veil the painful arch of brick or stone with fancies that make sport of its frowning labor! Such a parasitical use of iron, it must be admitted, is not its noblest use, nor do we fairly test its decorative capacities till it is made to illustrate its own constructive properties. Yet it is evident that in all cases this peculiar interstitial feature could be made one of the most important characteristics of the style. It is understood that architecture is in a great measure the art of shadows, and hitherto the *chiaroscuro*, as it were, of architectural design has been limited to contrasts of masses and lines of shade with masses and lines of light. It has been considered the peculiar privilege of the painter to break lights into the mass of his shadows, and by these quick and sparkling touches to enhance its repose and depth, and give brilliancy and life to his subject. Now, the use of interstitial decoration would at once place this power in the hands of the architect, and open to him a large field for new and delicate effects in his designs.[48]

The various references to Saracenic art which follow this statement and the stress laid on decoration announce the arrival in America of a new English authority, Owen Jones's *Grammar of Ornament*, which was published in 1856. Van Brunt's final contribution was to see that iron could release architects from "very many old axioms and laws." Its use would "admit masses over voids as well as voids over masses . . . almost any width of aperture . . . almost any slenderness of supports . . . to meet all the strange exigencies of modern buildings."

Through this lecture the Gothic revival theorists may be heard in the distance. Van Brunt had accepted Ruskin's language and imagery, and the principles of architecture which *The Crayon* had intelligently summarized were present in his work. Though rejecting eclecticism, Van Brunt punctuated his lecture with references to the architecture of the past, knowledge to which the scholars of the Gothic revival had made a distinguished contribution. Part of the power possessed by the revival was certainly negative, in the sense that those opposed to its conclusions were moved by its dogmatism to develop ideas to contradict it. This Van Brunt also fairly represents. He knew what he thought in part because he disagreed with the revivalists. Americans had neither the responsibility nor the wish to accept the past. They were sure that

[48] *Ibid.*, p. 19.

the nineteenth century was bringing the future into being. The belief that architecture involved social obligation and the conviction that building was an expression of the society which produced it were present in the United States as they were in England, but there were vast differences in the conclusions each nation derived from them. Though William Morris found that "as a condition of life, production by machinery is altogether an evil," Van Brunt, as we have seen, regarded "the iron age," the age of "aggregates," with optimism, for he felt it possessed humane and artistic possibilities different from but richer than those that would be realized through an attempt to resuscitate the past.

Intense study of the magnificent structure of Gothic and an admiring understanding of the social matrix out of which it came provided the "true principles" and the definition of "reality" disclosed by Pugin and refined and amplified by Ruskin, Fergusson, Owen Jones, and others. In this flowering of architectural ideas in the mid-nineteenth century, Gothic was comprehended and explained in the abstract language of the Classical theory and aesthetics of building. The word "propriety," for example, had a long and honorable history when Pugin first used it. Characteristically, the nineteenth-century search for a synthesis of the many and diverse facts presented by history had provided not only the feeling that a new style should be created but the material and standards of design upon which that style would be founded when it appeared. The expanded view of what had gone before enforced a search for order. Pugin's Catholicism, the dogmatism of the ecclesiologists, and the determination of the Americans not to accept everything they were told were varied reflections of this compelling need.

In March, 1886, when he was fifty-three years old and a successful architect and critic, Henry Van Brunt wrote an article, "On the Present Condition and Prospects of Architecture,"[49] in which he looked back as he appraised the present. The high hopes he held in 1859 had not been realized, but he was still melioristic. Though the two centuries that lay behind had been "an era of books, prints, and photographs," of analysis and the invention of "a science of aesthetics," he was forced to report that architectural "chaos" had been the result. The best he could say was that the men who came after him might be

---

[49] *The Atlantic Monthly*, 57 (March, 1886):374–84.

able to perceive in its "inchoate, nebulous mass . . . not a style . . . but . . . a sort of architectural constellation, in which may be seen . . . some reflection of the spirit of the times in which we live." In earlier great ages of building, changes and refinements had been possible because architects worked within "an orderly, intelligible, and harmonious evolution of styles." Eighteenth- and nineteenth-century architects were not so fortunate. In France, said Van Brunt, where originality was discouraged and schools were a "Propaganda of faith in an arbitrary type of art," distracting revivals were not tolerated but refinement was approved. Even Viollet le Duc had not been able to displace the authority of this "official system." England was still "groping" for a style which suited her national needs. She had no controls such as those which limited but stabilized French design. In England details were not as elegant, mistakes were made, varieties of styles flourished side by side, but "the elements of design . . . find the fullest expression." For all its turbulence, England had demonstrated "sincerity and zeal on pure questions of principles in art which are unparalleled in history." Revivals of all sorts had washed over her architecture, and of them only three—the Gothic, Queen Anne, and "free classical"—had left enduring results, though their possibilities in terms of the architecture of the future were limited because they aimed to restore "completed systems, of forms incapable of further progression." These revivals, however, had left a valuable heritage. It was "noteworthy," said Van Brunt, "that the first and greatest of the English revivals, that of medieval art, had its basis in an awakened conscience." Pugin and Ruskin had preached the gospel of this revival; they had asked for a return to the era of truth in art; they had asked that architectural expression should be controlled by structure and that decoration should follow the methods of nature. "The Gothic revival," said Van Brunt, was "the only instance in history of a moral revolution in art." But for all the encouragement and enrichment it brought to England, it had contributed only "sterile incidents."

American architects had made intelligent use of these English experiments, liberated by their "national genius . . . and their freedom from the tyranny of historic precedent." Improvements in architectural education were being made, and a more literate and discriminating public was emerging.

We have had good practice and experience in following the English fashions, but here their reign has never been undisputed. By the entire absence of local traditions;

by the entire absence of monuments more ancient than those which we call 'old colonial' . . . by the entire absence of any official prejudice, of any venerable conventionalities, of any national system of instruction in architecture, we are left in a condition of freedom which is fatal to art while we are ignorant, but capable of great developments when we are educated. . . . If our heritage of liberty has made us impatient of academical discipline, it has made us peculiarly hospitable to unprejudiced impressions of beauty and fitness.

In passing, Van Brunt had summarized the history of the parish church revival and assigned it a place in American architecture. Concluding his article with praise for H. H. Richardson, he affirmed America's special architectural genius, which he felt sure would, in the end, accomplish more than England's archeological diversity and the "academical discipline" of France.

The English Gothic revival and its ecclesiological specialists served as catalysts for change in American architecture. The "moral revolution" and the "awakened conscience," which Van Brunt recognized, heightened the impact of the revival, for they encouraged Americans to contemplate not medieval buildings but their architectural principles, which were the revival's most constructive and enduring contribution.

Index

INDEX

INDEX

287, 289, 293, 296, 300, 305; biography, 127, 128, 148, 296, 321; and development of revival, 191–93; influence, 287, 293n, 296; influences on, 188–90, 191, 192, 193, 296; and *NYE,* 161, 180, 181, 182–85; and NYES, 280, 284, 286, 287, 289, 296; and wooden churches, 154, 258n, 268–69, 287, 293n; writings, 13n, 191–93, 320
Wilmington, New Hanover County, N.C.: St. James', 221n
Windrim, John T., 107n
Withers, Frederick C., 280n, 322

Wood: as building material. *See* Materials, use of
Woolsthorpe, Lincolnshire: St. James', 76, 78, 97, 113
Wyatt, T. H., 322

Yorkville, N.Y.: All Angels', 184–85

Zion Church, Rome, N.Y. (R. Upjohn), 185